TOMB RAIDER™

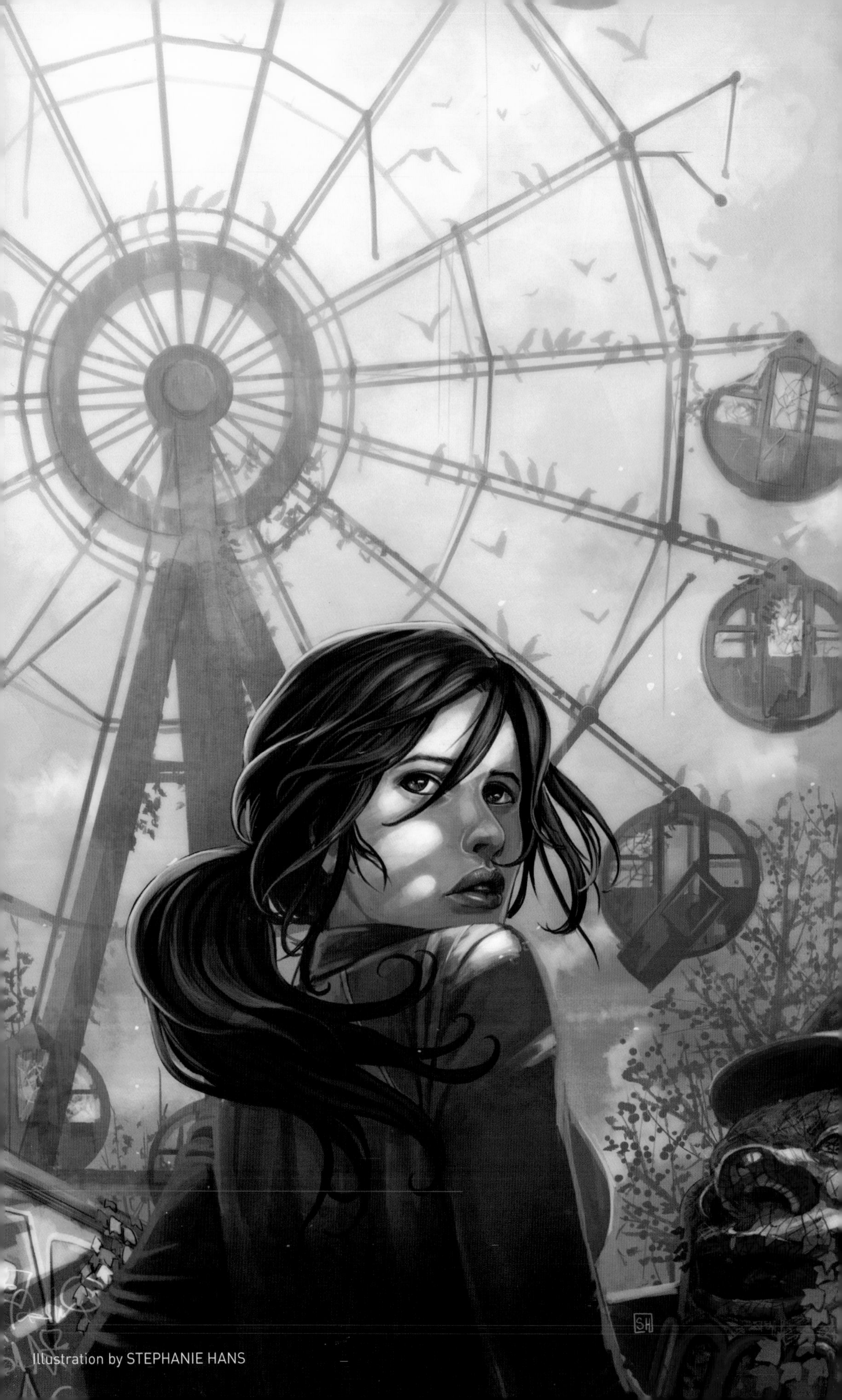
SH

Illustration by STEPHANIE HANS

TOMB RAIDER™

SECRETS AND LIES

VOLUME 2

SCRIPT
RHIANNA PRATCHETT
AND **GAIL SIMONE**

PENCILS
DERLIS SANTACRUZ (PAGES 7–72)
NICOLÁS DANIEL SELMA (PAGES 73–140)

INKS
ANDY OWENS (PAGES 7–72)
JUAN GEDEON (PAGES 73–140)

COLORS
MICHAEL ATIYEH

LETTERING
MICHAEL HEISLER

FRONT COVER ART
ANDY PARK

DARK HORSE BOOKS

PUBLISHER
MIKE RICHARDSON

COLLECTION DESIGNER
KAT LARSON

ASSISTANT EDITORS
ROXY POLK
AARON WALKER

EDITOR
DAVE MARSHALL

Special thanks to Crystal Dynamics and Square Enix, including
Rich Briggs, Brian Horton, and Noah Hughes.

TOMB RAIDER VOLUME 2: SECRETS AND LIES

This volume collects issues #7–#12 of the Dark Horse comic-book series *Tomb Raider*.

Published by
Dark Horse Books
A division of
Dark Horse Comics, Inc.
10956 SE Main Street
Milwaukie, OR 97222

DarkHorse.com
TombRaider.com

First edition: May 2015
ISBN 978-1-61655-639-6

1 3 5 7 9 10 8 6 4 2
Printed in China

Illustration by STEPHANIE HANS

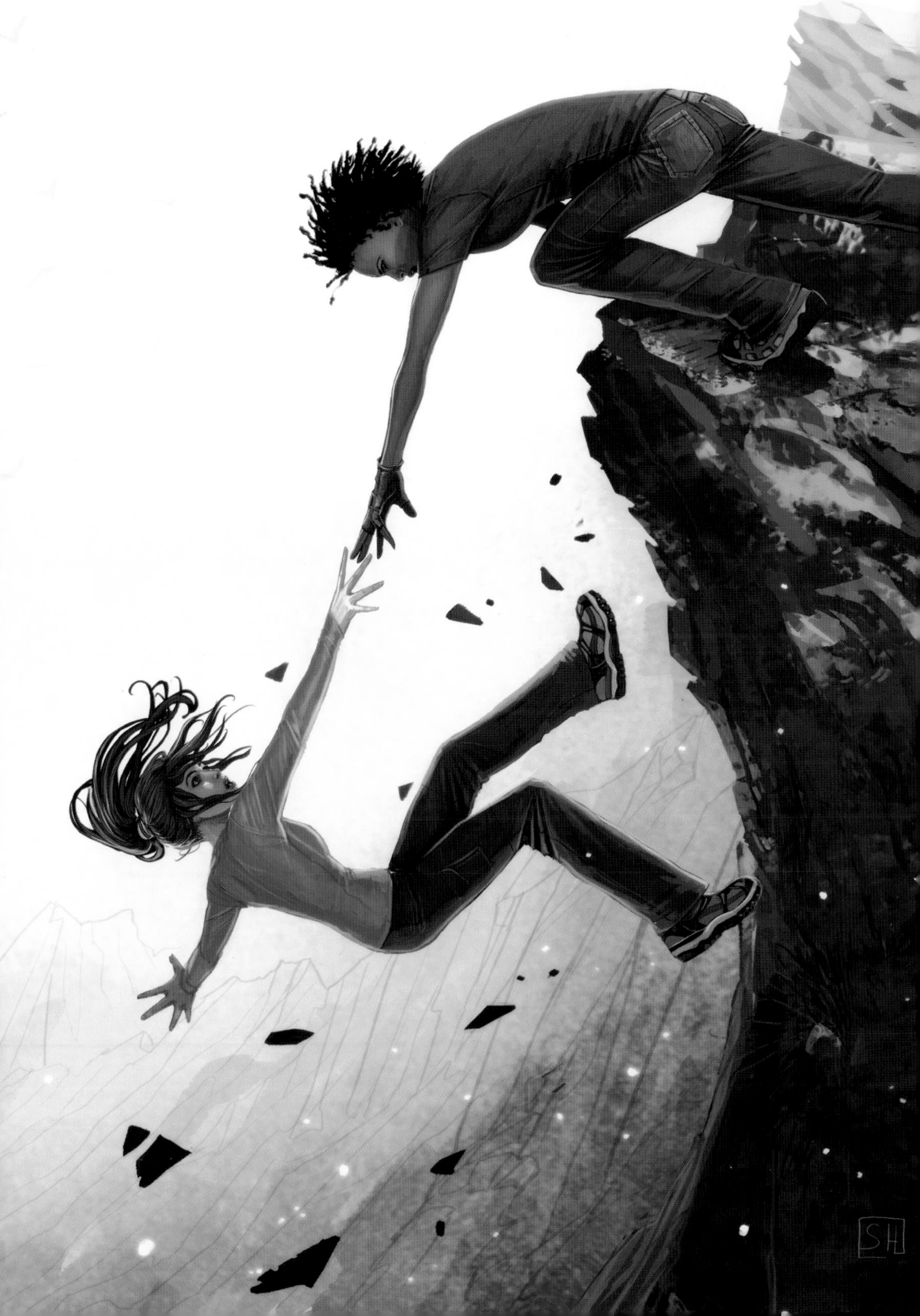
SH

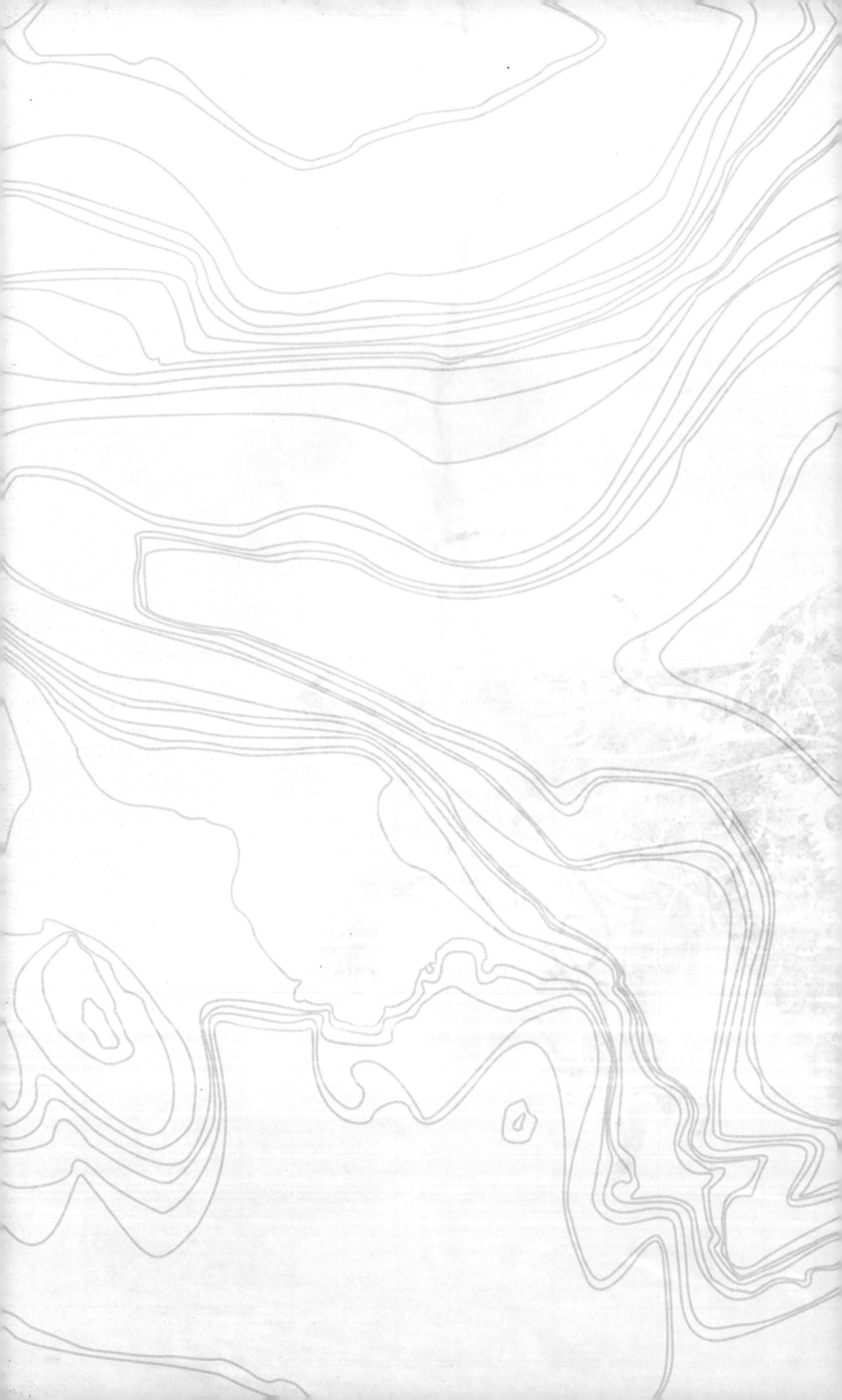

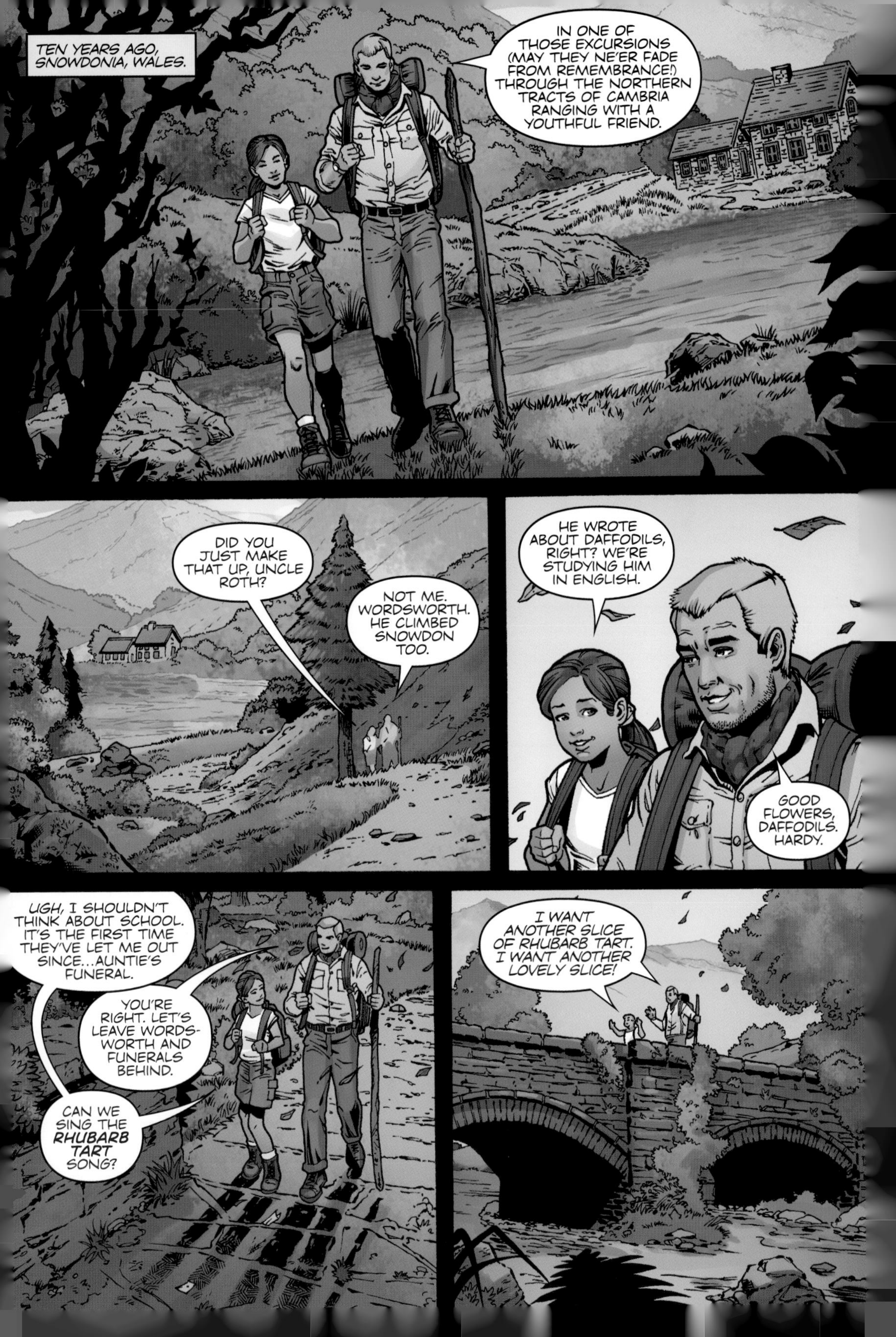

TEN YEARS AGO, SNOWDONIA, WALES.
IN ONE OF THOSE EXCURSIONS (MAY THEY NE'ER FADE FROM REMEMBRANCE!) THROUGH THE NORTHERN TRACTS OF CAMBRIA RANGING WITH A YOUTHFUL FRIEND.
DID YOU JUST MAKE THAT UP, UNCLE ROTH?
NOT ME. WORDSWORTH. HE CLIMBED SNOWDON TOO.
HE WROTE ABOUT DAFFODILS, RIGHT? WE'RE STUDYING HIM IN ENGLISH.
GOOD FLOWERS, DAFFODILS. HARDY.
UGH, I SHOULDN'T THINK ABOUT SCHOOL. IT'S THE FIRST TIME THEY'VE LET ME OUT SINCE...AUNTIE'S FUNERAL.
YOU'RE RIGHT. LET'S LEAVE WORDS-WORTH AND FUNERALS BEHIND.
CAN WE SING THE RHUBARB TART SONG?
I WANT ANOTHER SLICE OF RHUBARB TART. I WANT ANOTHER LOVELY SLICE!

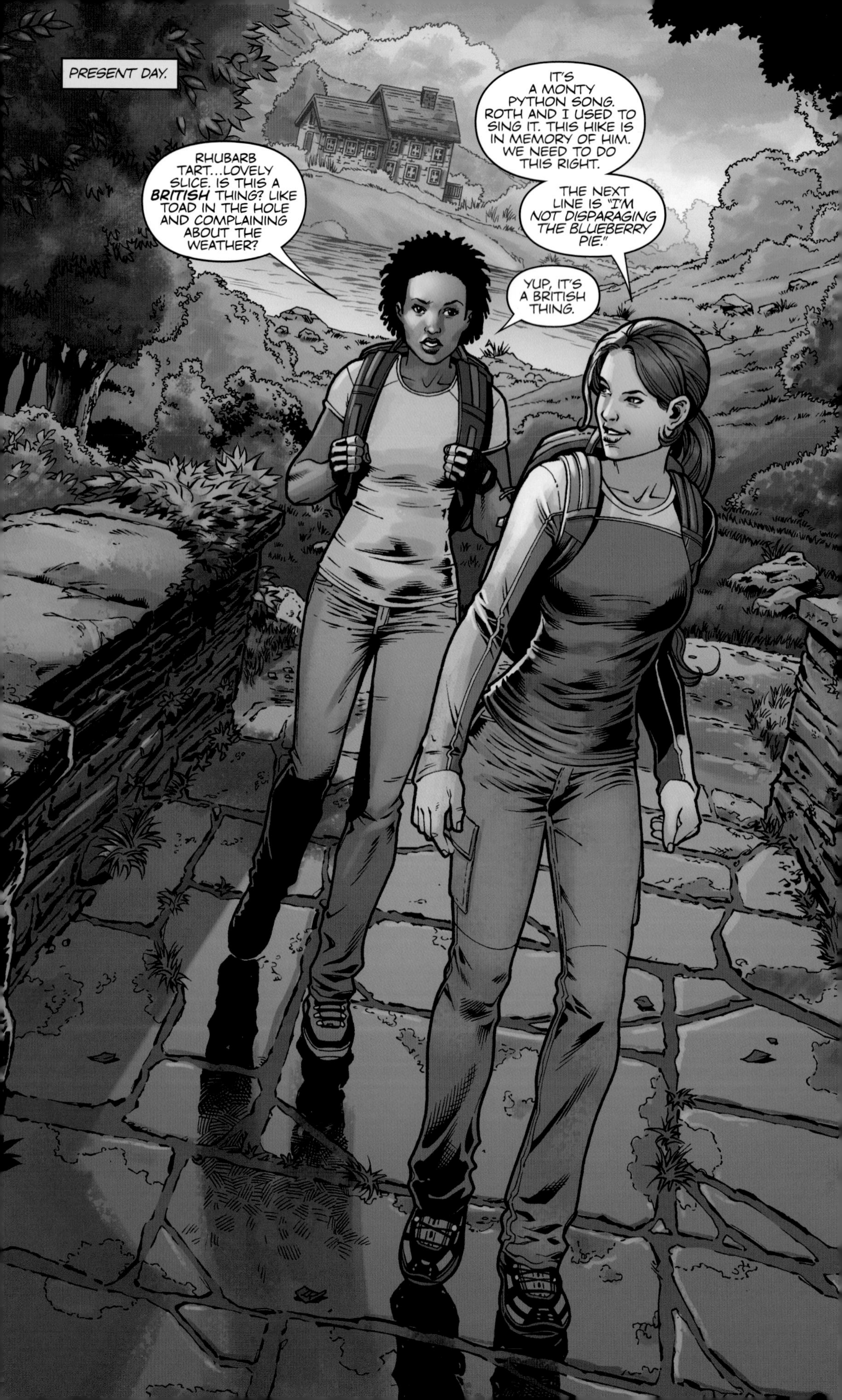
PRESENT DAY.
RHUBARB TART...LOVELY SLICE. IS THIS A **BRITISH** THING? LIKE TOAD IN THE HOLE AND COMPLAINING ABOUT THE WEATHER?
IT'S A MONTY PYTHON SONG. ROTH AND I USED TO SING IT. THIS HIKE IS IN MEMORY OF HIM. WE NEED TO DO THIS RIGHT.
THE NEXT LINE IS *"I'M NOT DISPARAGING THE BLUEBERRY PIE."*
YUP, IT'S A BRITISH THING.

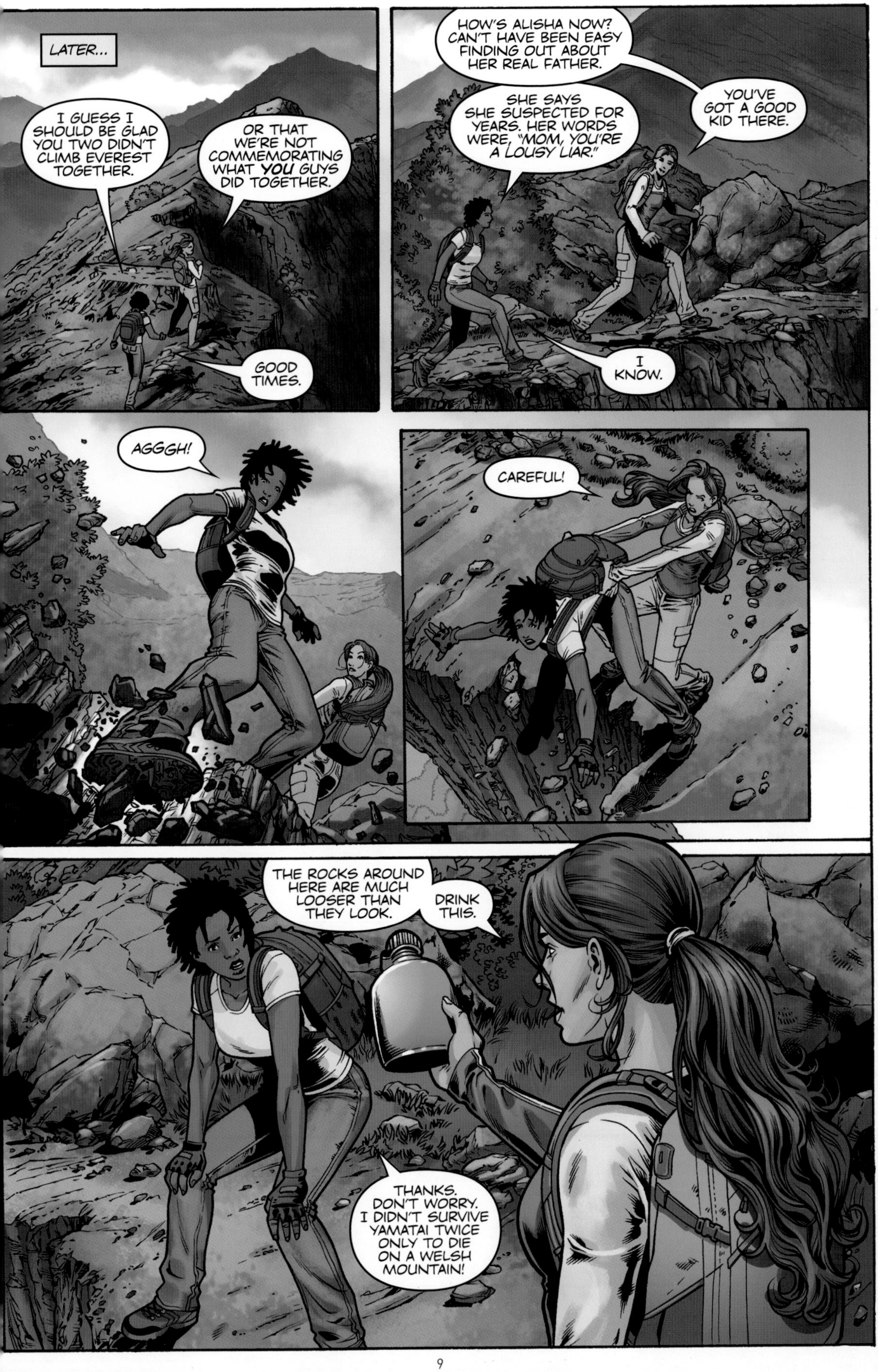
LATER...
I GUESS I SHOULD BE GLAD YOU TWO DIDN'T CLIMB EVEREST TOGETHER.
OR THAT WE'RE NOT COMMEMORATING WHAT *YOU* GUYS DID TOGETHER.
GOOD TIMES.
HOW'S ALISHA NOW? CAN'T HAVE BEEN EASY FINDING OUT ABOUT HER REAL FATHER.
SHE SAYS SHE SUSPECTED FOR YEARS. HER WORDS WERE, *"MOM, YOU'RE A LOUSY LIAR."*
YOU'VE GOT A GOOD KID THERE.
I KNOW.
AGGGH!
CAREFUL!
THE ROCKS AROUND HERE ARE MUCH LOOSER THAN THEY LOOK.
DRINK THIS.
THANKS. DON'T WORRY. I DIDN'T SURVIVE YAMATAI TWICE ONLY TO DIE ON A WELSH MOUNTAIN!

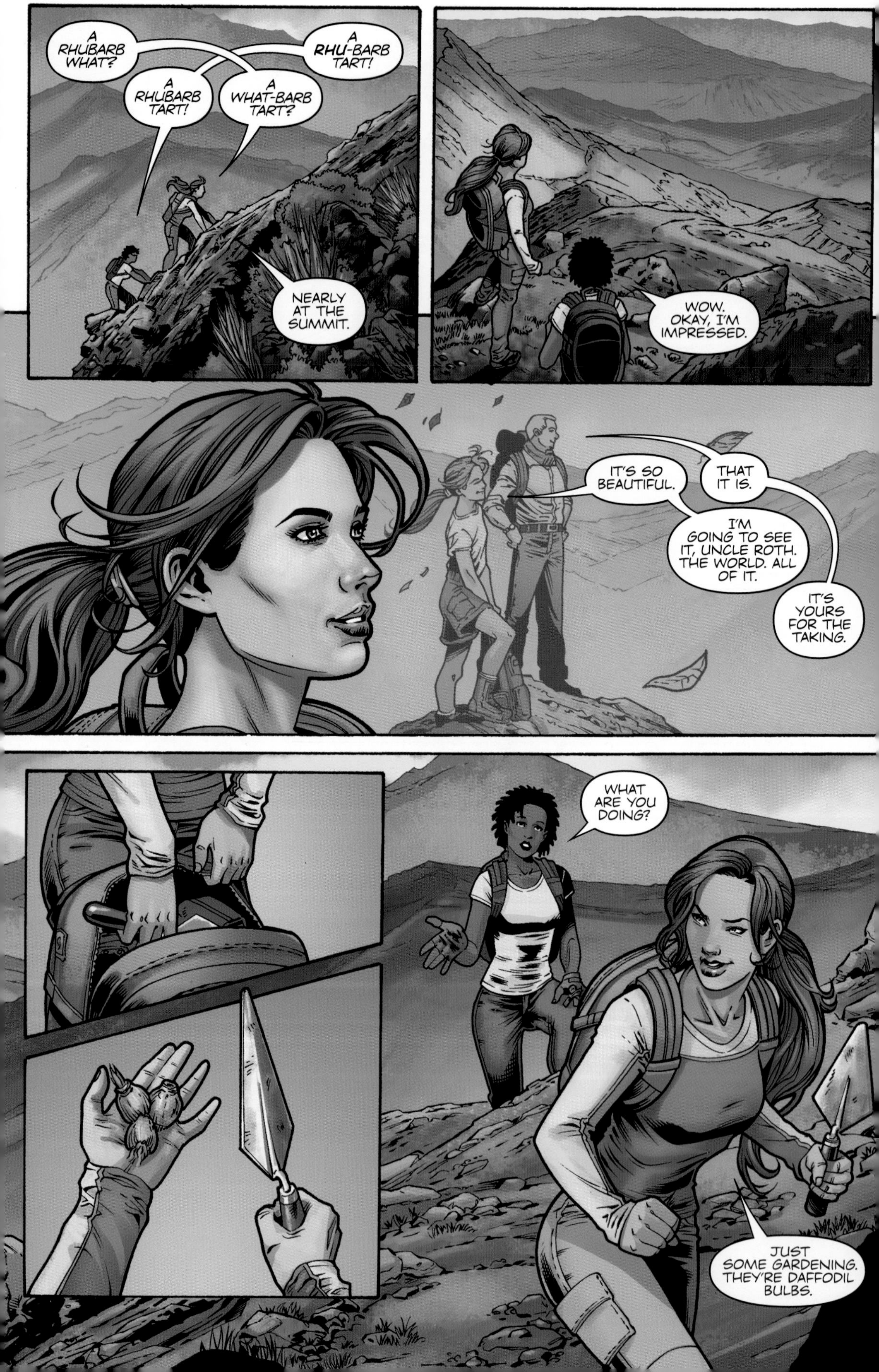
A RHUBARB WHAT?
A RHUBARB TART!
A WHAT-BARB TART?
A **RHU**-BARB TART!
NEARLY AT THE SUMMIT.
WOW. OKAY, I'M IMPRESSED.
IT'S SO BEAUTIFUL.
THAT IT IS.
I'M GOING TO SEE IT, UNCLE ROTH. THE WORLD. ALL OF IT.
IT'S YOURS FOR THE TAKING.
WHAT ARE YOU DOING?
JUST SOME GARDENING. THEY'RE DAFFODIL BULBS.

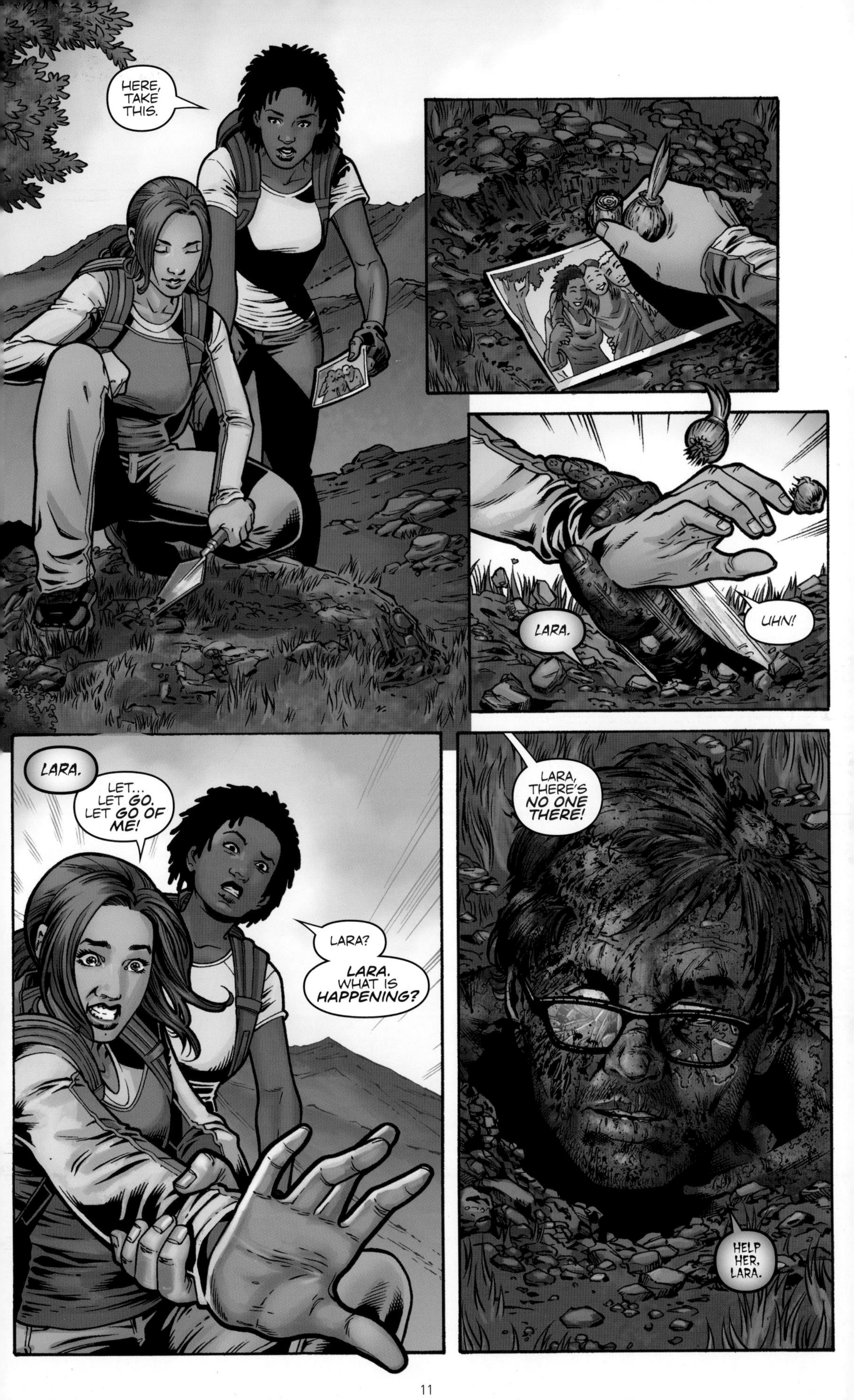
HERE, TAKE THIS.
LARA.
UHN!
LARA.
LET... LET GO. LET GO OF ME!
LARA?
LARA. WHAT IS HAPPENING?
LARA, THERE'S NO ONE THERE!
HELP HER, LARA.

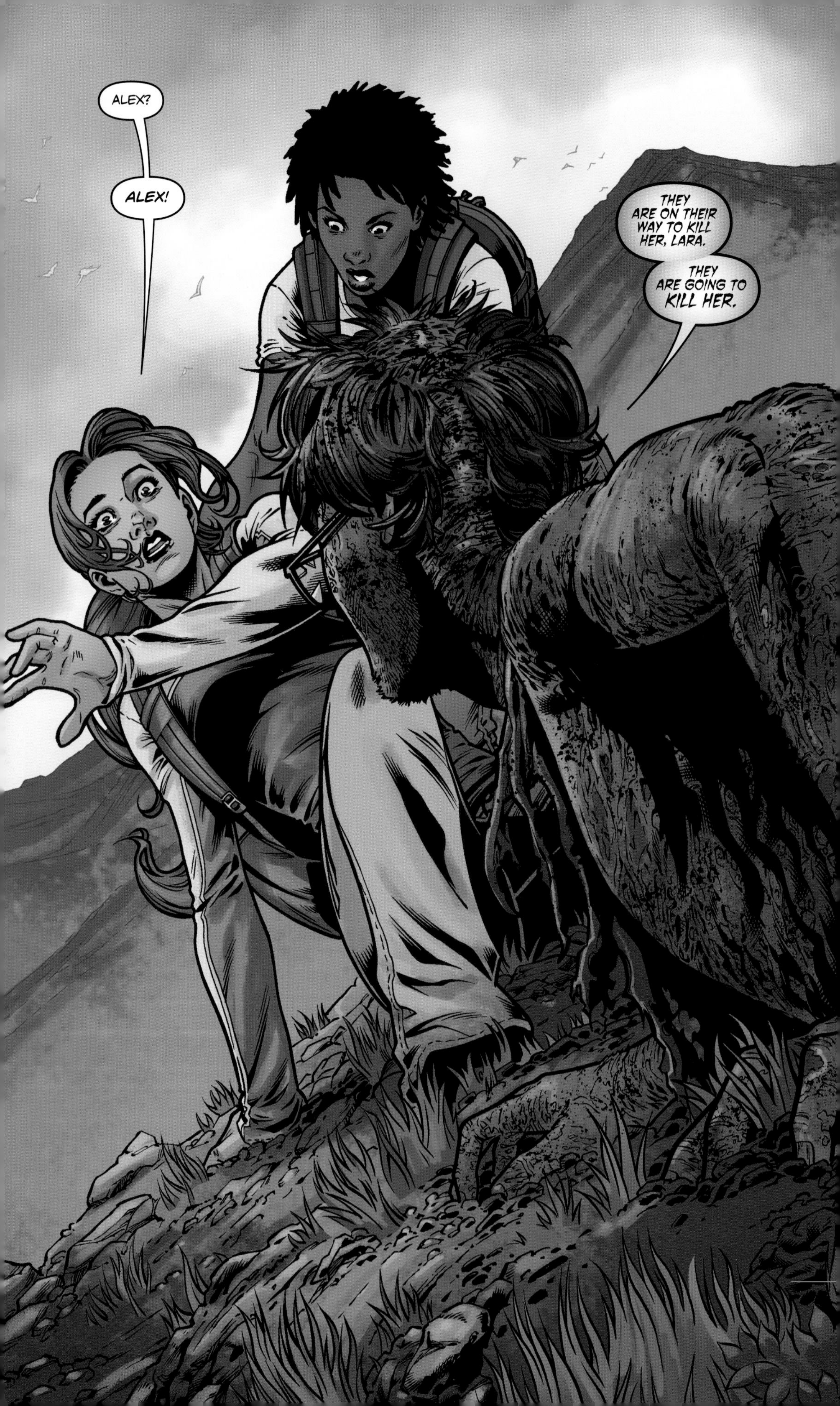
ALEX?
ALEX!
THEY ARE ON THEIR WAY TO KILL HER, LARA.
THEY ARE GOING TO KILL HER.

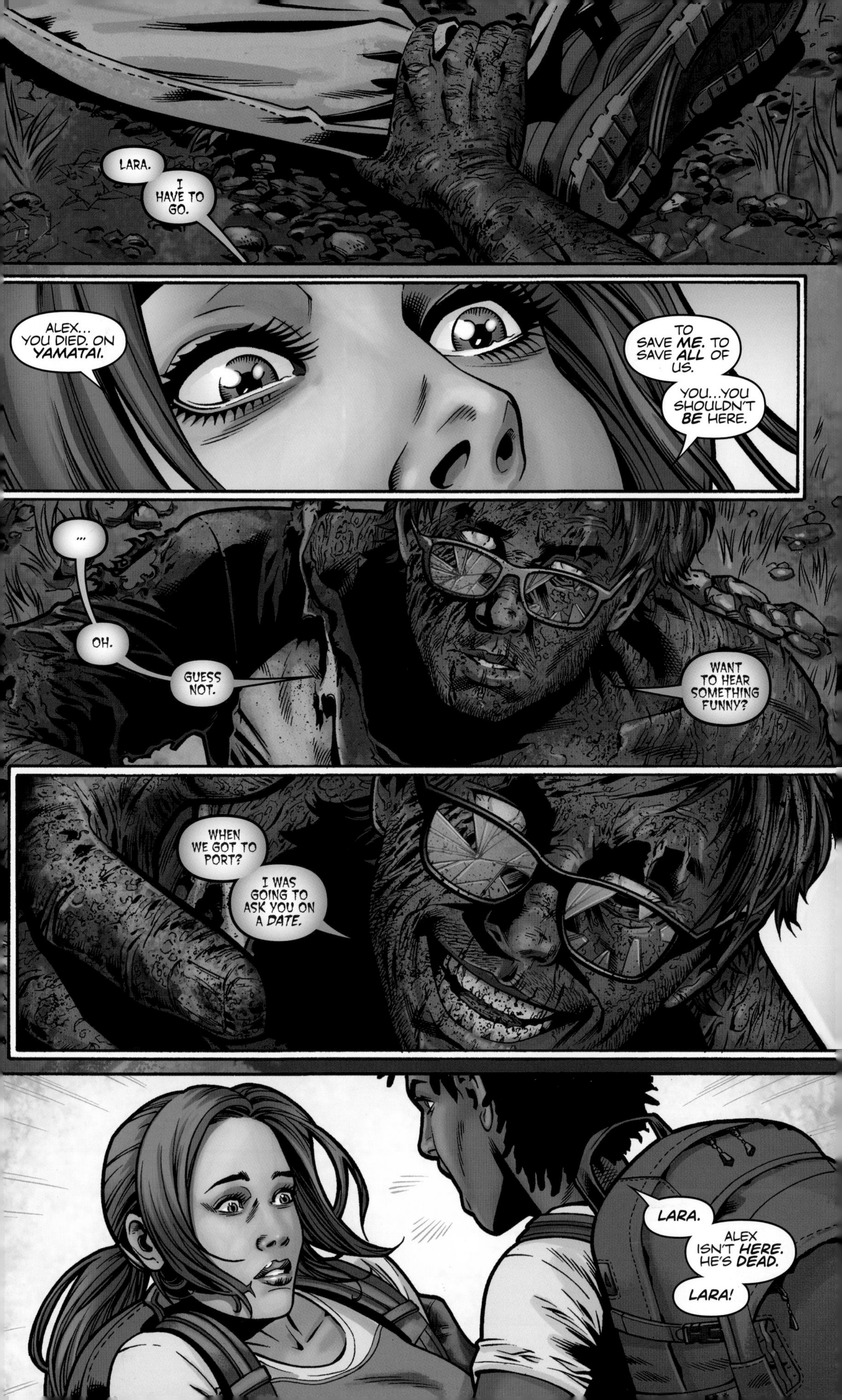
LARA.
I HAVE TO GO.
ALEX... YOU DIED. ON YAMATAI.
TO SAVE ME. TO SAVE ALL OF US.
YOU...YOU SHOULDN'T BE HERE.
...
OH.
GUESS NOT.
WANT TO HEAR SOMETHING FUNNY?
WHEN WE GOT TO PORT?
I WAS GOING TO ASK YOU ON A DATE.
LARA.
ALEX ISN'T HERE. HE'S DEAD.
LARA!

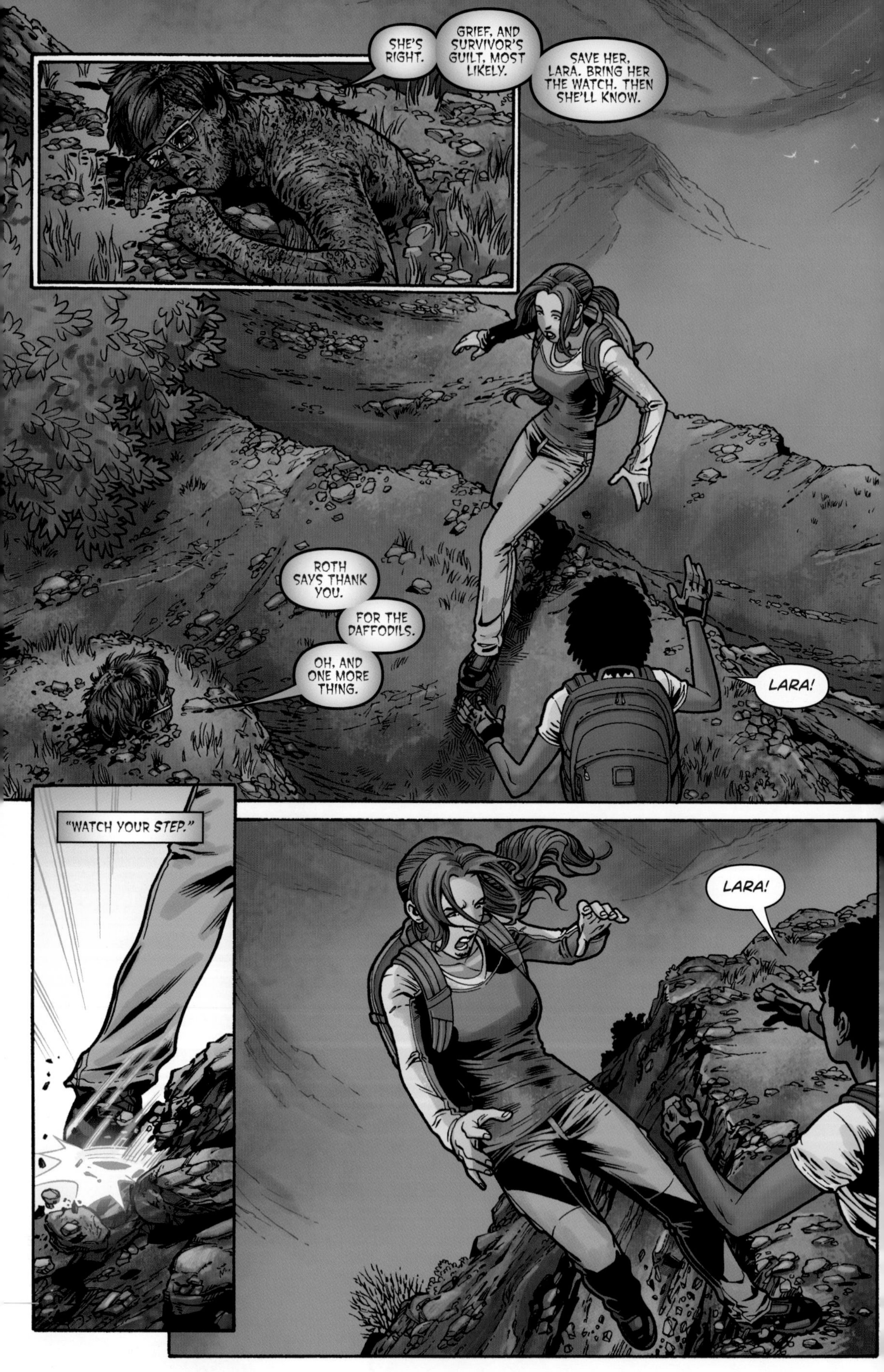
SHE'S RIGHT.
GRIEF, AND SURVIVOR'S GUILT, MOST LIKELY.
SAVE HER, LARA. BRING HER THE WATCH. THEN SHE'LL KNOW.
ROTH SAYS THANK YOU.
FOR THE DAFFODILS.
OH, AND ONE MORE THING.
LARA!
"WATCH YOUR STEP."
LARA!

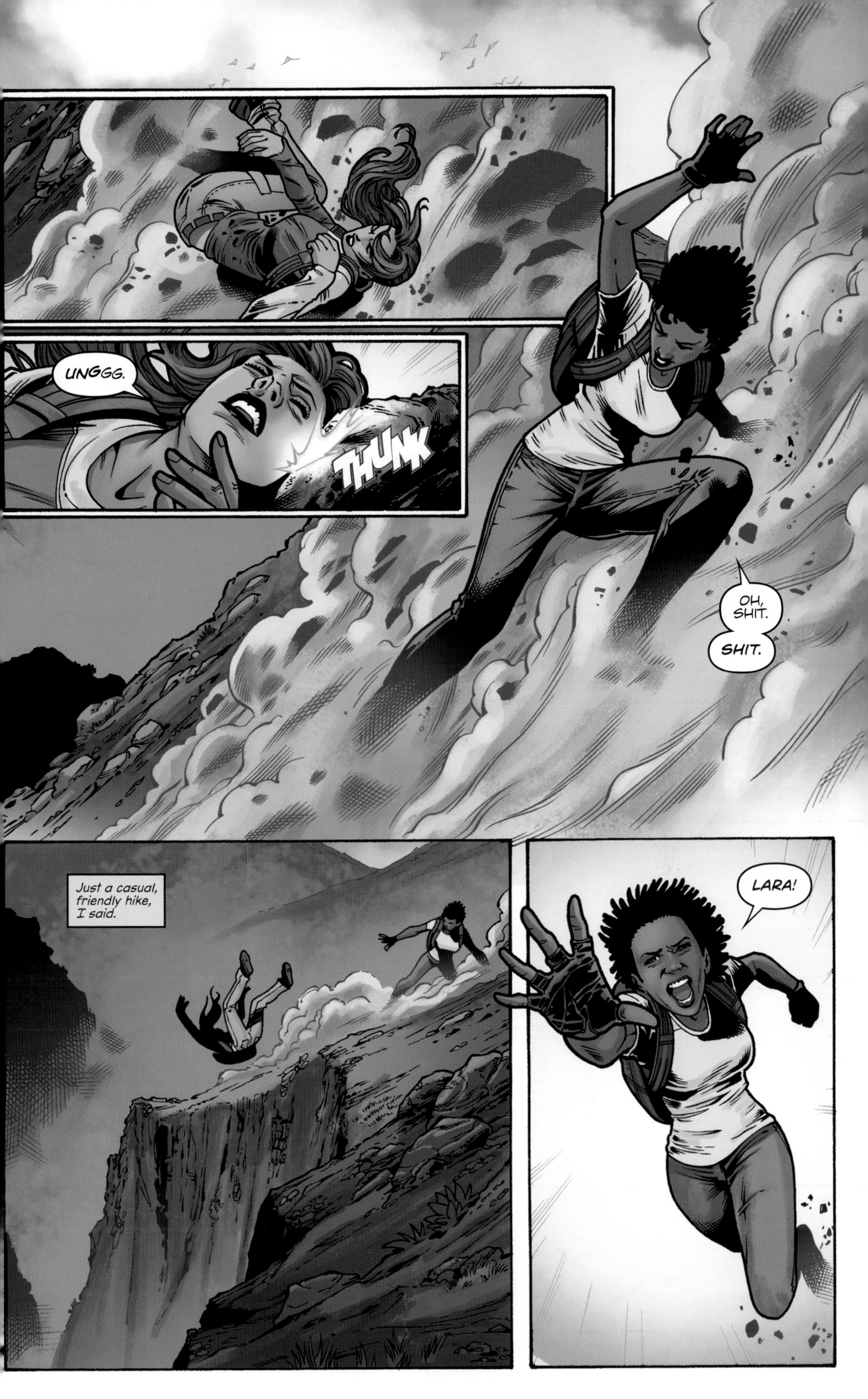

UNGGG.
THUNK
OH, SHIT.
SHIT.
Just a casual, friendly hike, I said.
LARA!

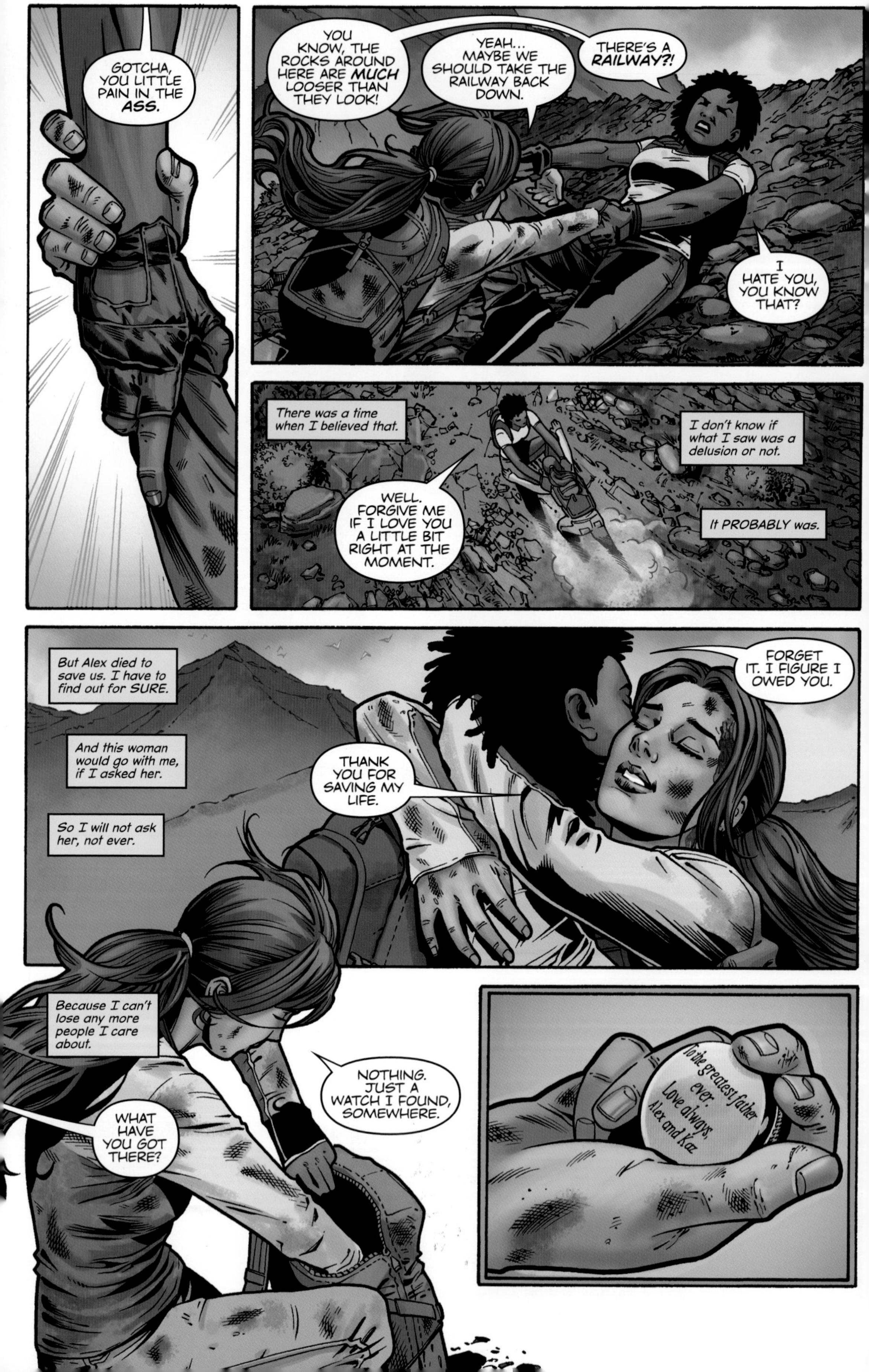

GOTCHA, YOU LITTLE PAIN IN THE ASS.
YOU KNOW, THE ROCKS AROUND HERE ARE MUCH LOOSER THAN THEY LOOK!
YEAH... MAYBE WE SHOULD TAKE THE RAILWAY BACK DOWN.
THERE'S A RAILWAY?!
I HATE YOU, YOU KNOW THAT?
There was a time when I believed that.
WELL. FORGIVE ME IF I LOVE YOU A LITTLE BIT RIGHT AT THE MOMENT.
I don't know if what I saw was a delusion or not.
It PROBABLY was.
But Alex died to save us. I have to find out for SURE.
And this woman would go with me, if I asked her.
So I will not ask her, not ever.
THANK YOU FOR SAVING MY LIFE.
FORGET IT. I FIGURE I OWED YOU.
Because I can't lose any more people I care about.
WHAT HAVE YOU GOT THERE?
NOTHING. JUST A WATCH I FOUND, SOMEWHERE.
To the greatest father ever. Love always, Alex and Kaz

REYKJAVIK, ICELAND.

<WELCOME TO MY BAR, MY FRIEND! WE'RE NOT *QUITE* OPEN YET, BUT NEVER MIND! WHAT CAN I GET YOU?>

I DON'T SPEAK THAT DRIVEL.

AH. WELL. WOULD YOU LIKE A WHEATGRASS TEA, OR --

IN A MOMENT.

I'M LOOKING FOR *THIS* WOMAN.

I KNOW SHE COMES HERE.

I...I DON'T KNOW. I SEE A LOT OF PEOPLE.

PLACE LIKE THIS, WITH WHEATGRASS TEA AS THE SPECIAL? I'M SURE YOU'RE SWAMPED.

SO, I'LL ASK AGAIN. HAVE YOU SEEN THIS WOMAN?

LOOK, I DON'T KNOW WHO YOU ARE.

BUT HASN'T SHE HAD *ENOUGH* TROUBLE?

SHE'S A GOOD GIRL. CAN'T YOU JUST LEAVE HER *BE?*

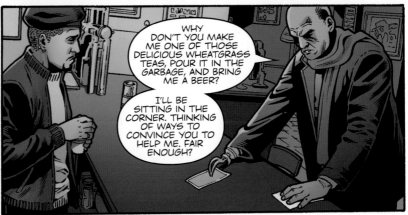

WHY DON'T YOU MAKE ME ONE OF THOSE DELICIOUS WHEATGRASS TEAS, POUR IT IN THE GARBAGE, AND BRING ME A BEER?

I'LL BE SITTING IN THE CORNER. THINKING OF WAYS TO CONVINCE YOU TO HELP ME. FAIR ENOUGH?

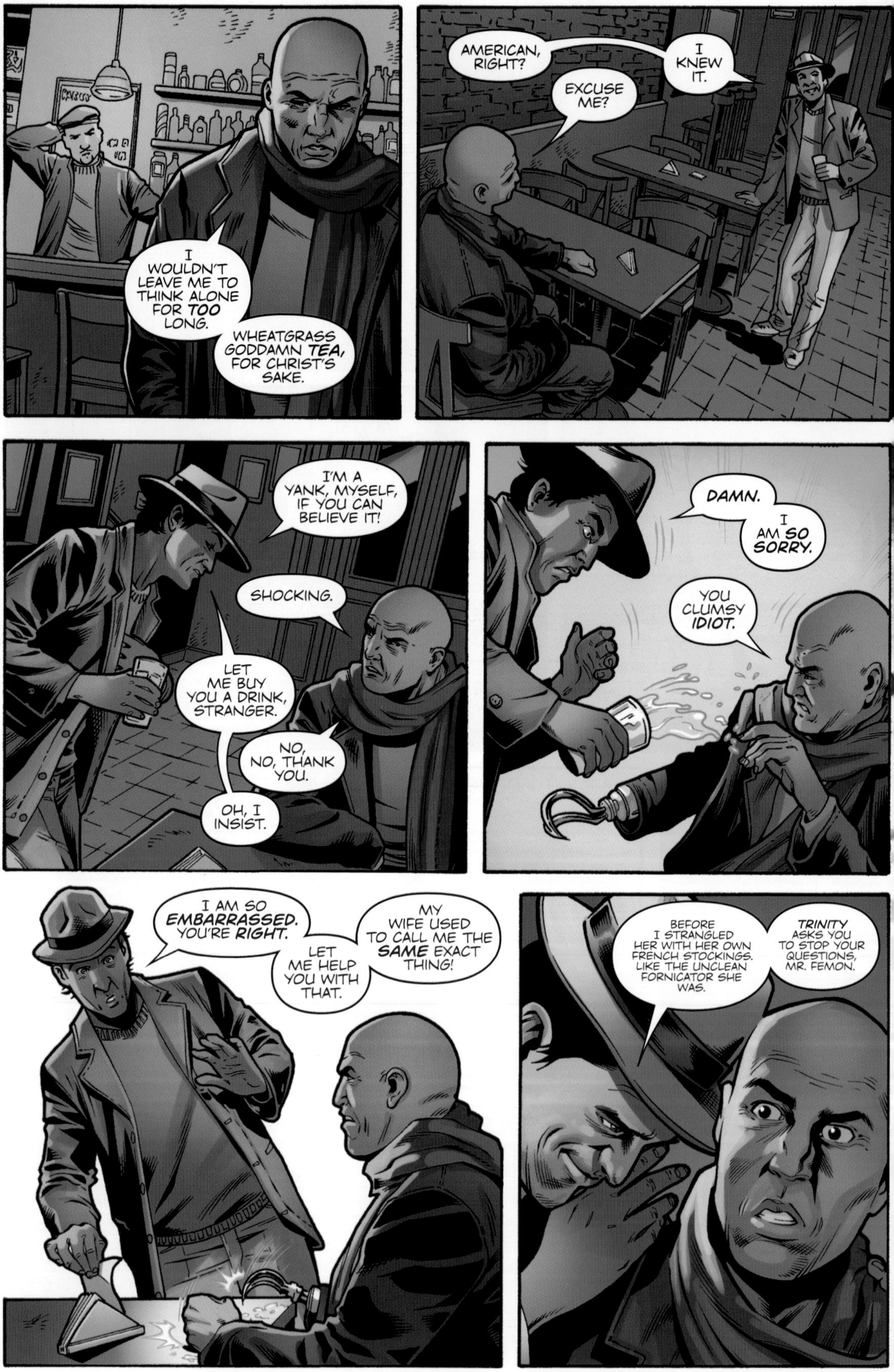

I WOULDN'T LEAVE ME TO THINK ALONE FOR TOO LONG.
WHEATGRASS GODDAMN TEA, FOR CHRIST'S SAKE.
AMERICAN, RIGHT?
EXCUSE ME?
I KNEW IT.
I'M A YANK, MYSELF, IF YOU CAN BELIEVE IT!
SHOCKING.
LET ME BUY YOU A DRINK, STRANGER.
NO, NO, THANK YOU.
OH, I INSIST.
DAMN.
I AM SO SORRY.
YOU CLUMSY IDIOT.
I AM SO EMBARRASSED. YOU'RE RIGHT.
LET ME HELP YOU WITH THAT.
MY WIFE USED TO CALL ME THE SAME EXACT THING!
BEFORE I STRANGLED HER WITH HER OWN FRENCH STOCKINGS. LIKE THE UNCLEAN FORNICATOR SHE WAS.
TRINITY ASKS YOU TO STOP YOUR QUESTIONS, MR. FEMON.

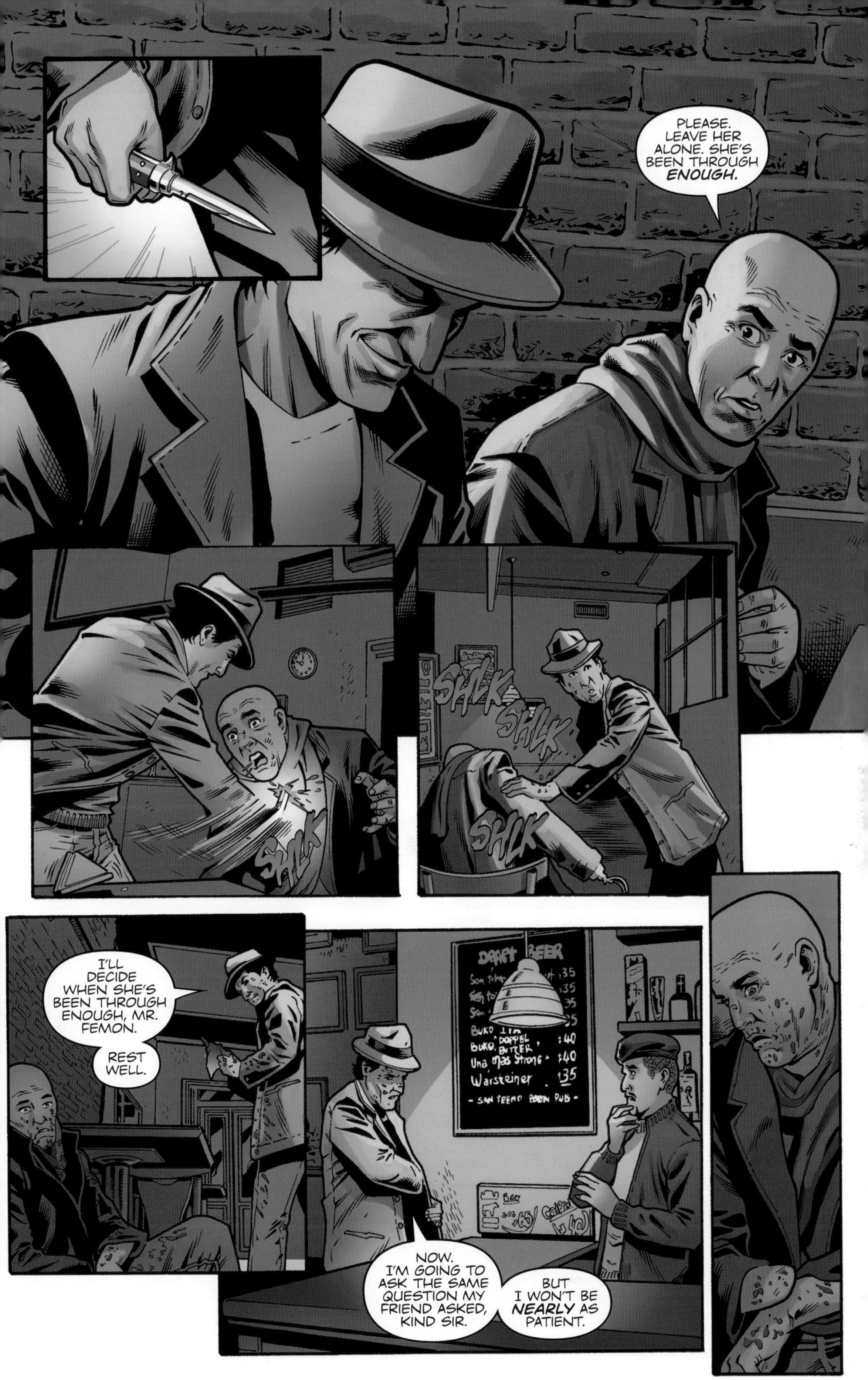
PLEASE. LEAVE HER ALONE. SHE'S BEEN THROUGH *ENOUGH*.
SHLK
SHLK
SHLK
SHLK
I'LL DECIDE WHEN SHE'S BEEN THROUGH ENOUGH, MR. FEMON.
REST WELL.
NOW. I'M GOING TO ASK THE SAME QUESTION MY FRIEND ASKED, KIND SIR.
BUT I WON'T BE *NEARLY* AS PATIENT.

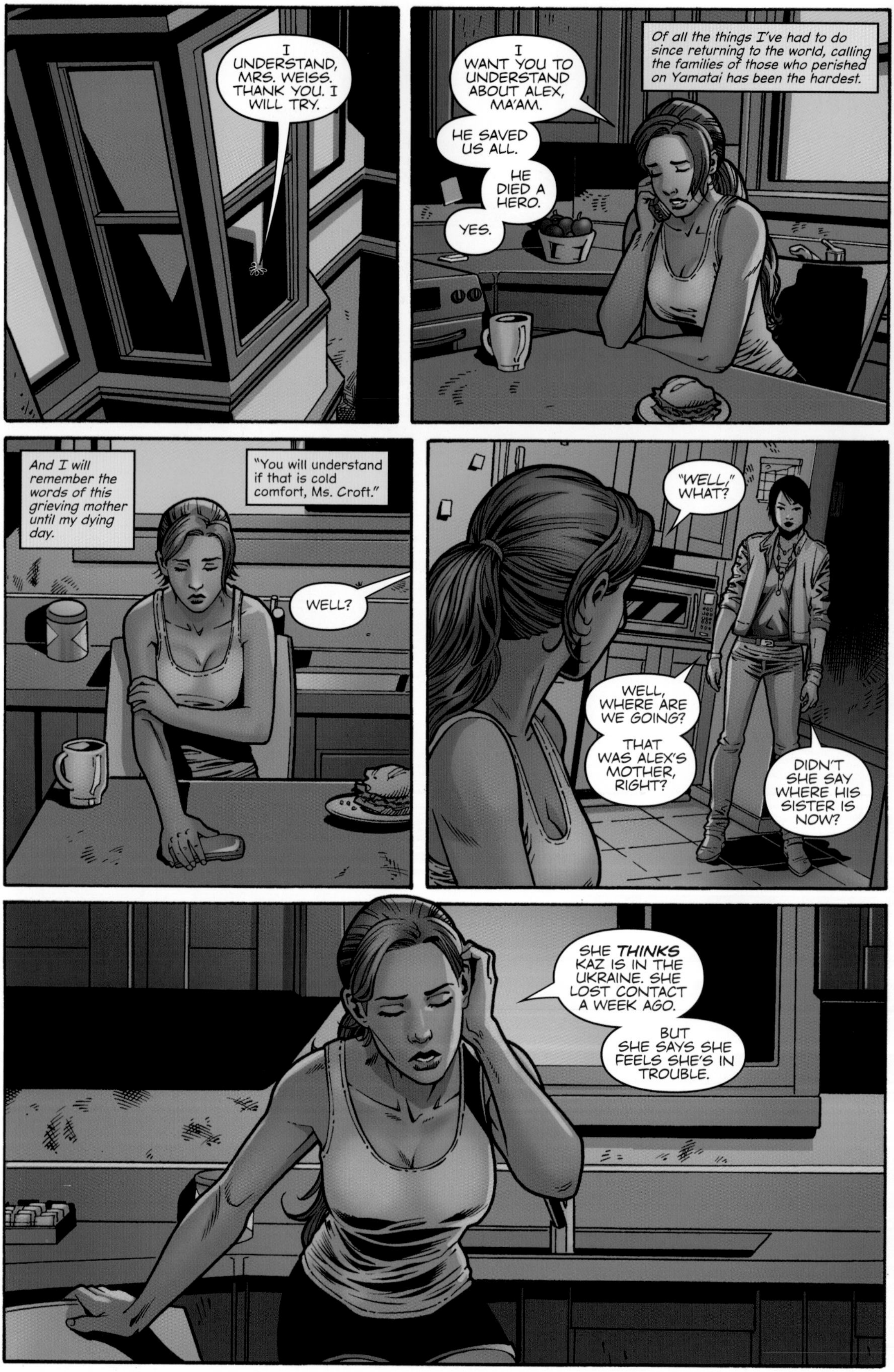
I UNDERSTAND, MRS. WEISS. THANK YOU. I WILL TRY.
Of all the things I've had to do since returning to the world, calling the families of those who perished on Yamatai has been the hardest.
I WANT YOU TO UNDERSTAND ABOUT ALEX, MA'AM.
HE SAVED US ALL.
HE DIED A HERO.
YES.
And I will remember the words of this grieving mother until my dying day.
"You will understand if that is cold comfort, Ms. Croft."
WELL?
"WELL," WHAT?
WELL, WHERE ARE WE GOING?
THAT WAS ALEX'S MOTHER, RIGHT?
DIDN'T SHE SAY WHERE HIS SISTER IS NOW?
SHE THINKS KAZ IS IN THE UKRAINE. SHE LOST CONTACT A WEEK AGO.
BUT SHE SAYS SHE FEELS SHE'S IN TROUBLE.

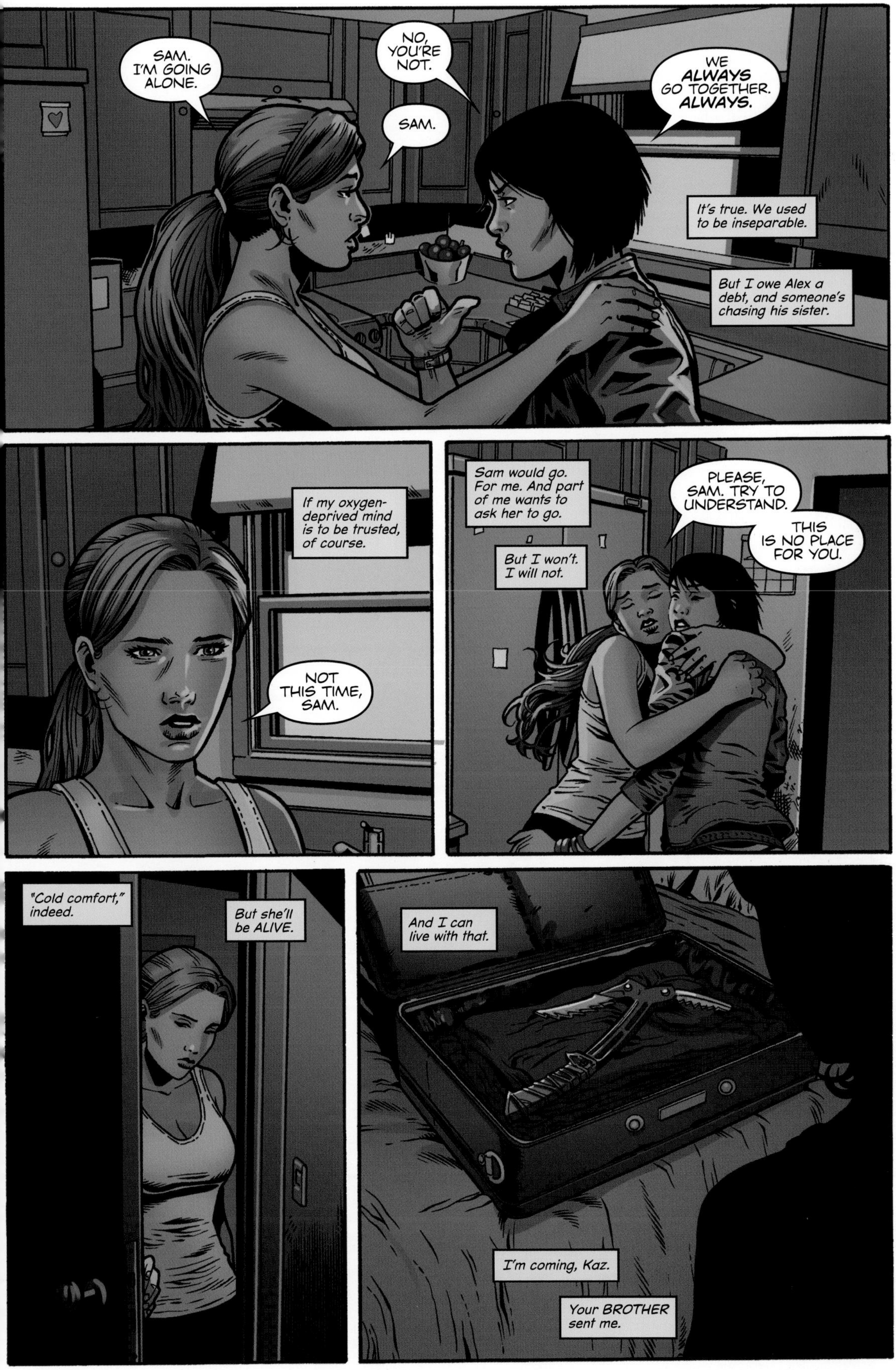
SAM. I'M GOING ALONE.
NO, YOU'RE NOT.
SAM.
WE ALWAYS GO TOGETHER. ALWAYS.
It's true. We used to be inseparable.
But I owe Alex a debt, and someone's chasing his sister.
If my oxygen-deprived mind is to be trusted, of course.
NOT THIS TIME, SAM.
Sam would go. For me. And part of me wants to ask her to go.
But I won't. I will not.
PLEASE, SAM. TRY TO UNDERSTAND.
THIS IS NO PLACE FOR YOU.
"Cold comfort," indeed.
But she'll be ALIVE.
And I can live with that.
I'm coming, Kaz.
Your BROTHER sent me.

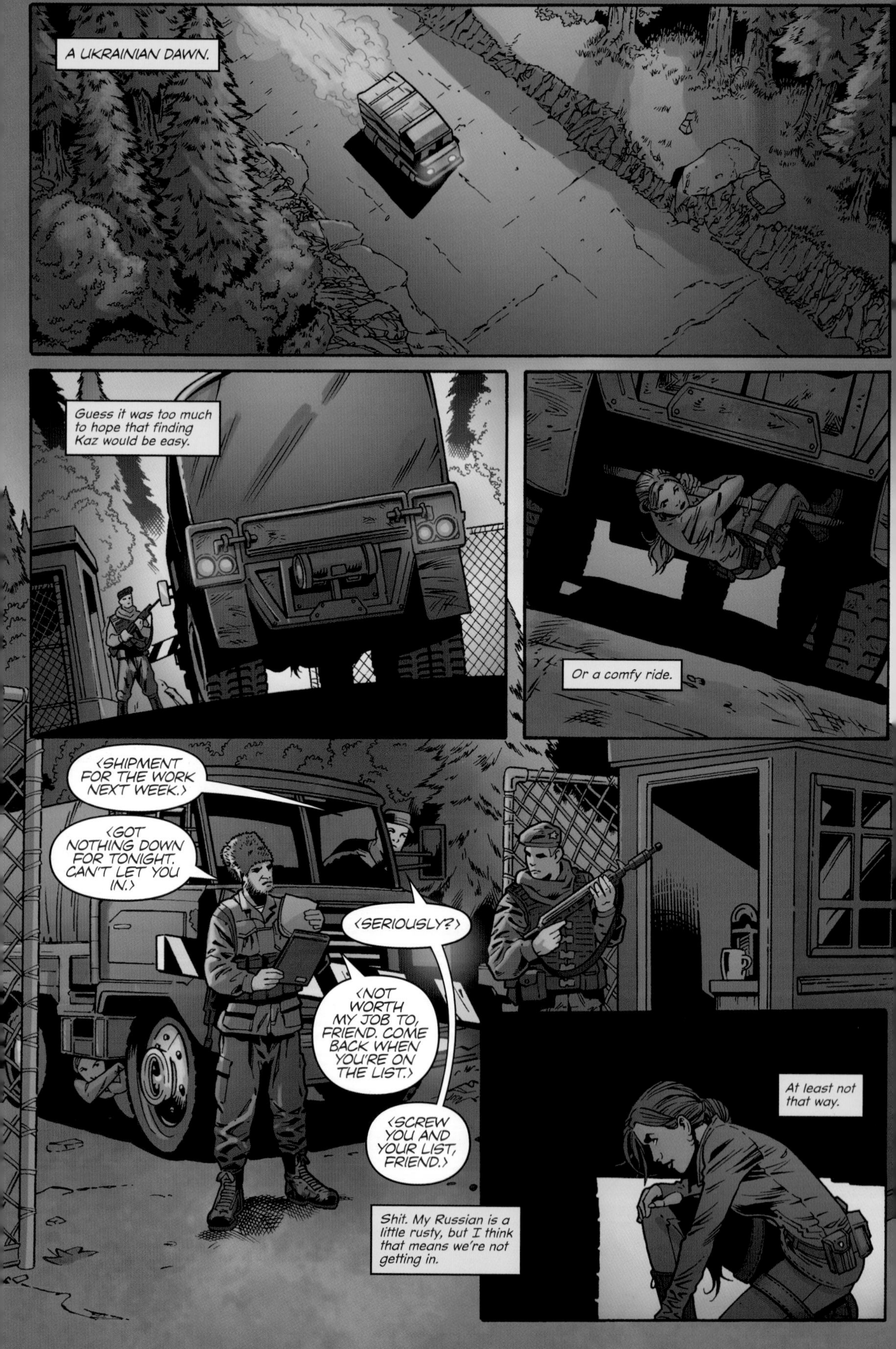
A UKRAINIAN DAWN.
Guess it was too much to hope that finding Kaz would be easy.
Or a comfy ride.
<SHIPMENT FOR THE WORK NEXT WEEK.>
<GOT NOTHING DOWN FOR TONIGHT. CAN'T LET YOU IN.>
<SERIOUSLY?>
<NOT WORTH MY JOB TO, FRIEND. COME BACK WHEN YOU'RE ON THE LIST.>
<SCREW YOU AND YOUR LIST, FRIEND.>
Shit. My Russian is a little rusty, but I think that means we're not getting in.
At least not that way.

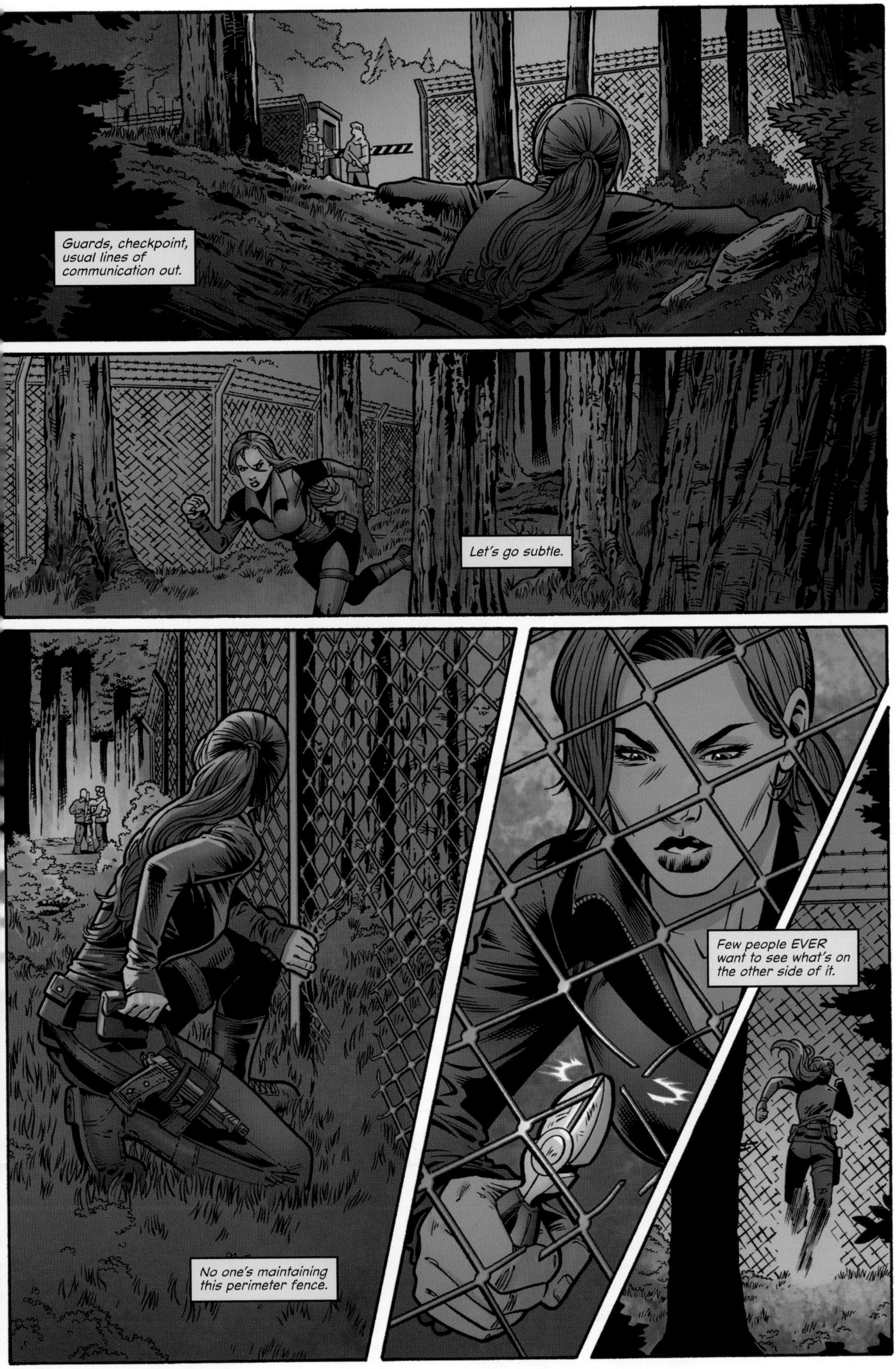
Guards, checkpoint, usual lines of communication out.
Let's go subtle.
No one's maintaining this perimeter fence.
Few people EVER want to see what's on the other side of it.

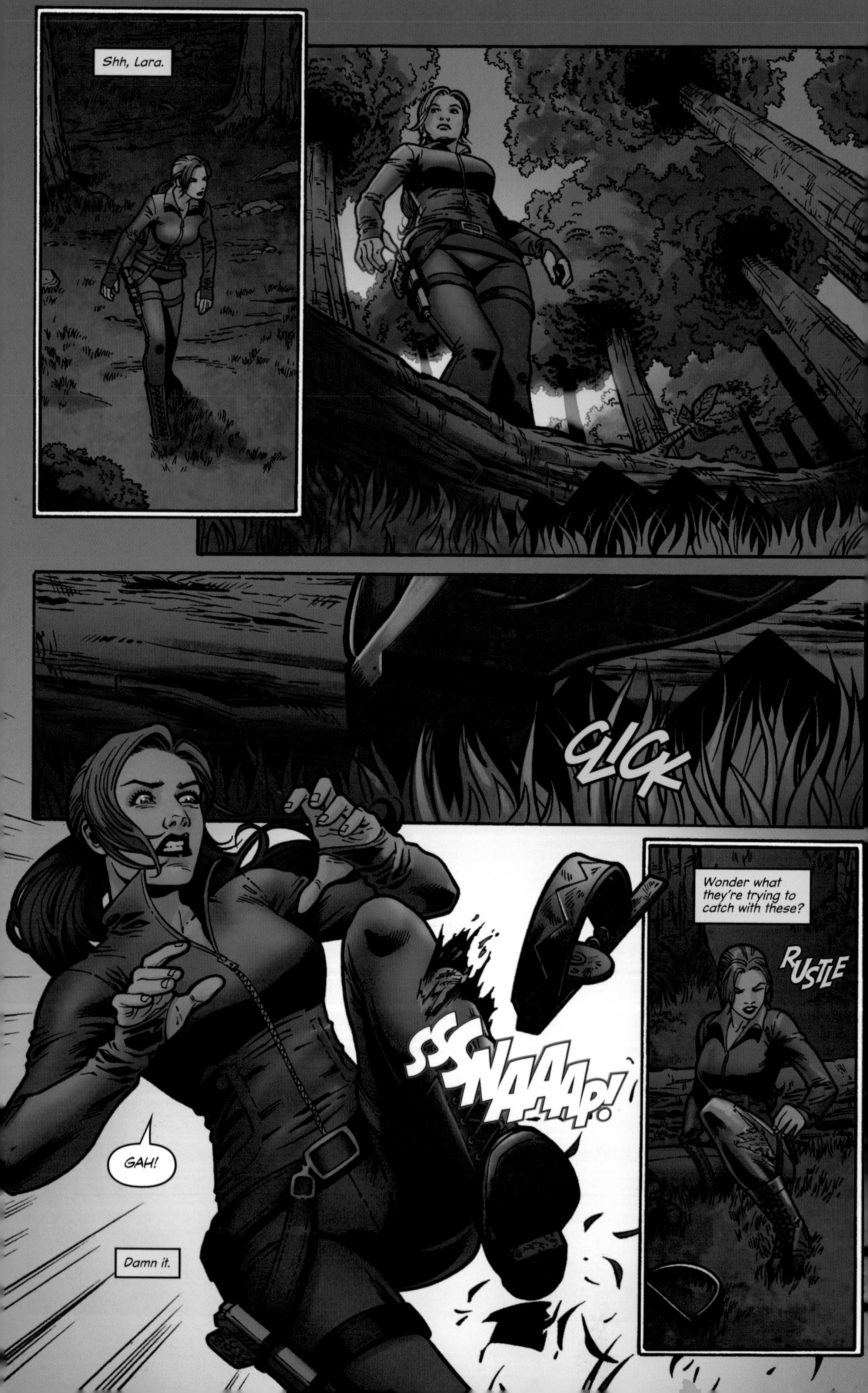
Shh, Lara.
CLICK
GAH!
SSSNAAAAP!
Damn it.
Wonder what they're trying to catch with these?
RUSTLE

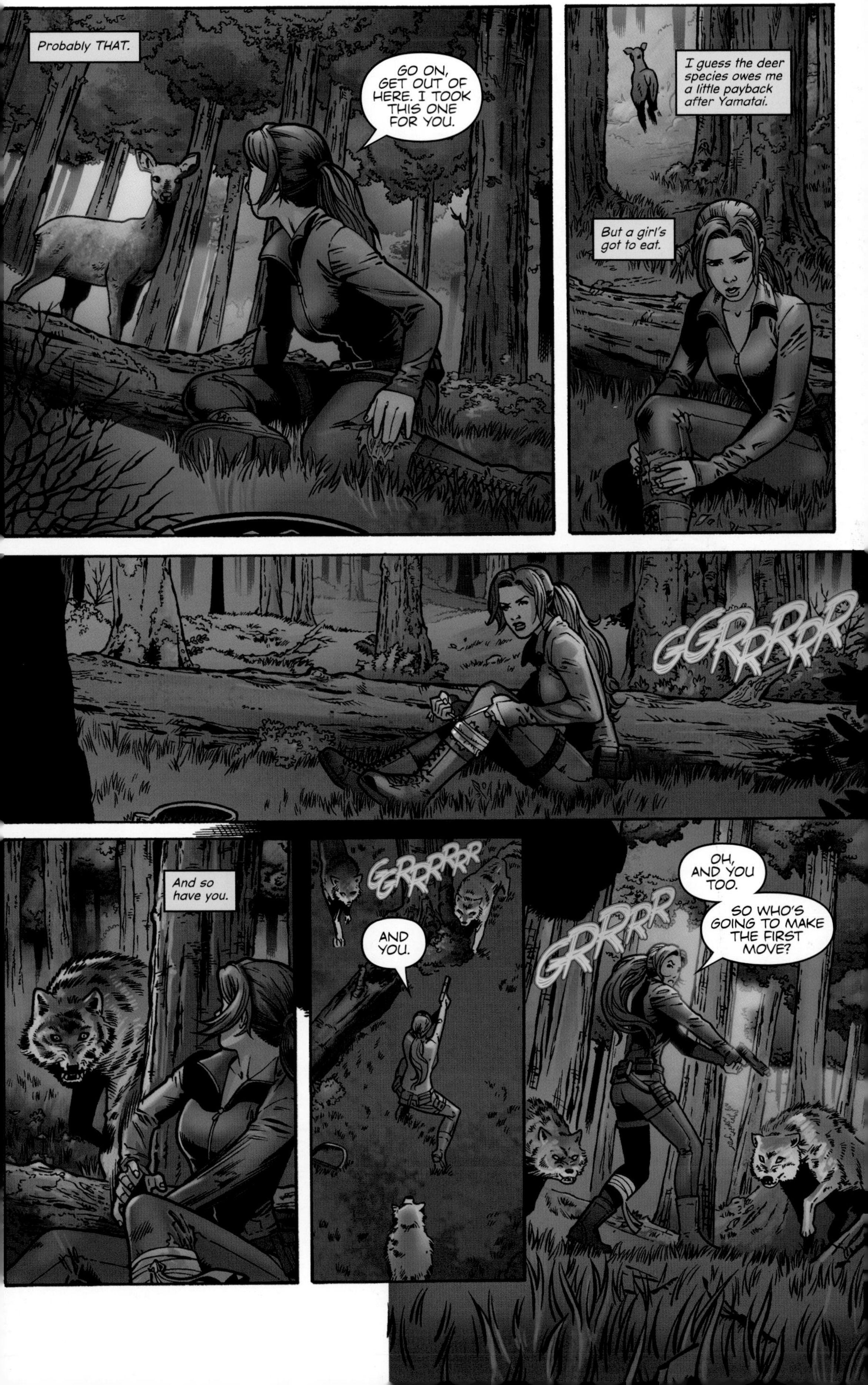

Probably THAT.
GO ON, GET OUT OF HERE. I TOOK THIS ONE FOR YOU.
I guess the deer species owes me a little payback after Yamatai.
But a girl's got to eat.
GGRRRRR
And so have you.
GGRRRRR
AND YOU.
OH, AND YOU TOO.
SO WHO'S GOING TO MAKE THE FIRST MOVE?
GRRRR

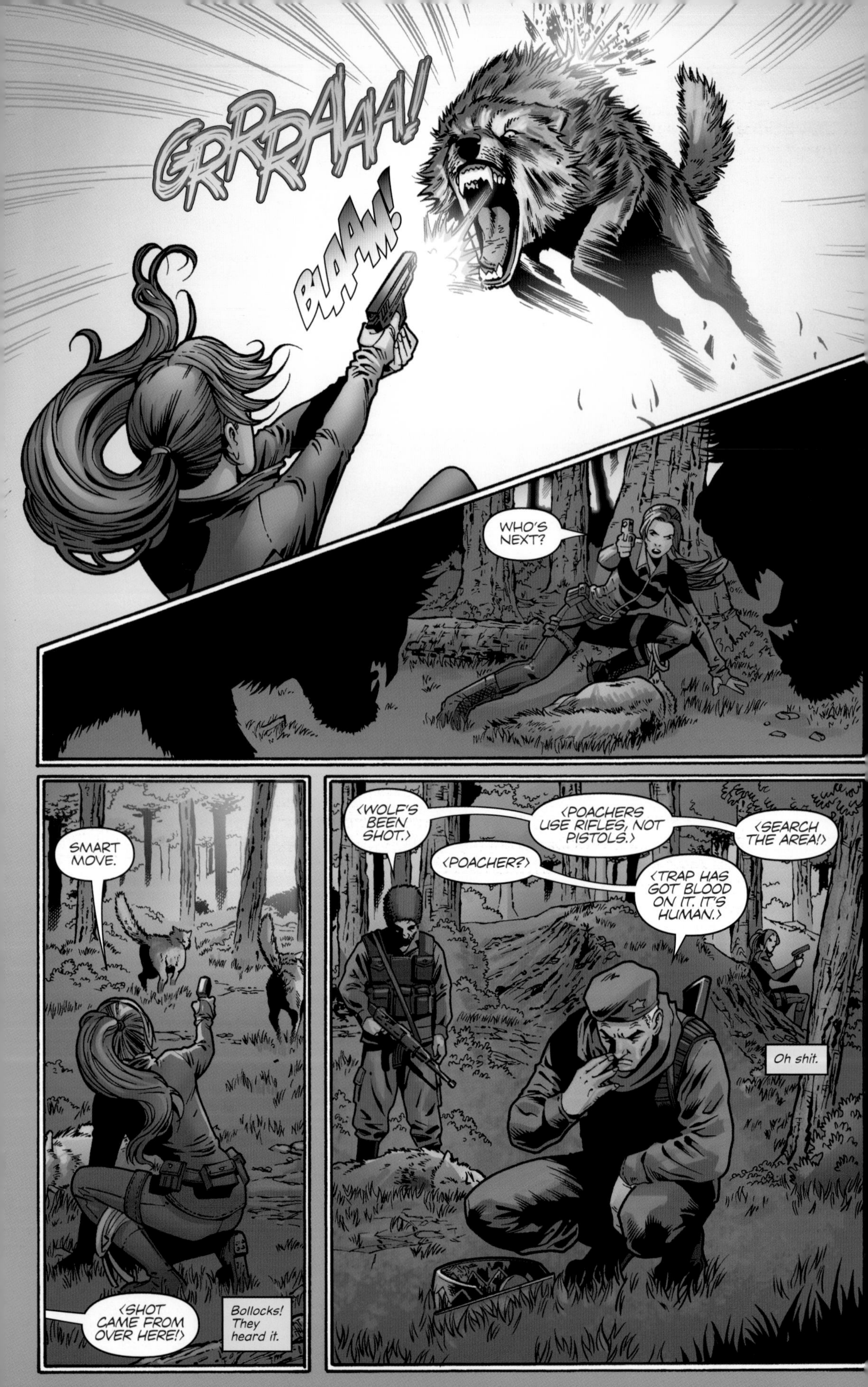
GRRRAAA!
BLAAM!
WHO'S NEXT?
SMART MOVE.
‹SHOT CAME FROM OVER HERE!›
Bollocks! They heard it.
‹WOLF'S BEEN SHOT.›
‹POACHER?›
‹POACHERS USE RIFLES, NOT PISTOLS.›
‹TRAP HAS GOT BLOOD ON IT. IT'S HUMAN.›
‹SEARCH THE AREA!›
Oh shit.

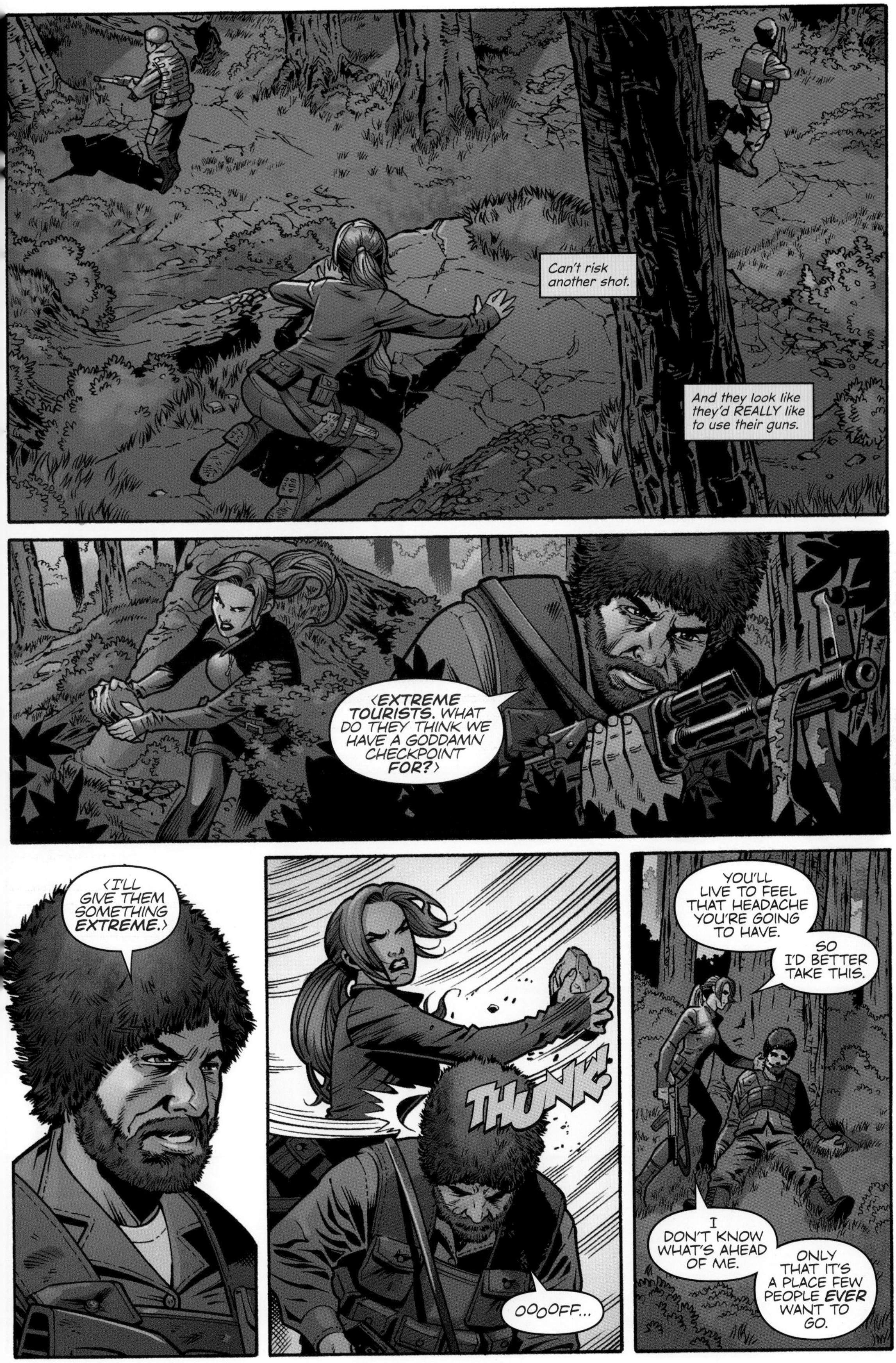
Can't risk another shot.
And they look like they'd REALLY like to use their guns.
‹EXTREME TOURISTS. WHAT DO THEY THINK WE HAVE A GODDAMN CHECKPOINT FOR?›
‹I'LL GIVE THEM SOMETHING EXTREME.›
THUNK!
OOOOFF...
YOU'LL LIVE TO FEEL THAT HEADACHE YOU'RE GOING TO HAVE.
SO I'D BETTER TAKE THIS.
I DON'T KNOW WHAT'S AHEAD OF ME.
ONLY THAT IT'S A PLACE FEW PEOPLE EVER WANT TO GO.

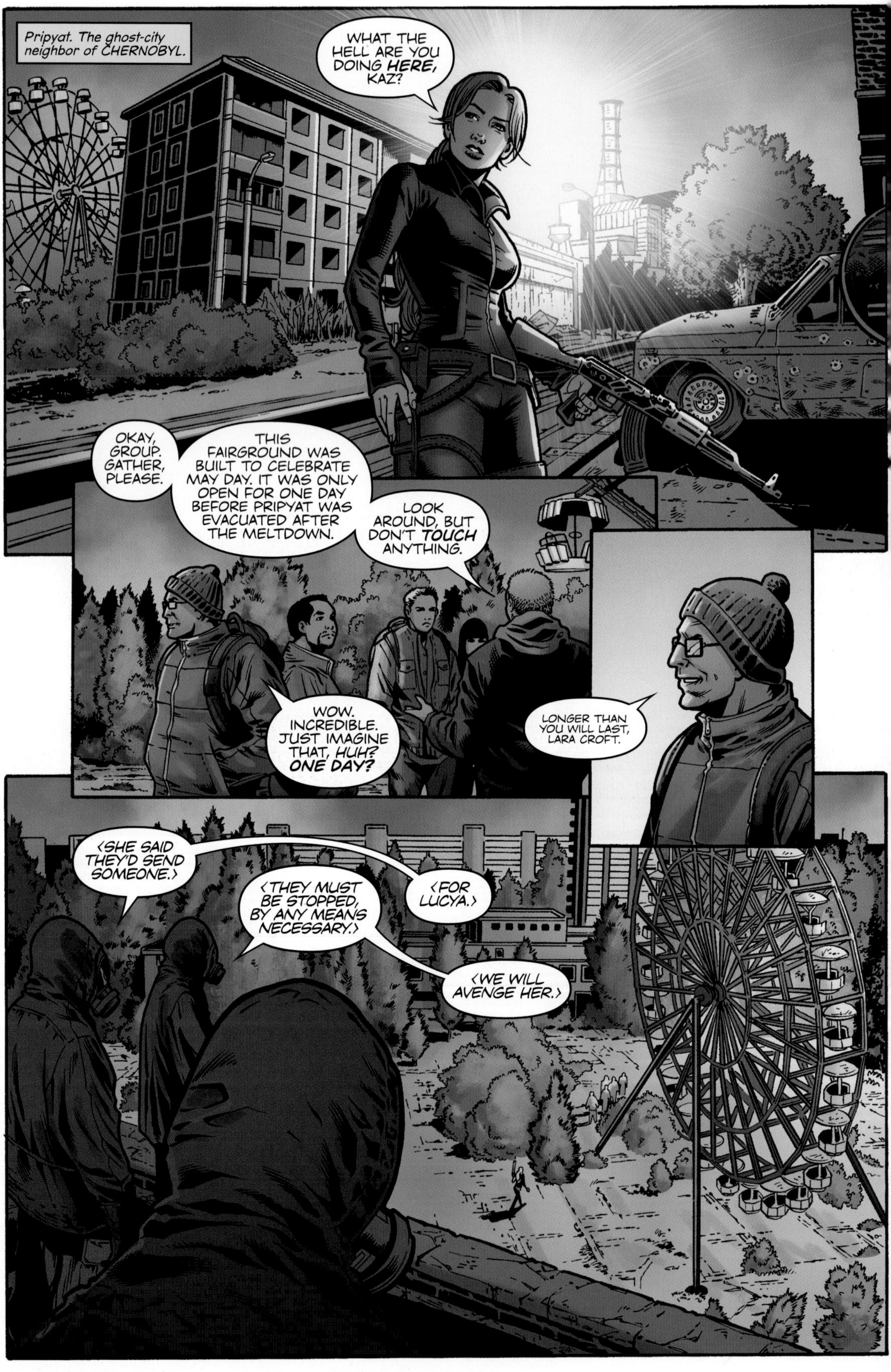
Pripyat. The ghost-city neighbor of CHERNOBYL.
WHAT THE HELL ARE YOU DOING HERE, KAZ?
OKAY, GROUP. GATHER, PLEASE.
THIS FAIRGROUND WAS BUILT TO CELEBRATE MAY DAY. IT WAS ONLY OPEN FOR ONE DAY BEFORE PRIPYAT WAS EVACUATED AFTER THE MELTDOWN.
LOOK AROUND, BUT DON'T TOUCH ANYTHING.
WOW. INCREDIBLE. JUST IMAGINE THAT, HUH? ONE DAY?
LONGER THAN YOU WILL LAST, LARA CROFT.
<SHE SAID THEY'D SEND SOMEONE.>
<THEY MUST BE STOPPED, BY ANY MEANS NECESSARY.>
<FOR LUCYA.>
<WE WILL AVENGE HER.>

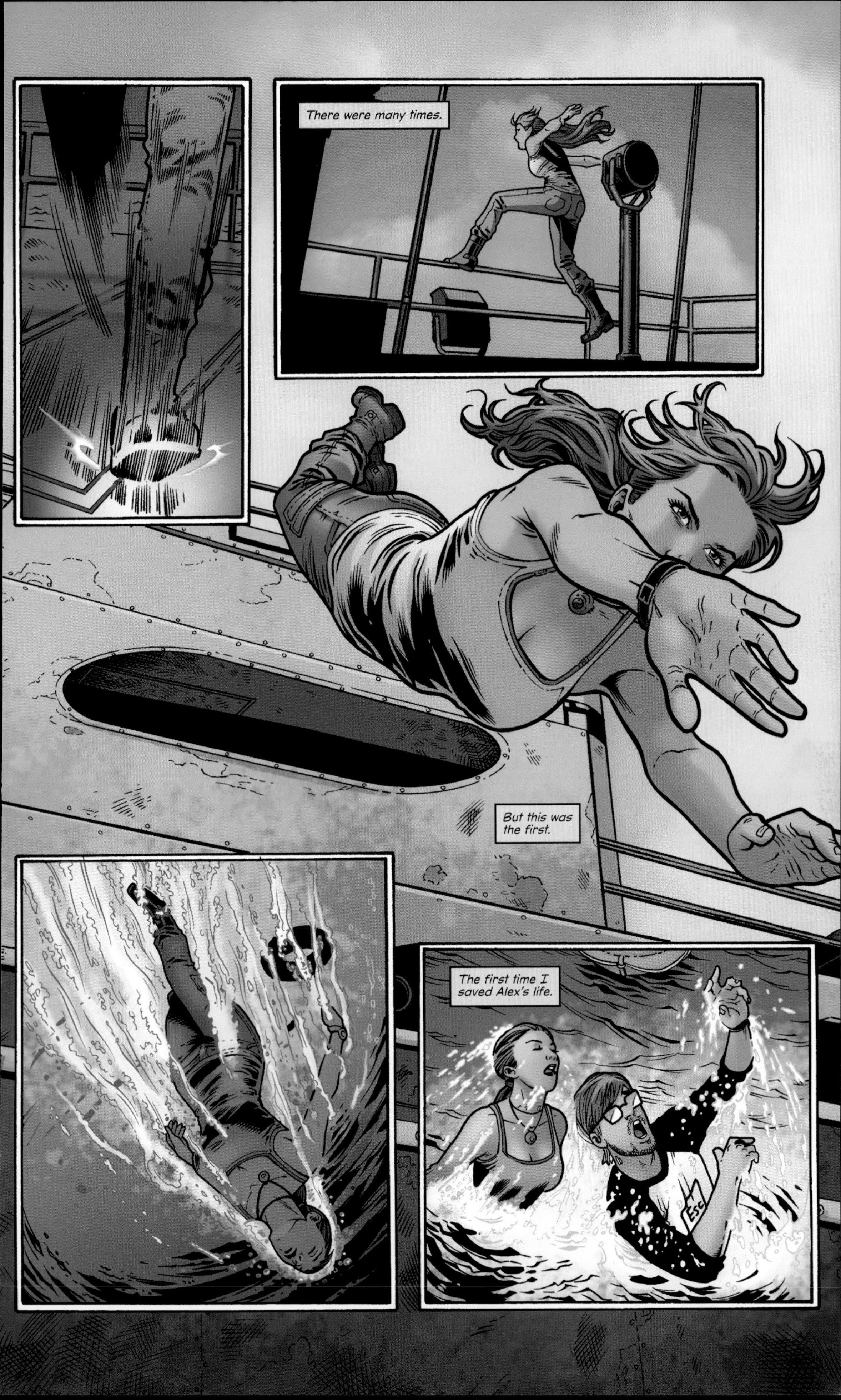
There were many times.
But this was the first.
The first time I saved Alex's life.
Esc

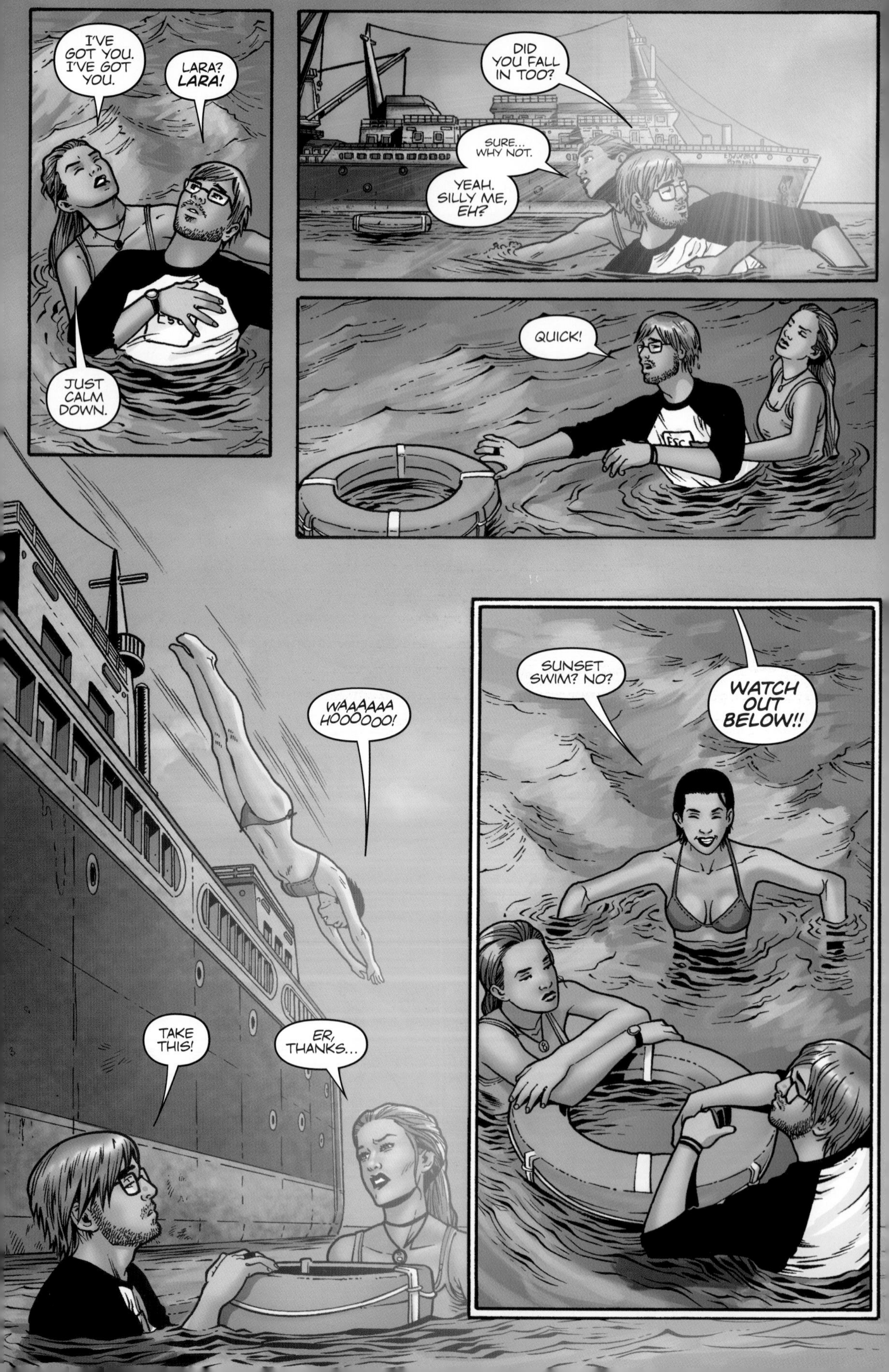
I'VE GOT YOU. I'VE GOT YOU.
LARA? LARA!
JUST CALM DOWN.
DID YOU FALL IN TOO?
SURE... WHY NOT.
YEAH. SILLY ME, EH?
QUICK!
WAAAAAA HOOOOOO!
TAKE THIS!
ER, THANKS...
SUNSET SWIM? NO?
WATCH OUT BELOW!!

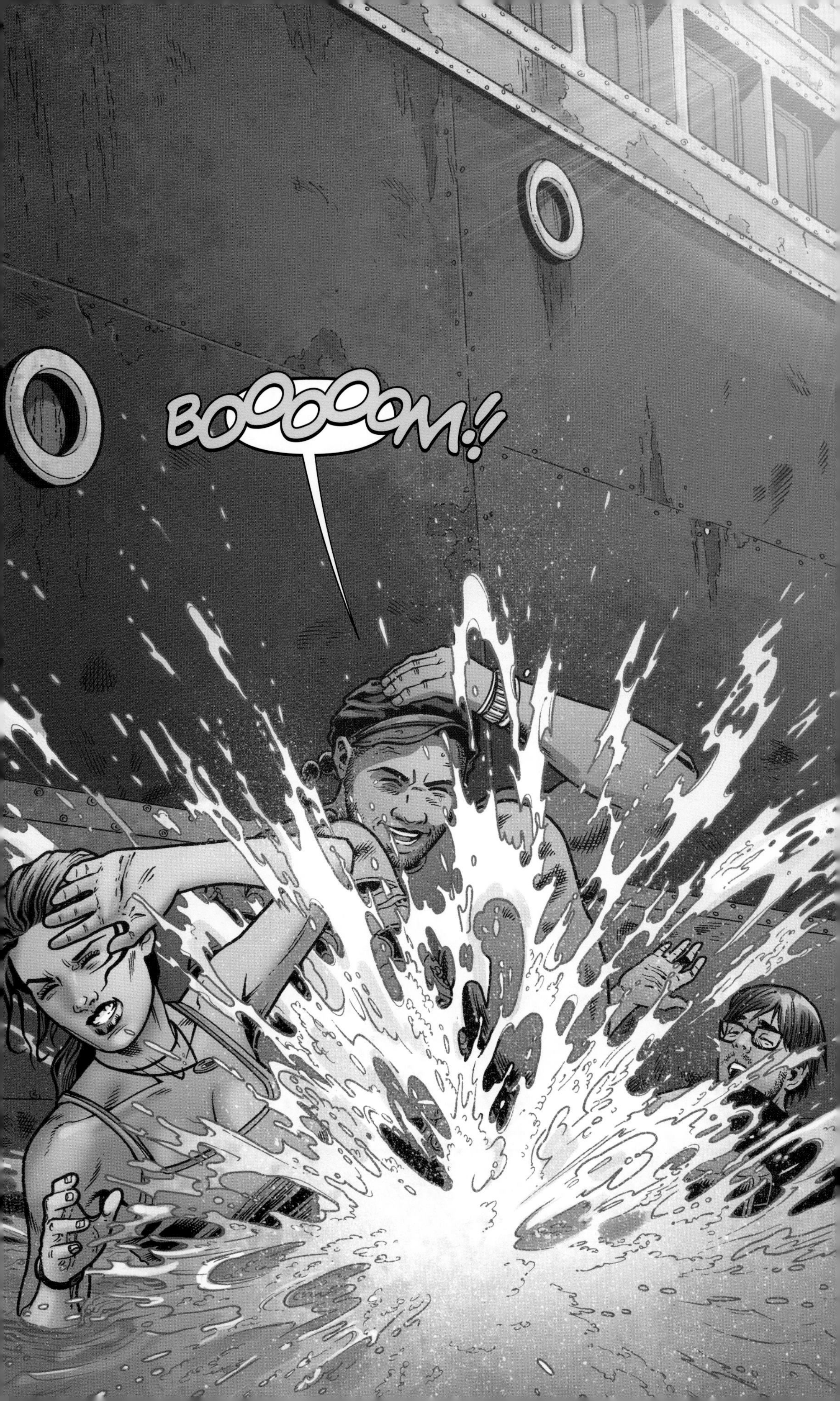
BOOOOOOM!!

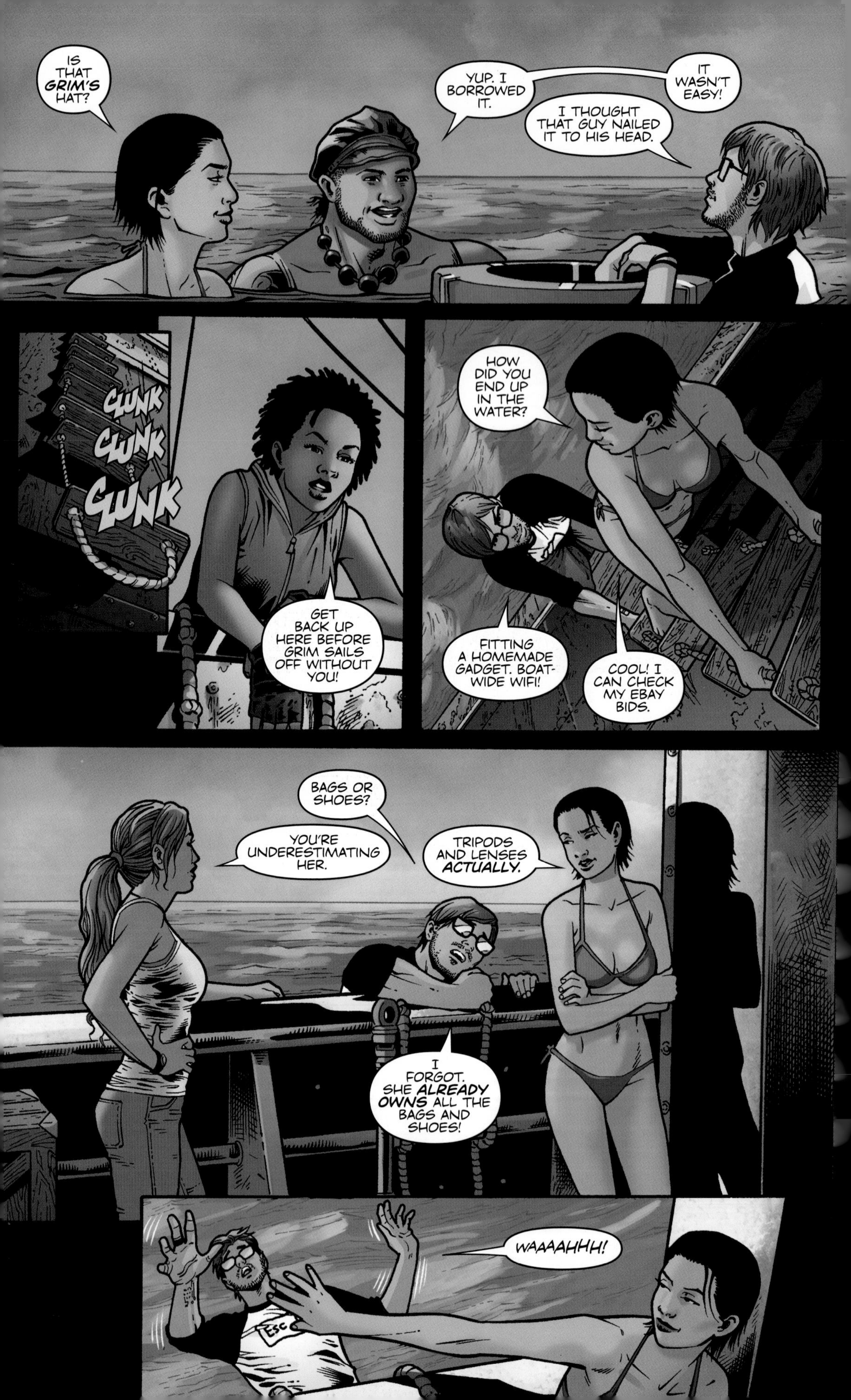
IS THAT GRIM'S HAT?
YUP. I BORROWED IT.
IT WASN'T EASY!
I THOUGHT THAT GUY NAILED IT TO HIS HEAD.
CLUNK
CLUNK
CLUNK
GET BACK UP HERE BEFORE GRIM SAILS OFF WITHOUT YOU!
HOW DID YOU END UP IN THE WATER?
FITTING A HOMEMADE GADGET. BOAT-WIDE WIFI!
COOL! I CAN CHECK MY EBAY BIDS.
BAGS OR SHOES?
YOU'RE UNDERESTIMATING HER.
TRIPODS AND LENSES ACTUALLY.
I FORGOT. SHE ALREADY OWNS ALL THE BAGS AND SHOES!
WAAAAHHH!

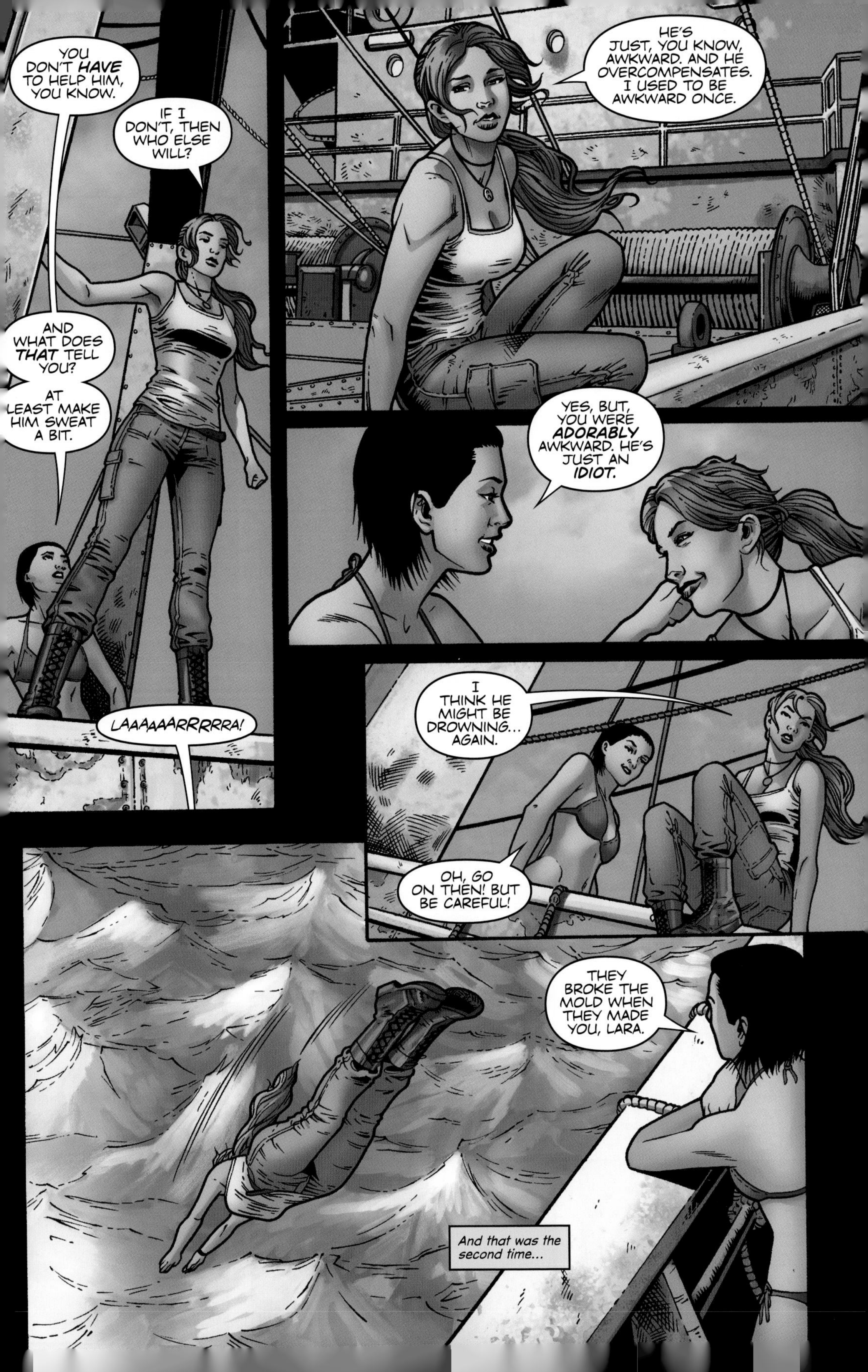

YOU DON'T HAVE TO HELP HIM, YOU KNOW.
IF I DON'T, THEN WHO ELSE WILL?
AND WHAT DOES THAT TELL YOU?
AT LEAST MAKE HIM SWEAT A BIT.
LAAAAAARRRRRA!
HE'S JUST, YOU KNOW, AWKWARD. AND HE OVERCOMPENSATES. I USED TO BE AWKWARD ONCE.
YES, BUT, YOU WERE ADORABLY AWKWARD. HE'S JUST AN IDIOT.
I THINK HE MIGHT BE DROWNING... AGAIN.
OH, GO ON THEN! BUT BE CAREFUL!
THEY BROKE THE MOLD WHEN THEY MADE YOU, LARA.
And that was the second time...

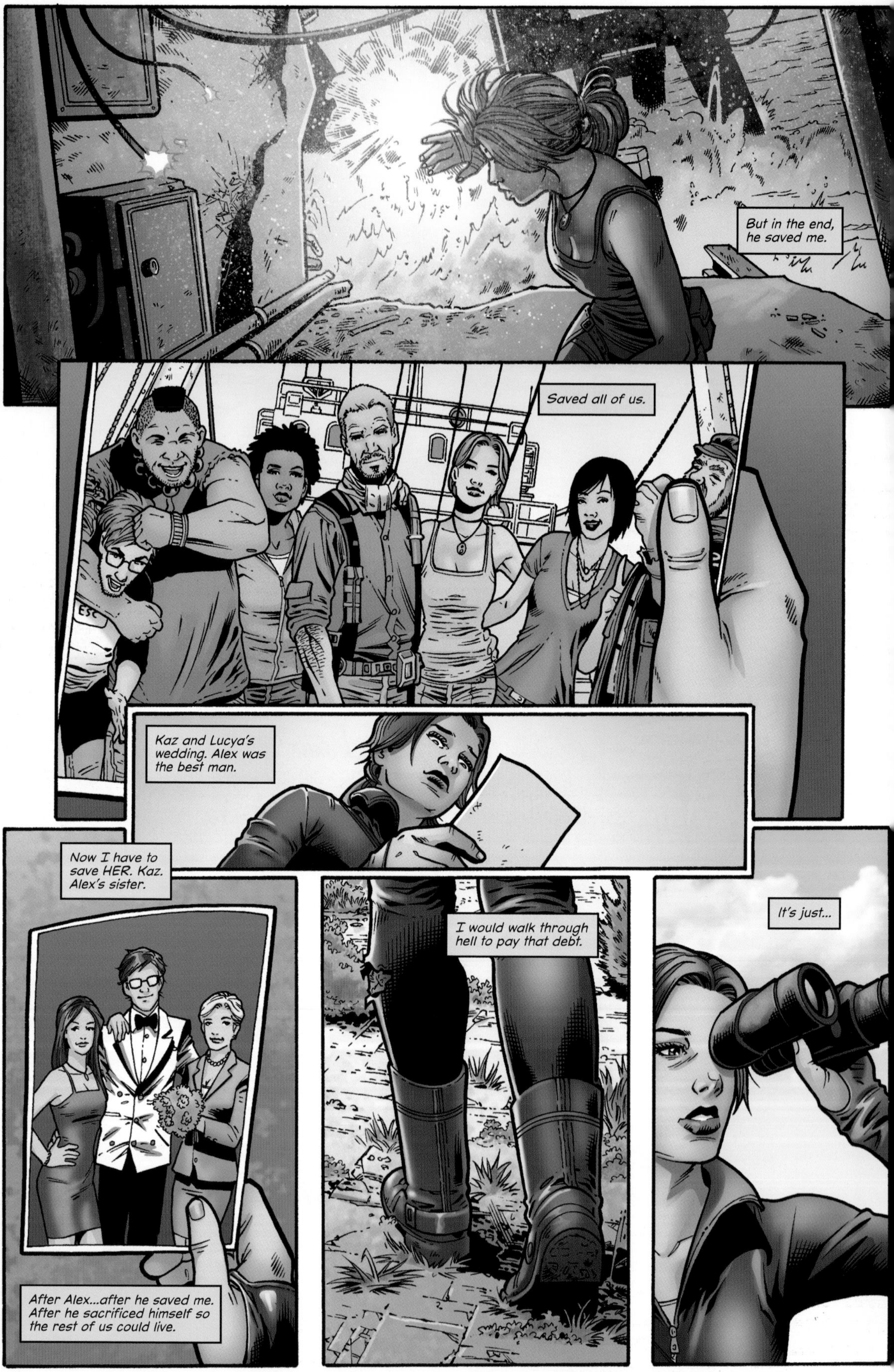

But in the end, he saved me.
Saved all of us.
Kaz and Lucya's wedding. Alex was the best man.
Now I have to save HER. Kaz. Alex's sister.
After Alex...after he saved me. After he sacrificed himself so the rest of us could live.
I would walk through hell to pay that debt.
It's just...

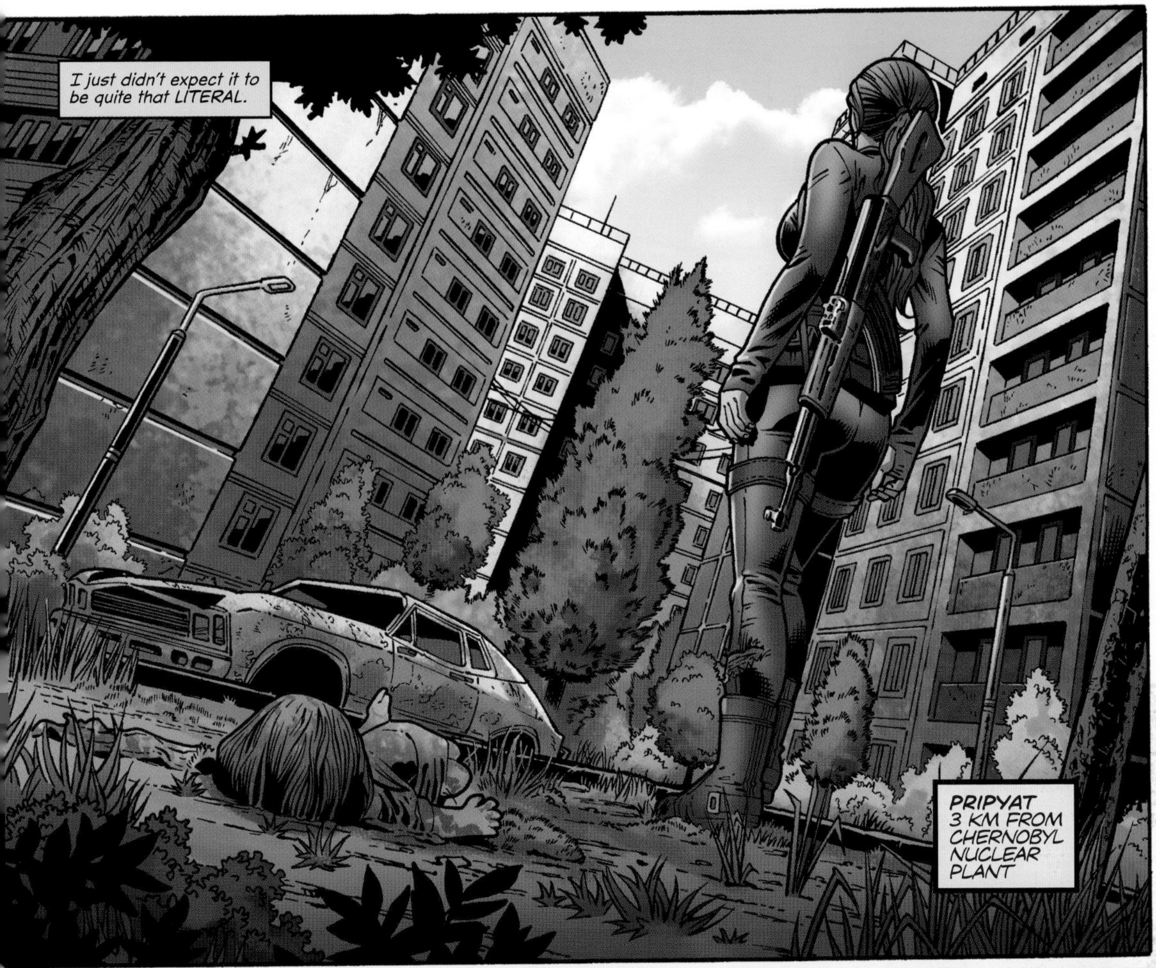
I just didn't expect it to be quite that LITERAL.
PRIPYAT 3 KM FROM CHERNOBYL NUCLEAR PLANT

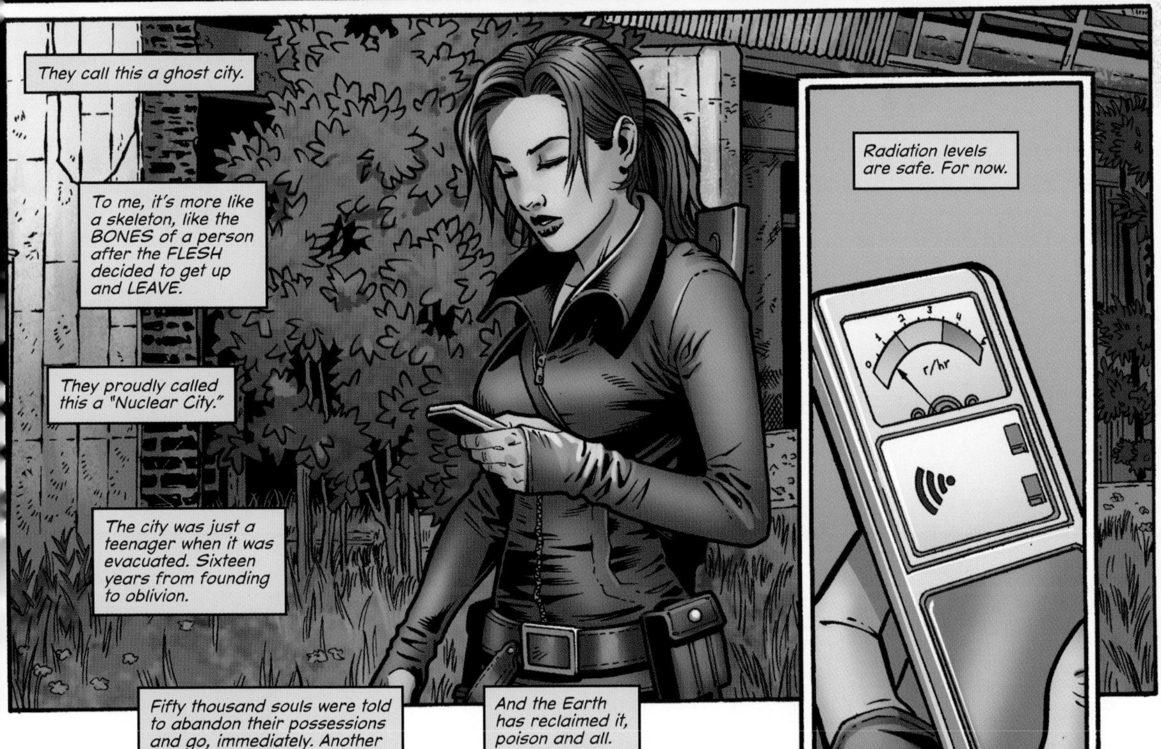
They call this a ghost city.
To me, it's more like a skeleton, like the BONES of a person after the FLESH decided to get up and LEAVE.
They proudly called this a "Nuclear City."
The city was just a teenager when it was evacuated. Sixteen years from founding to oblivion.
Fifty thousand souls were told to abandon their possessions and go, immediately. Another two hundred thousand from the surrounding area.
And the Earth has reclaimed it, poison and all.
Radiation levels are safe. For now.
r/hr

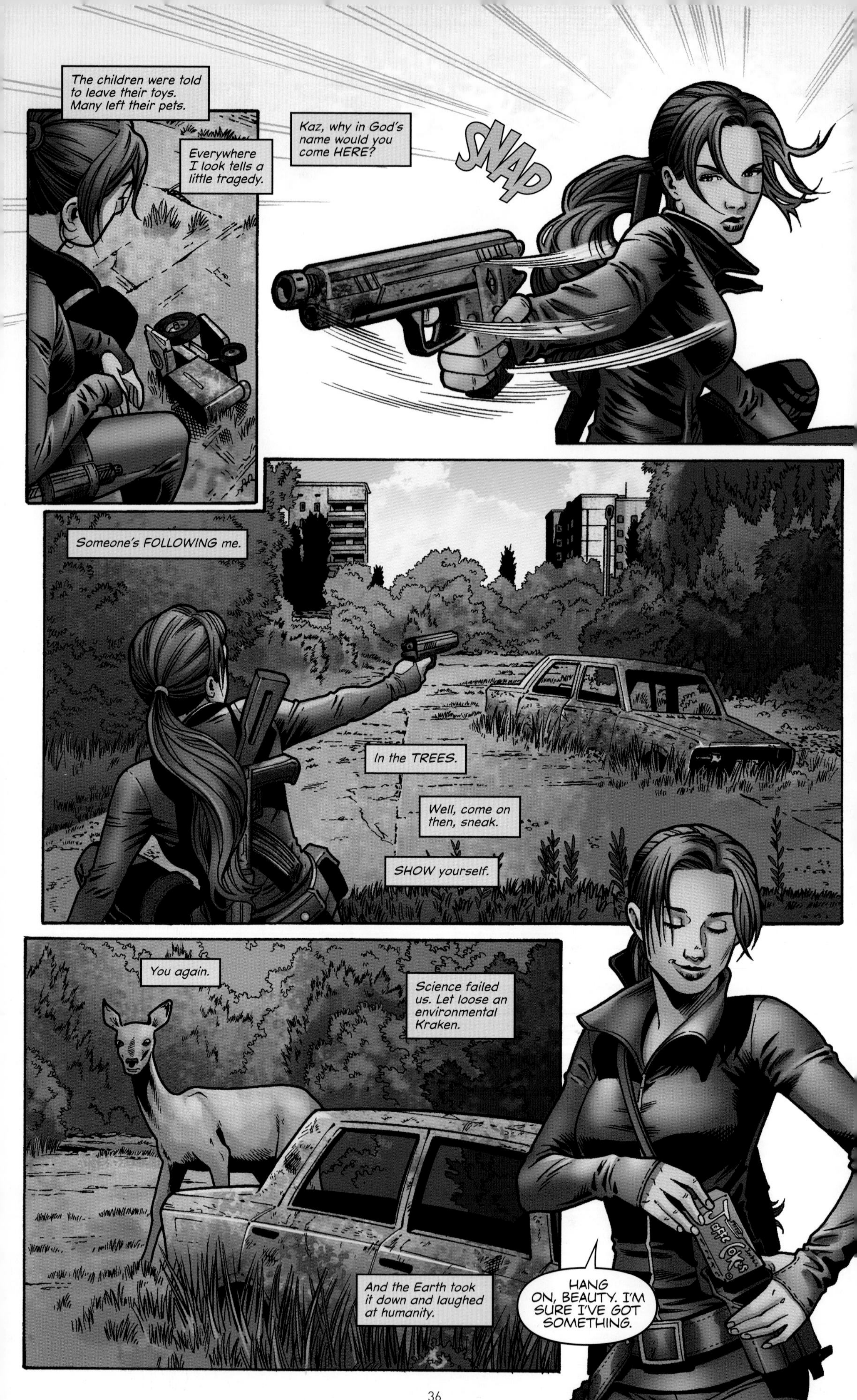
The children were told to leave their toys. Many left their pets.
Everywhere I look tells a little tragedy.
Kaz, why in God's name would you come HERE?
SNAP
Someone's FOLLOWING me.
In the TREES.
Well, come on then, sneak.
SHOW yourself.
You again.
Science failed us. Let loose an environmental Kraken.
And the Earth took it down and laughed at humanity.
HANG ON, BEAUTY. I'M SURE I'VE GOT SOMETHING.

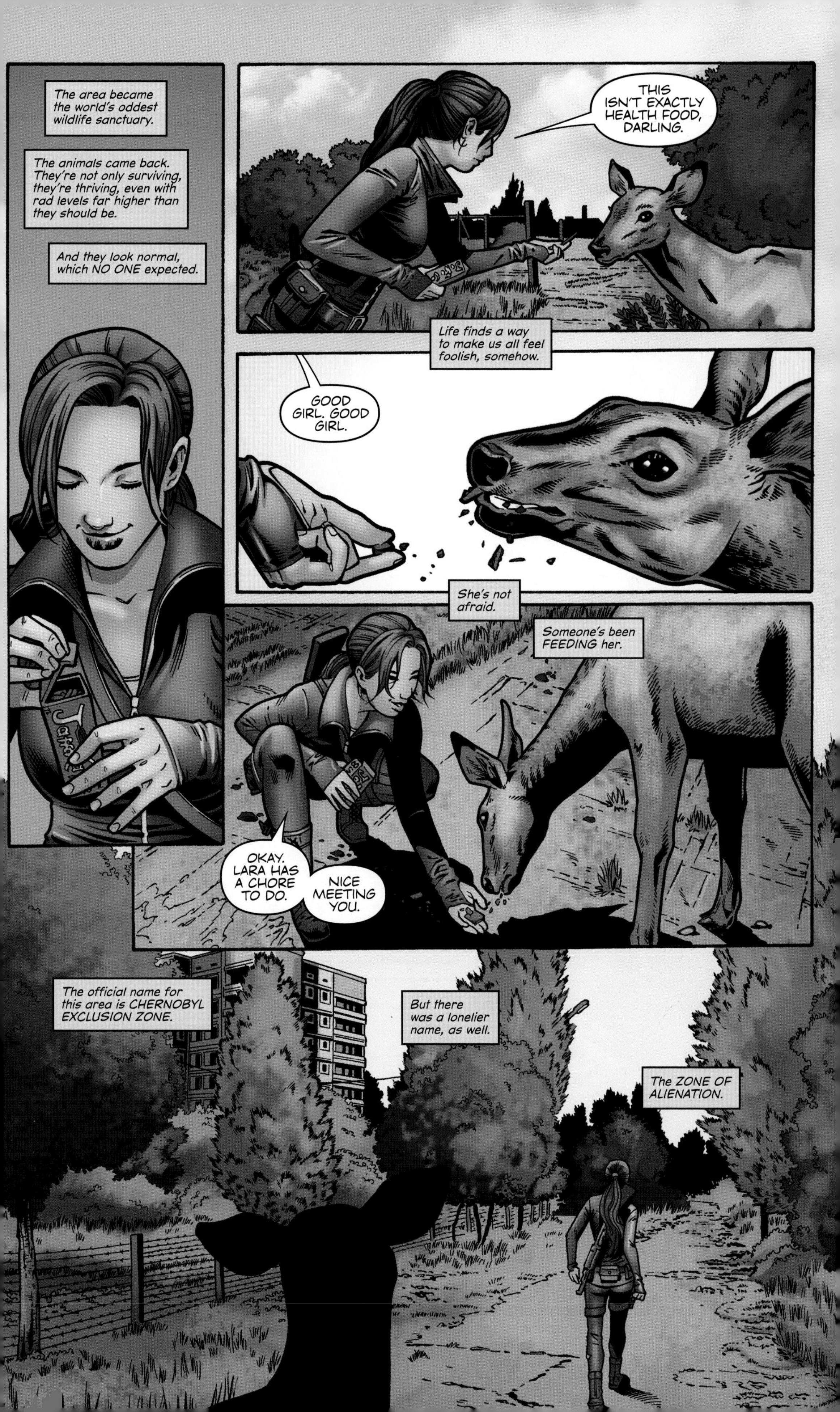
The area became the world's oddest wildlife sanctuary.
The animals came back. They're not only surviving, they're thriving, even with rad levels far higher than they should be.
And they look normal, which NO ONE expected.
THIS ISN'T EXACTLY HEALTH FOOD, DARLING.
Life finds a way to make us all feel foolish, somehow.
GOOD GIRL. GOOD GIRL.
She's not afraid.
Someone's been FEEDING her.
OKAY. LARA HAS A CHORE TO DO.
NICE MEETING YOU.
The official name for this area is CHERNOBYL EXCLUSION ZONE.
But there was a lonelier name, as well.
The ZONE OF ALIENATION.

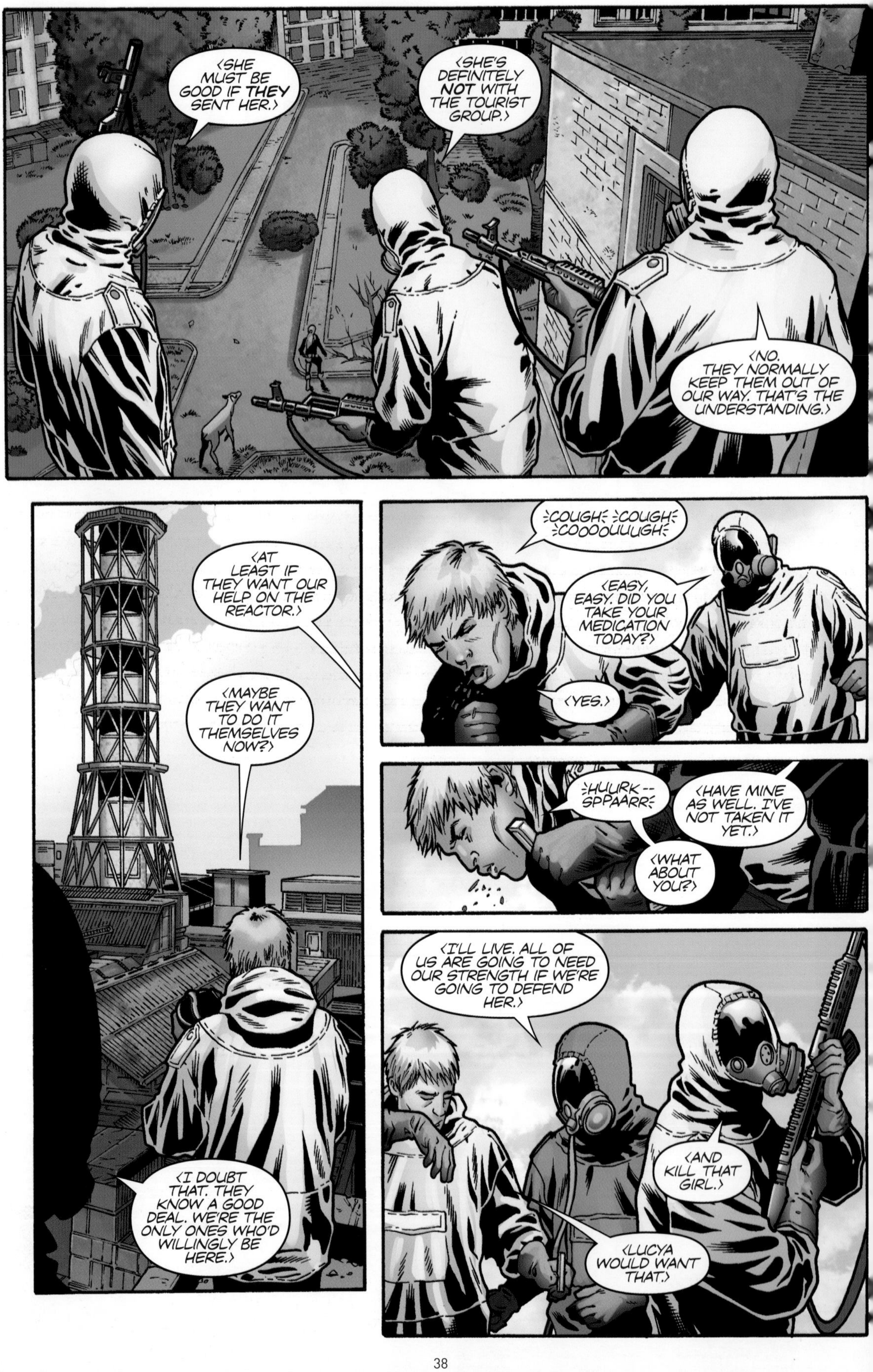

‹SHE MUST BE GOOD IF THEY SENT HER.›
‹SHE'S DEFINITELY NOT WITH THE TOURIST GROUP.›
‹NO. THEY NORMALLY KEEP THEM OUT OF OUR WAY. THAT'S THE UNDERSTANDING.›
‹AT LEAST IF THEY WANT OUR HELP ON THE REACTOR.›
‹MAYBE THEY WANT TO DO IT THEMSELVES NOW?›
‹I DOUBT THAT. THEY KNOW A GOOD DEAL. WE'RE THE ONLY ONES WHO'D WILLINGLY BE HERE.›
COUGH COUGH COOOOUUUGH
‹EASY, EASY. DID YOU TAKE YOUR MEDICATION TODAY?›
‹YES.›
HUURK-- SPPAARR
‹HAVE MINE AS WELL. I'VE NOT TAKEN IT YET.›
‹WHAT ABOUT YOU?›
‹I'LL LIVE. ALL OF US ARE GOING TO NEED OUR STRENGTH IF WE'RE GOING TO DEFEND HER.›
‹AND KILL THAT GIRL.›
‹LUCYA WOULD WANT THAT.›

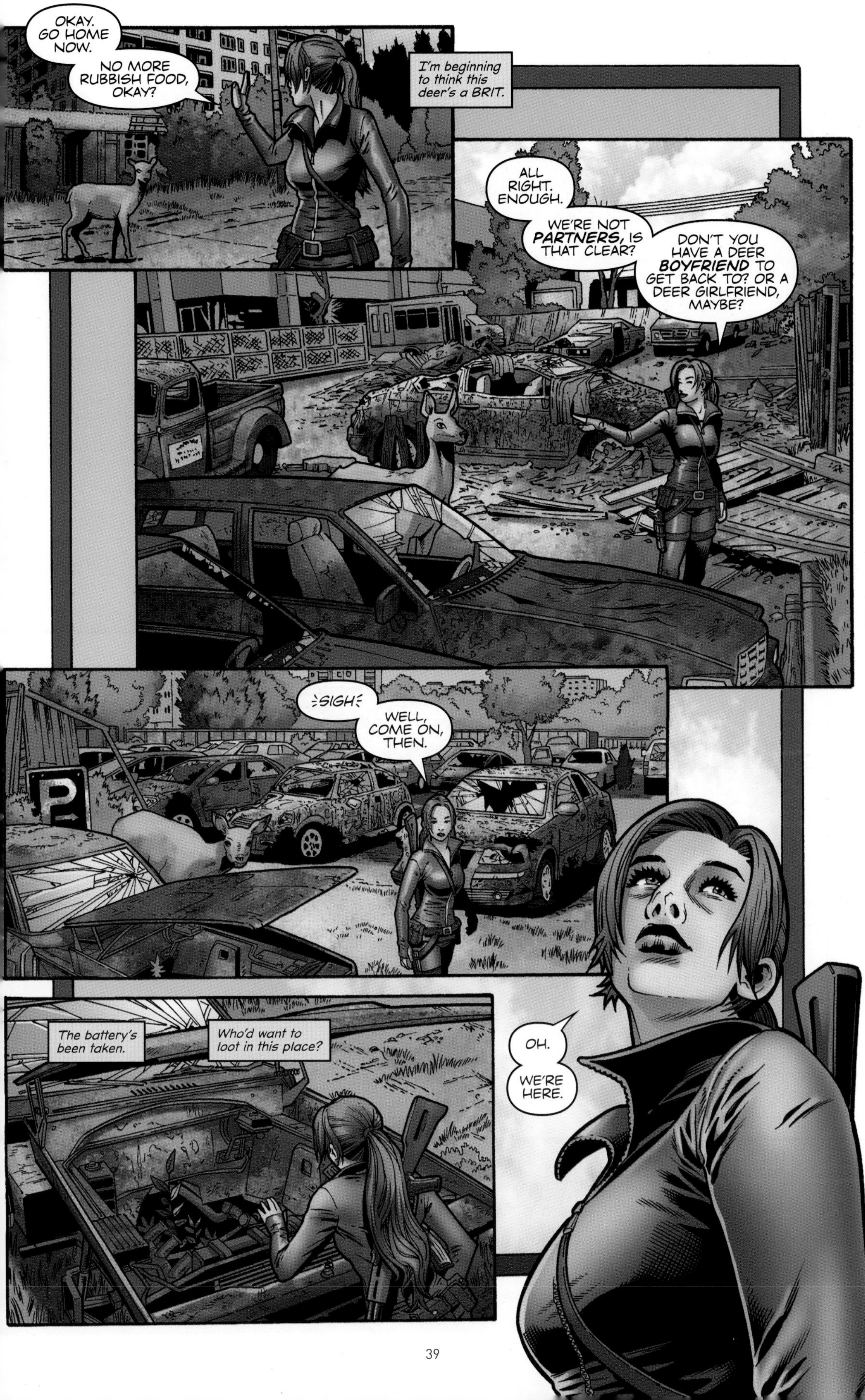

OKAY. GO HOME NOW.
NO MORE RUBBISH FOOD, OKAY?
I'm beginning to think this deer's a BRIT.
ALL RIGHT. ENOUGH.
WE'RE NOT PARTNERS, IS THAT CLEAR?
DON'T YOU HAVE A DEER BOYFRIEND TO GET BACK TO? OR A DEER GIRLFRIEND, MAYBE?
SIGH
WELL, COME ON, THEN.
The battery's been taken.
Who'd want to loot in this place?
OH.
WE'RE HERE.

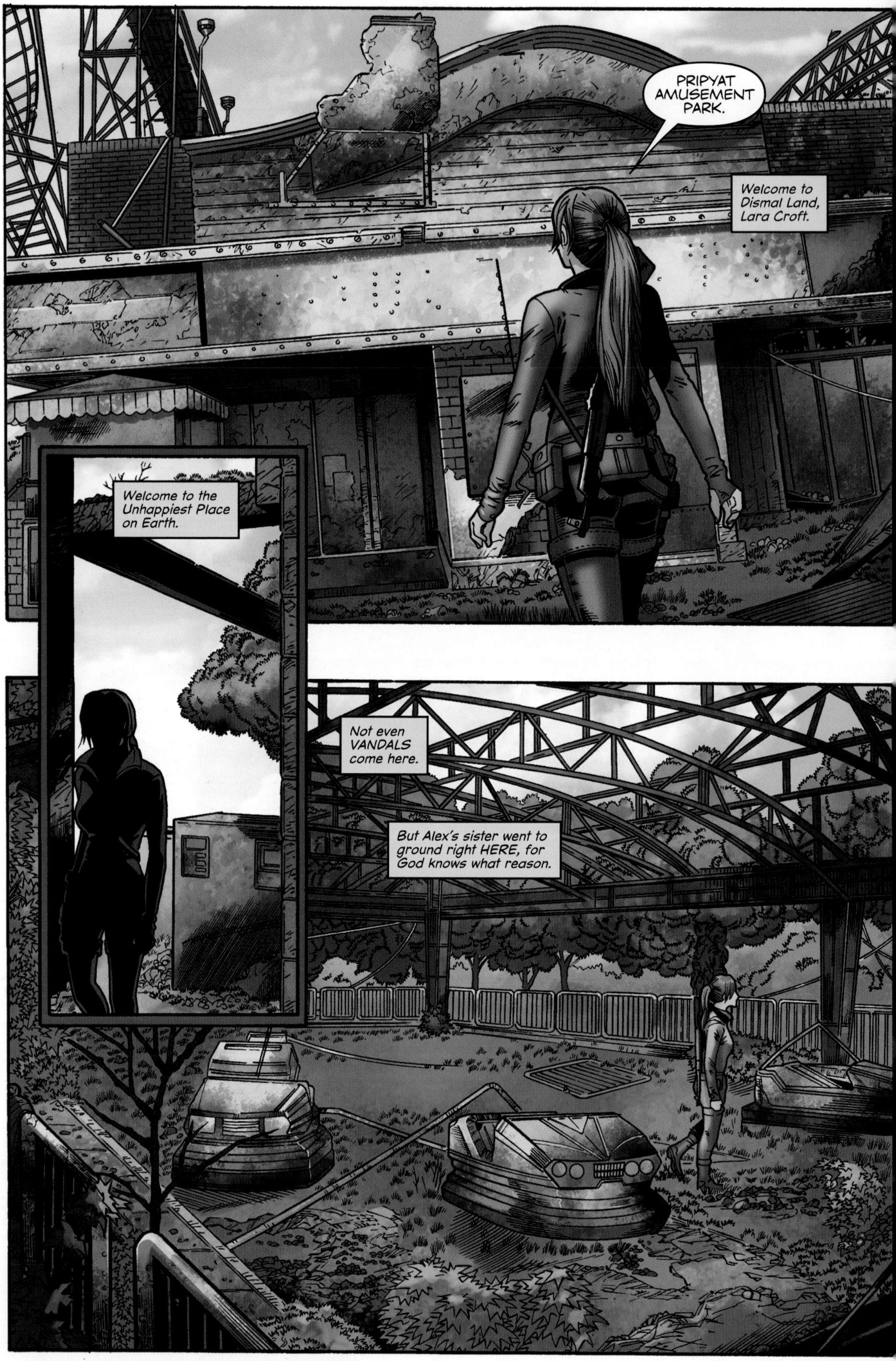
PRIPYAT AMUSEMENT PARK.
Welcome to Dismal Land, Lara Croft.
Welcome to the Unhappiest Place on Earth.
Not even VANDALS come here.
But Alex's sister went to ground right HERE, for God knows what reason.

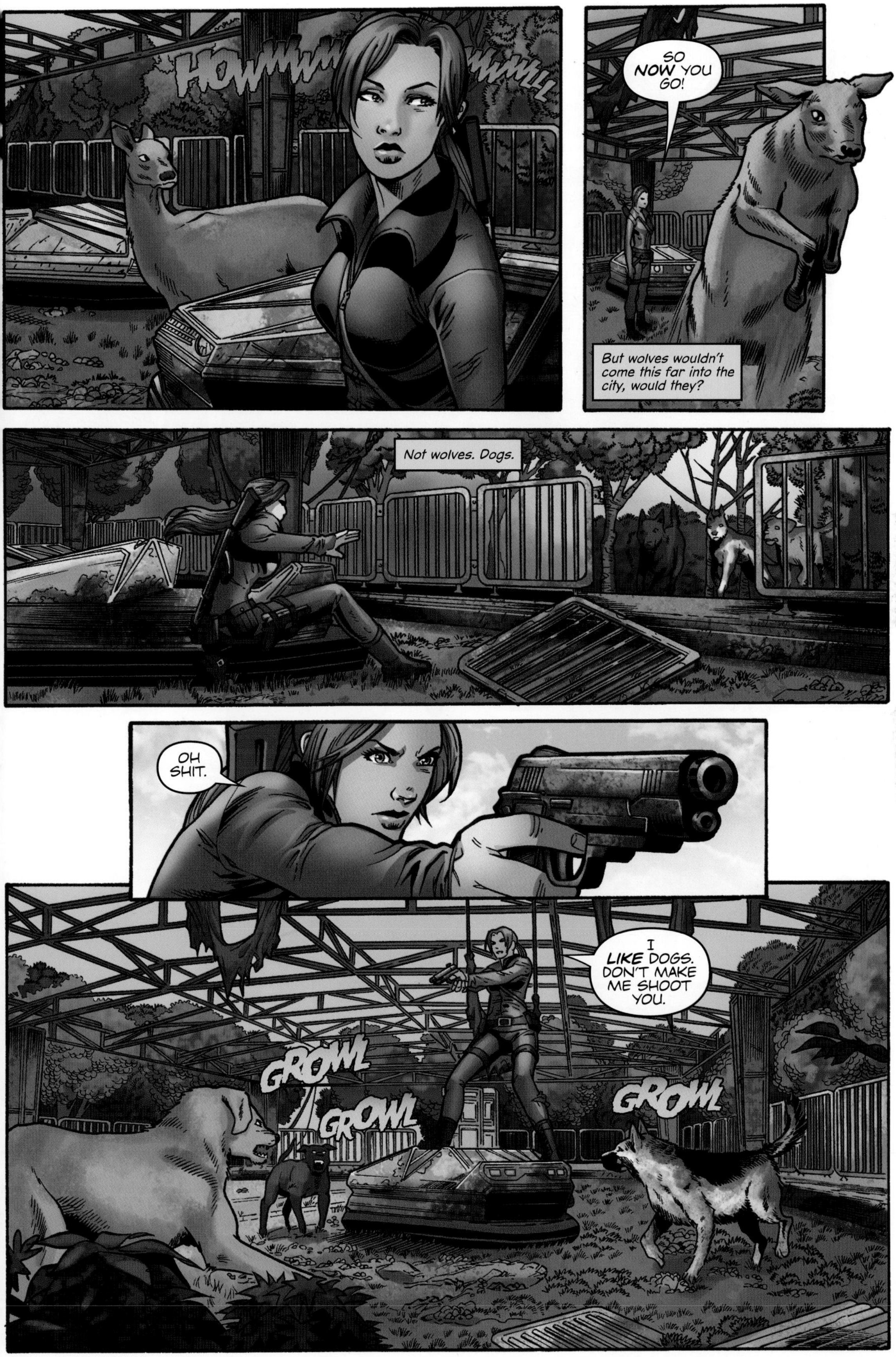
HOWWWWWWWWWLLL
SO NOW YOU GO!
But wolves wouldn't come this far into the city, would they?
Not wolves. Dogs.
OH SHIT.
I LIKE DOGS. DON'T MAKE ME SHOOT YOU.
GROWL
GROWL
GROWL

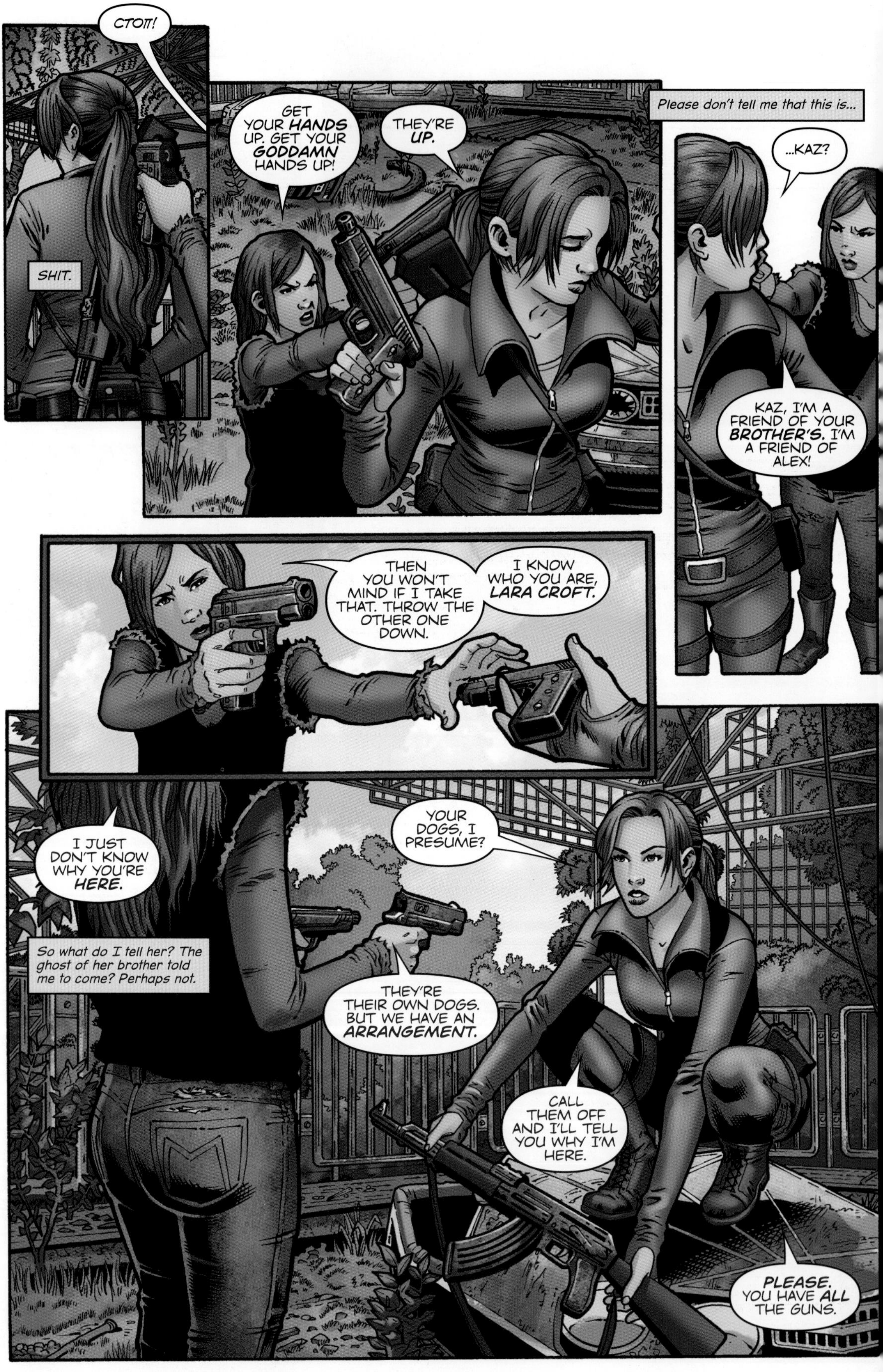

СТОП!
SHIT.
GET YOUR HANDS UP. GET YOUR GODDAMN HANDS UP!
THEY'RE UP.
Please don't tell me that this is...
...KAZ?
KAZ, I'M A FRIEND OF YOUR BROTHER'S. I'M A FRIEND OF ALEX!
I KNOW WHO YOU ARE, LARA CROFT.
THEN YOU WON'T MIND IF I TAKE THAT. THROW THE OTHER ONE DOWN.
I JUST DON'T KNOW WHY YOU'RE HERE.
So what do I tell her? The ghost of her brother told me to come? Perhaps not.
YOUR DOGS, I PRESUME?
THEY'RE THEIR OWN DOGS. BUT WE HAVE AN ARRANGEMENT.
CALL THEM OFF AND I'LL TELL YOU WHY I'M HERE.
PLEASE. YOU HAVE ALL THE GUNS.

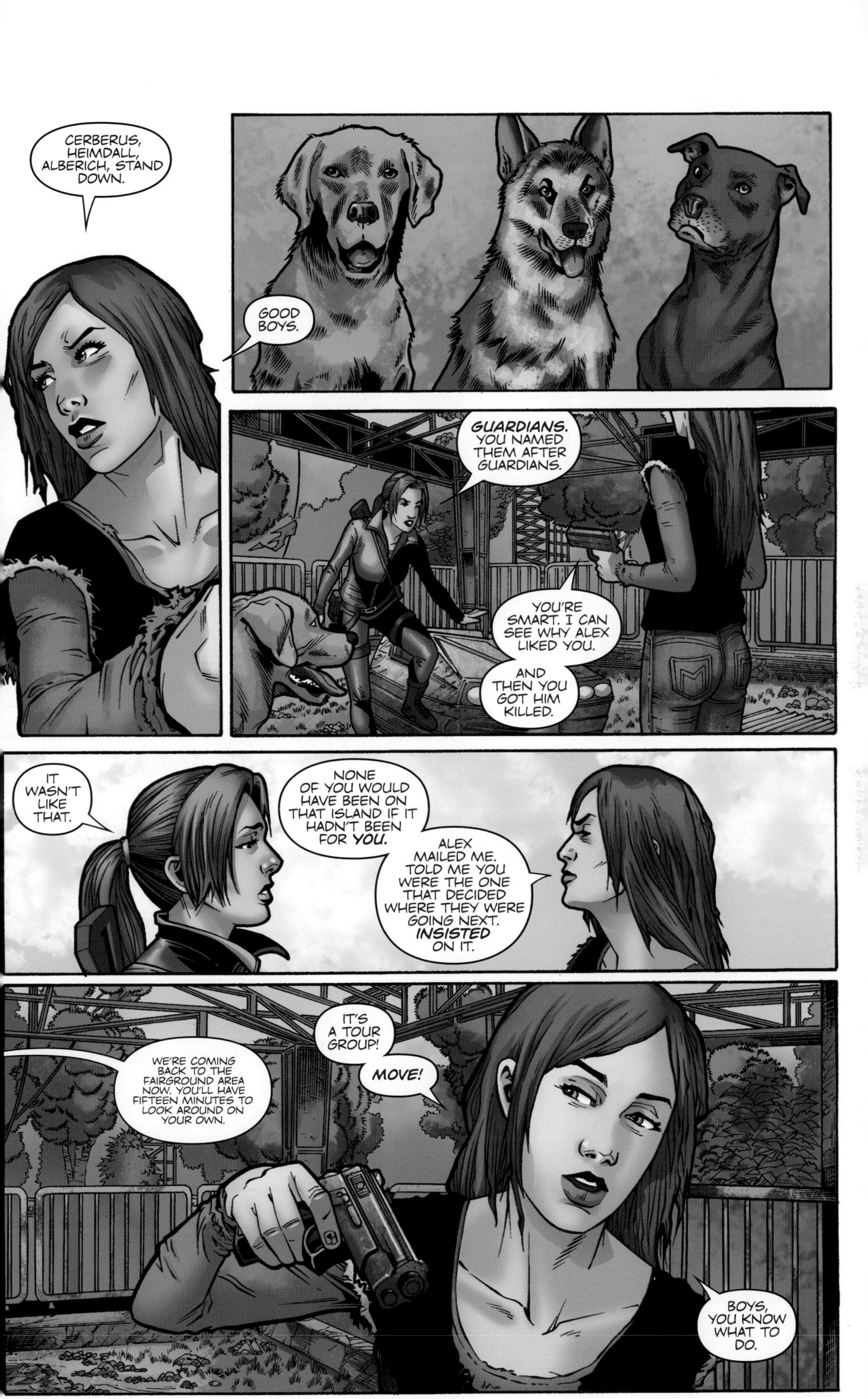

CERBERUS, HEIMDALL, ALBERICH, STAND DOWN.
GOOD BOYS.
GUARDIANS. YOU NAMED THEM AFTER GUARDIANS.
YOU'RE SMART. I CAN SEE WHY ALEX LIKED YOU.
AND THEN YOU GOT HIM KILLED.
IT WASN'T LIKE THAT.
NONE OF YOU WOULD HAVE BEEN ON THAT ISLAND IF IT HADN'T BEEN FOR YOU.
ALEX MAILED ME. TOLD ME YOU WERE THE ONE THAT DECIDED WHERE THEY WERE GOING NEXT. INSISTED ON IT.
WE'RE COMING BACK TO THE FAIRGROUND AREA NOW. YOU'LL HAVE FIFTEEN MINUTES TO LOOK AROUND ON YOUR OWN.
IT'S A TOUR GROUP!
MOVE!
BOYS, YOU KNOW WHAT TO DO.

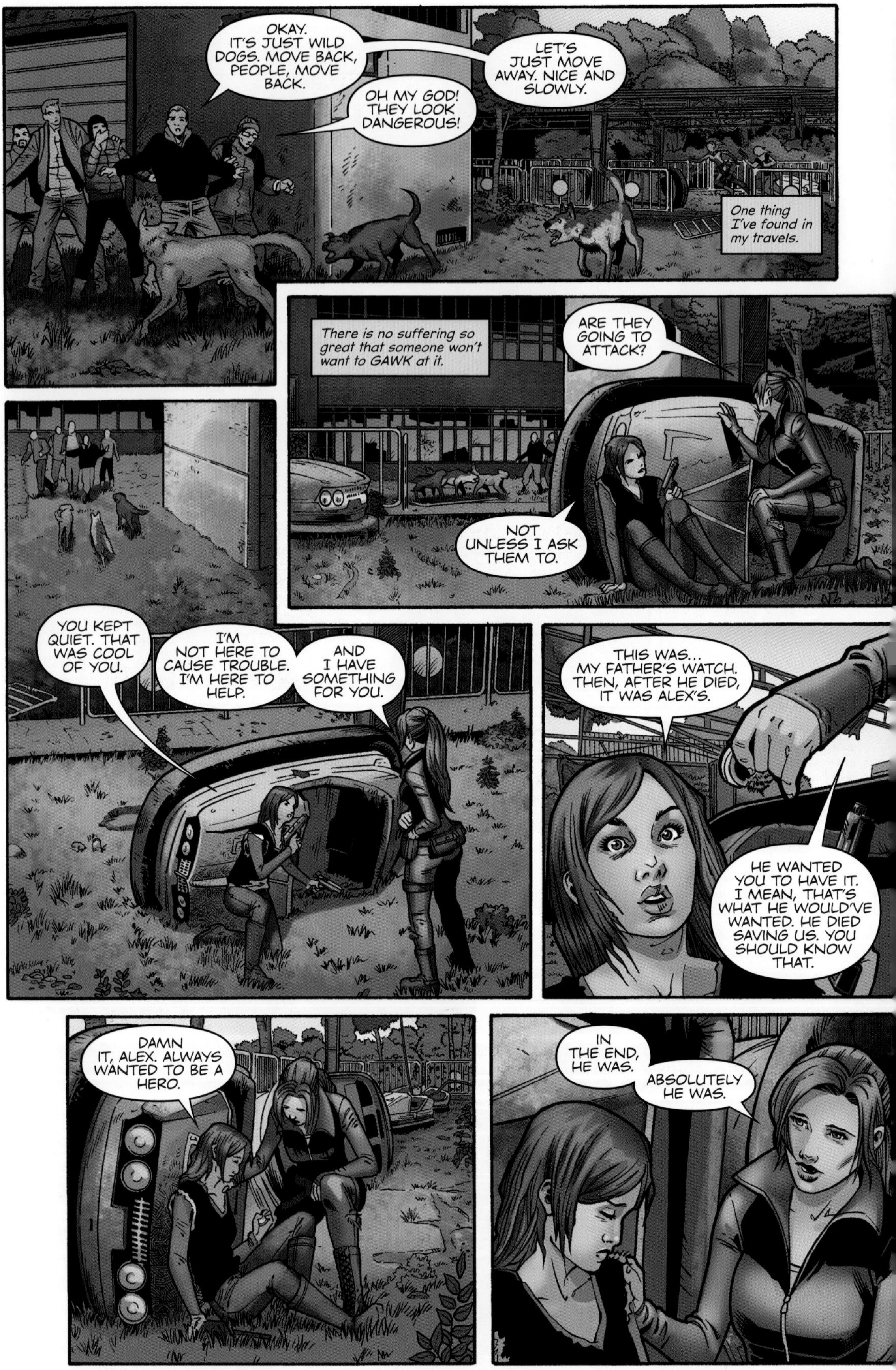
OKAY. IT'S JUST WILD DOGS. MOVE BACK, PEOPLE, MOVE BACK.
OH MY GOD! THEY LOOK DANGEROUS!
LET'S JUST MOVE AWAY. NICE AND SLOWLY.
One thing I've found in my travels.
There is no suffering so great that someone won't want to GAWK at it.
ARE THEY GOING TO ATTACK?
NOT UNLESS I ASK THEM TO.
YOU KEPT QUIET. THAT WAS COOL OF YOU.
I'M NOT HERE TO CAUSE TROUBLE. I'M HERE TO HELP.
AND I HAVE SOMETHING FOR YOU.
THIS WAS... MY FATHER'S WATCH. THEN, AFTER HE DIED, IT WAS ALEX'S.
HE WANTED YOU TO HAVE IT. I MEAN, THAT'S WHAT HE WOULD'VE WANTED. HE DIED SAVING US. YOU SHOULD KNOW THAT.
DAMN IT, ALEX. ALWAYS WANTED TO BE A HERO.
IN THE END, HE WAS.
ABSOLUTELY HE WAS.

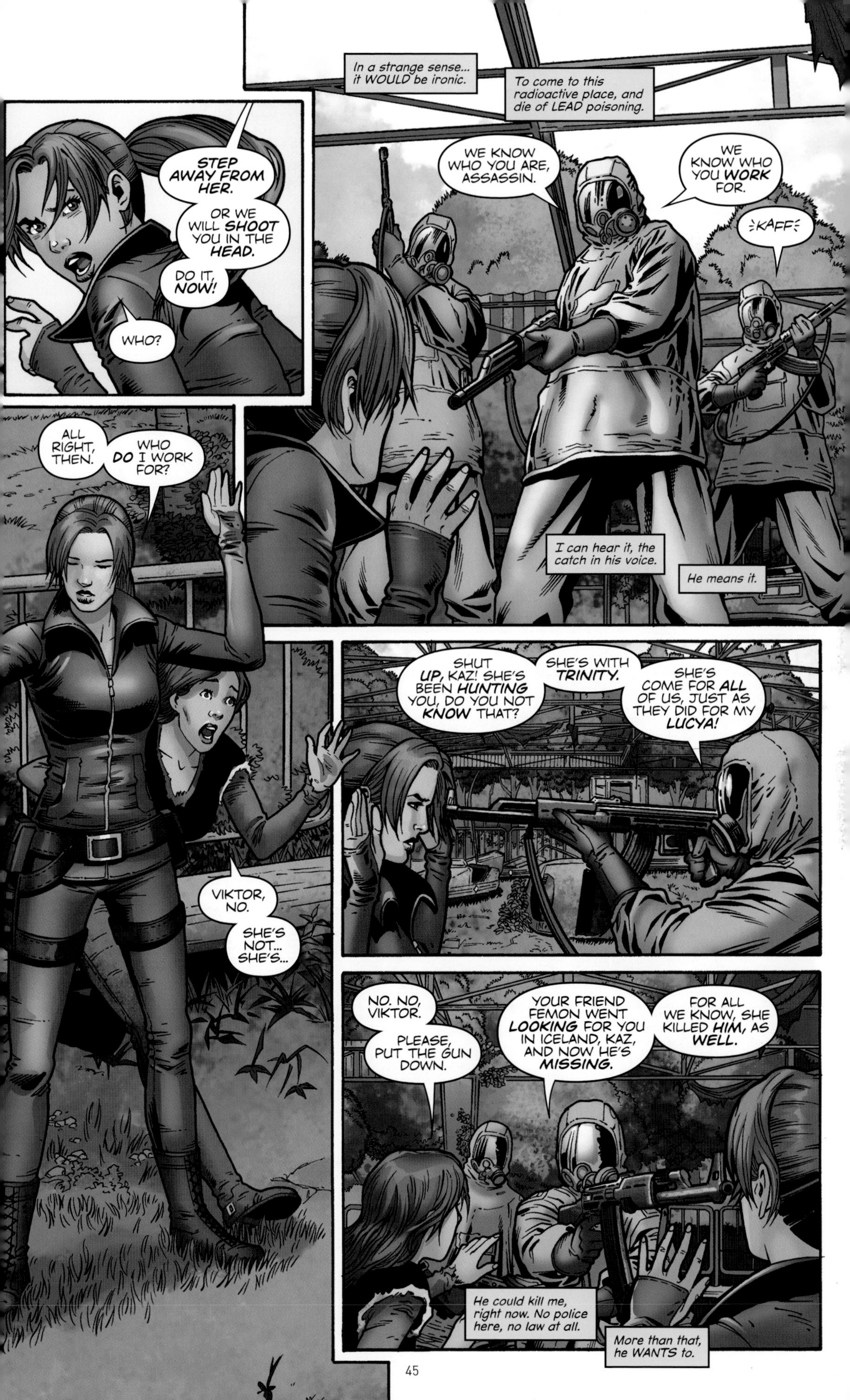
In a strange sense... it WOULD be ironic.
To come to this radioactive place, and die of LEAD poisoning.
STEP AWAY FROM HER.
OR WE WILL SHOOT YOU IN THE HEAD.
DO IT, NOW!
WHO?
WE KNOW WHO YOU ARE, ASSASSIN.
WE KNOW WHO YOU WORK FOR.
KAFF
ALL RIGHT, THEN.
WHO DO I WORK FOR?
I can hear it, the catch in his voice.
He means it.
VIKTOR, NO.
SHE'S NOT... SHE'S...
SHUT UP, KAZ! SHE'S BEEN HUNTING YOU, DO YOU NOT KNOW THAT?
SHE'S WITH TRINITY.
SHE'S COME FOR ALL OF US, JUST AS THEY DID FOR MY LUCYA!
NO. NO, VIKTOR.
PLEASE, PUT THE GUN DOWN.
YOUR FRIEND FEMON WENT LOOKING FOR YOU IN ICELAND, KAZ, AND NOW HE'S MISSING.
FOR ALL WE KNOW, SHE KILLED HIM, AS WELL.
He could kill me, right now. No police here, no law at all.
More than that, he WANTS to.

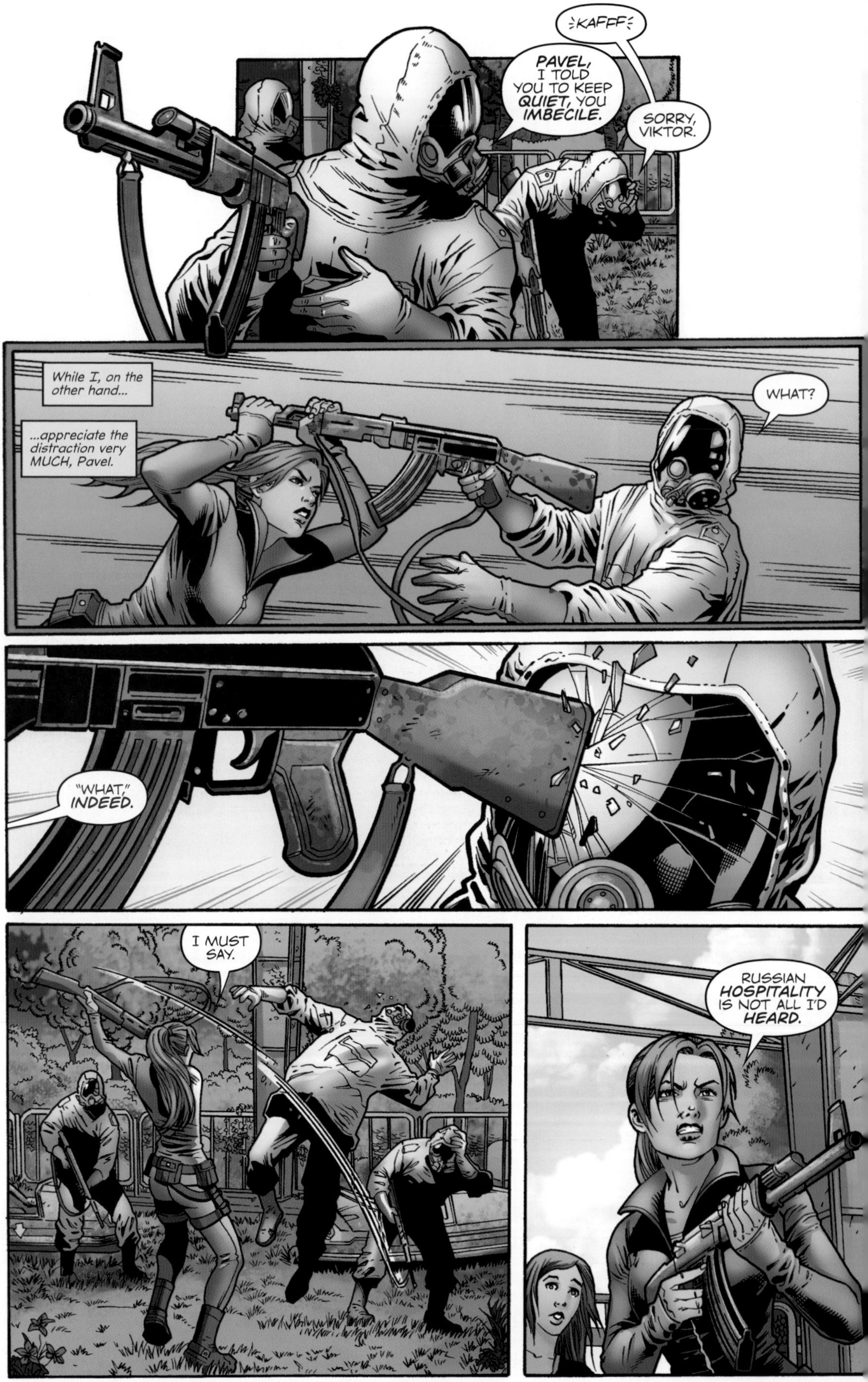

PAVEL, I TOLD YOU TO KEEP QUIET, YOU IMBECILE.
KAFFF
SORRY, VIKTOR.
While I, on the other hand...
...appreciate the distraction very MUCH, Pavel.
WHAT?
"WHAT," INDEED.
I MUST SAY.
RUSSIAN HOSPITALITY IS NOT ALL I'D HEARD.

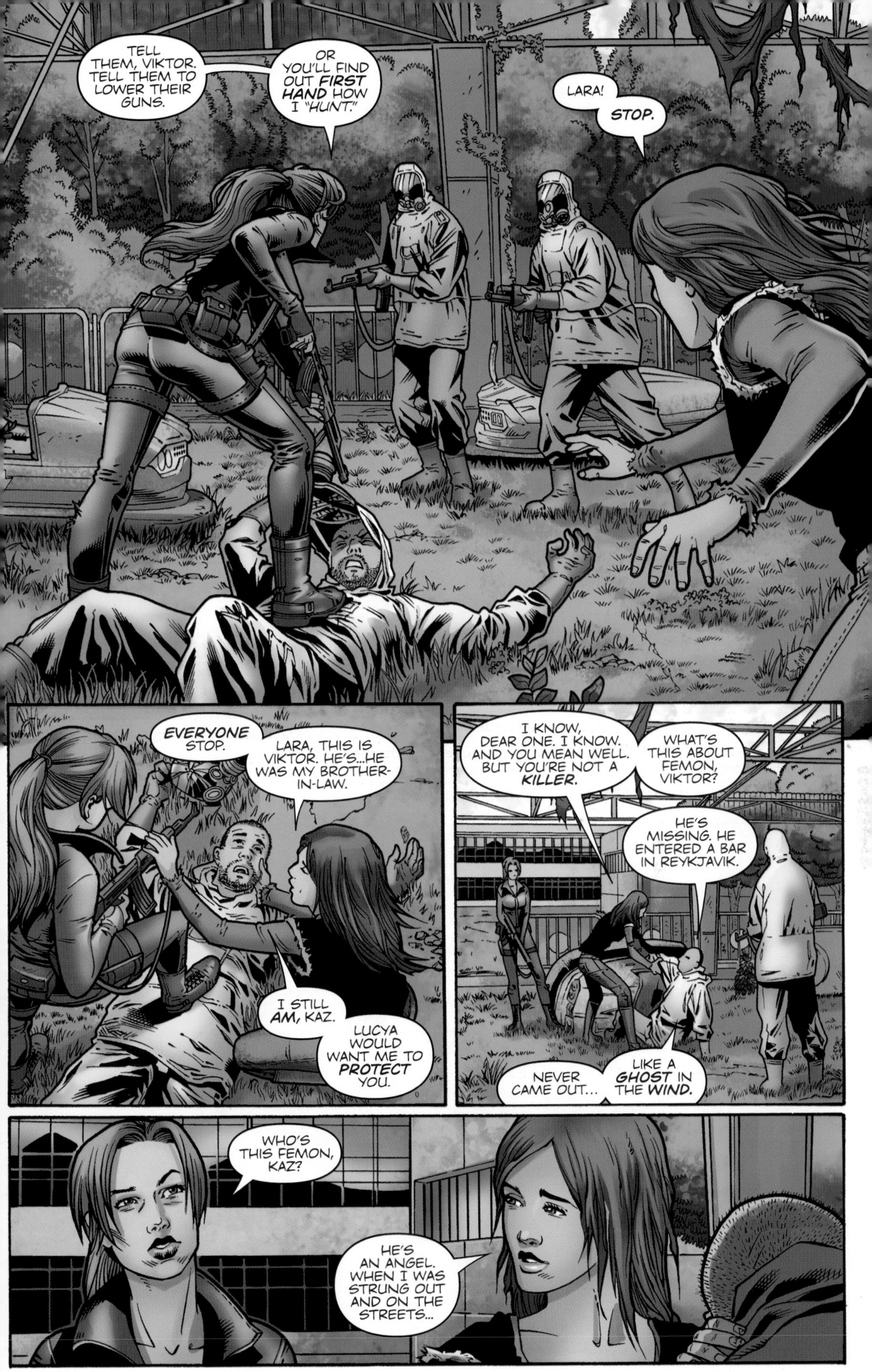

TELL THEM, VIKTOR. TELL THEM TO LOWER THEIR GUNS.
OR YOU'LL FIND OUT FIRST HAND HOW I "HUNT."
LARA!
STOP.
EVERYONE STOP.
LARA, THIS IS VIKTOR. HE'S...HE WAS MY BROTHER-IN-LAW.
I STILL AM, KAZ.
LUCYA WOULD WANT ME TO PROTECT YOU.
I KNOW, DEAR ONE. I KNOW. AND YOU MEAN WELL. BUT YOU'RE NOT A KILLER.
WHAT'S THIS ABOUT FEMON, VIKTOR?
HE'S MISSING. HE ENTERED A BAR IN REYKJAVIK.
NEVER CAME OUT...
LIKE A GHOST IN THE WIND.
WHO'S THIS FEMON, KAZ?
HE'S AN ANGEL. WHEN I WAS STRUNG OUT AND ON THE STREETS...

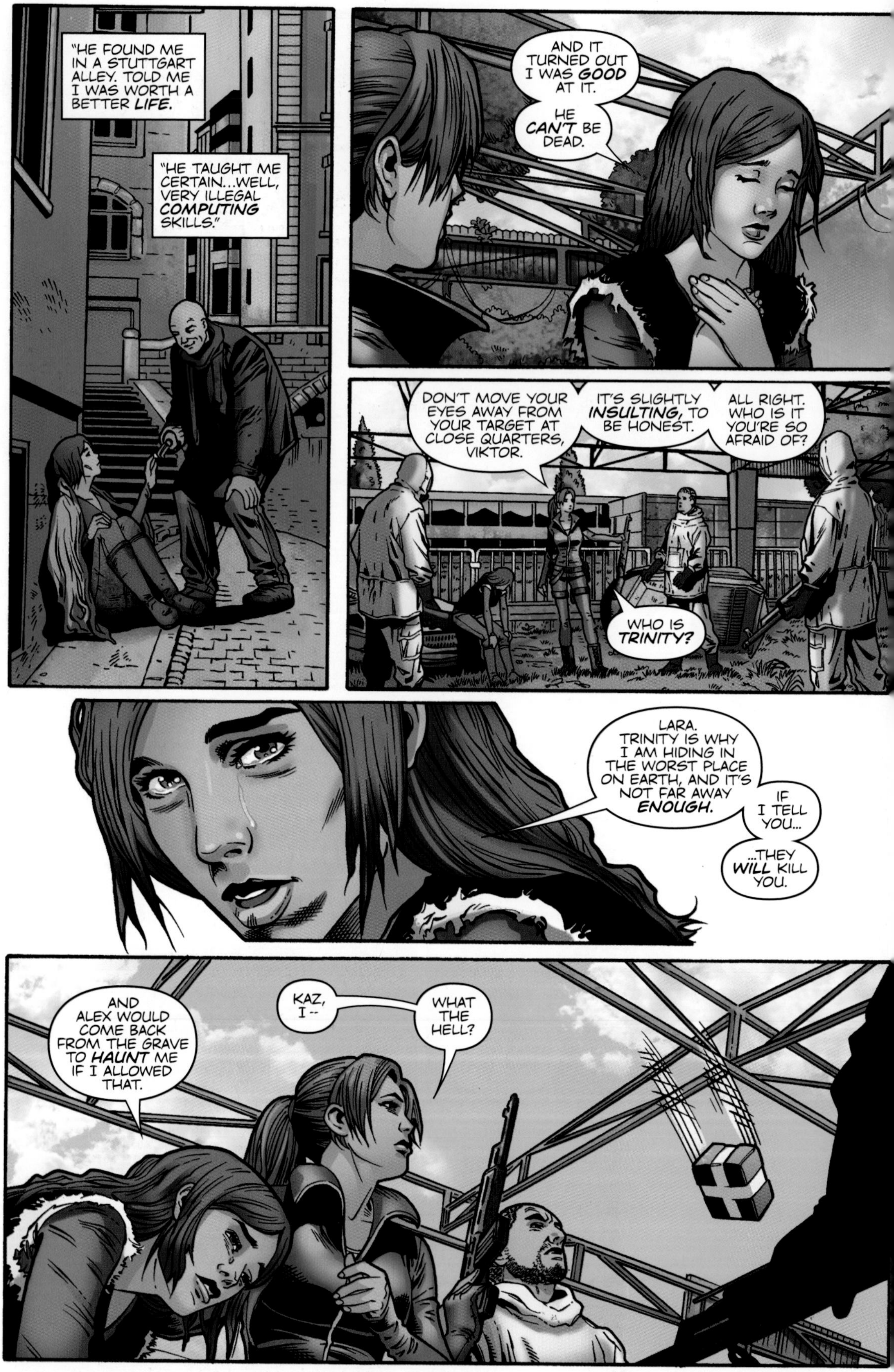
"HE FOUND ME IN A STUTTGART ALLEY. TOLD ME I WAS WORTH A BETTER LIFE.
"HE TAUGHT ME CERTAIN...WELL, VERY ILLEGAL COMPUTING SKILLS."
AND IT TURNED OUT I WAS GOOD AT IT.
HE CAN'T BE DEAD.
DON'T MOVE YOUR EYES AWAY FROM YOUR TARGET AT CLOSE QUARTERS, VIKTOR.
IT'S SLIGHTLY INSULTING, TO BE HONEST.
ALL RIGHT. WHO IS IT YOU'RE SO AFRAID OF?
WHO IS TRINITY?
LARA. TRINITY IS WHY I AM HIDING IN THE WORST PLACE ON EARTH, AND IT'S NOT FAR AWAY ENOUGH.
IF I TELL YOU...
...THEY WILL KILL YOU.
AND ALEX WOULD COME BACK FROM THE GRAVE TO HAUNT ME IF I ALLOWED THAT.
KAZ, I --
WHAT THE HELL?

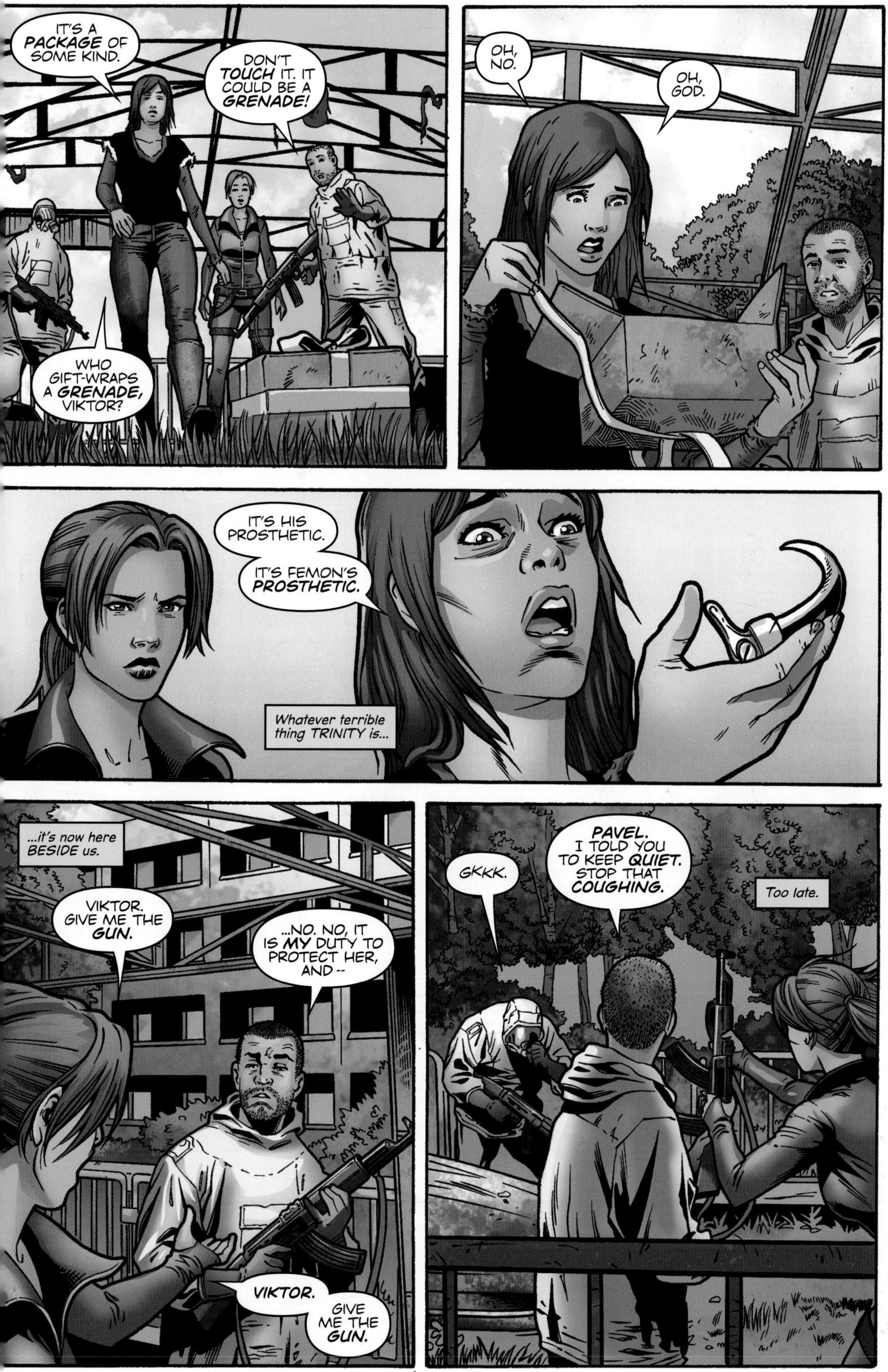
IT'S A PACKAGE OF SOME KIND.
DON'T TOUCH IT. IT COULD BE A GRENADE!
WHO GIFT-WRAPS A GRENADE, VIKTOR?
OH, NO.
OH, GOD.
IT'S HIS PROSTHETIC.
IT'S FEMON'S PROSTHETIC.
Whatever terrible thing TRINITY is...
...it's now here BESIDE us.
VIKTOR. GIVE ME THE GUN.
...NO. NO, IT IS MY DUTY TO PROTECT HER, AND --
VIKTOR.
GIVE ME THE GUN.
GKKK.
PAVEL. I TOLD YOU TO KEEP QUIET. STOP THAT COUGHING.
Too late.

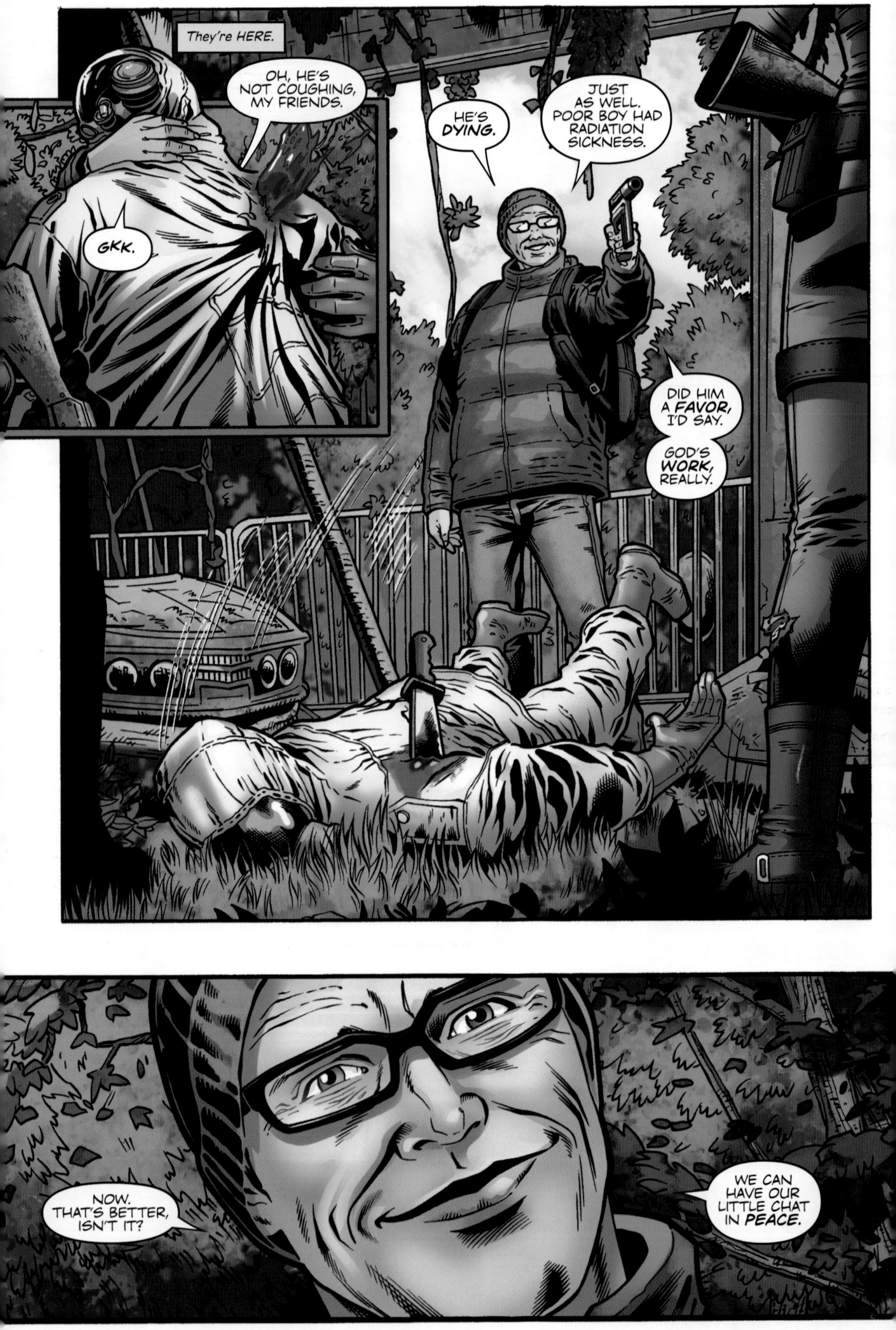

They're HERE.
OH, HE'S NOT COUGHING, MY FRIENDS.
GKK.
HE'S DYING.
JUST AS WELL. POOR BOY HAD RADIATION SICKNESS.
DID HIM A FAVOR, I'D SAY.
GOD'S WORK, REALLY.
NOW. THAT'S BETTER, ISN'T IT?
WE CAN HAVE OUR LITTLE CHAT IN PEACE.

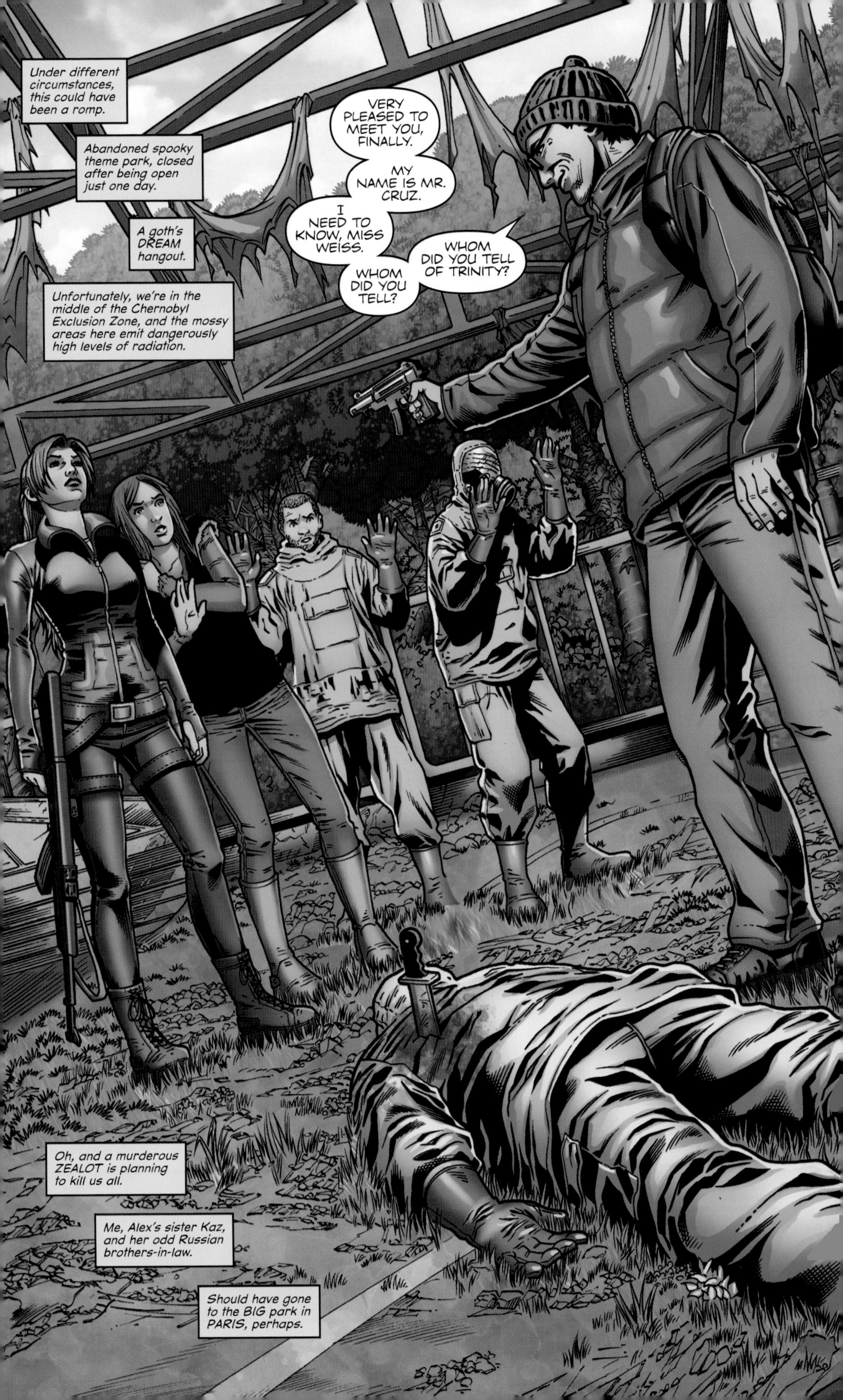

Under different circumstances, this could have been a romp.
Abandoned spooky theme park, closed after being open just one day.
A goth's DREAM hangout.
Unfortunately, we're in the middle of the Chernobyl Exclusion Zone, and the mossy areas here emit dangerously high levels of radiation.
VERY PLEASED TO MEET YOU, FINALLY.
MY NAME IS MR. CRUZ.
I NEED TO KNOW, MISS WEISS.
WHOM DID YOU TELL?
WHOM DID YOU TELL OF TRINITY?
Oh, and a murderous ZEALOT is planning to kill us all.
Me, Alex's sister Kaz, and her odd Russian brothers-in-law.
Should have gone to the BIG park in PARIS, perhaps.

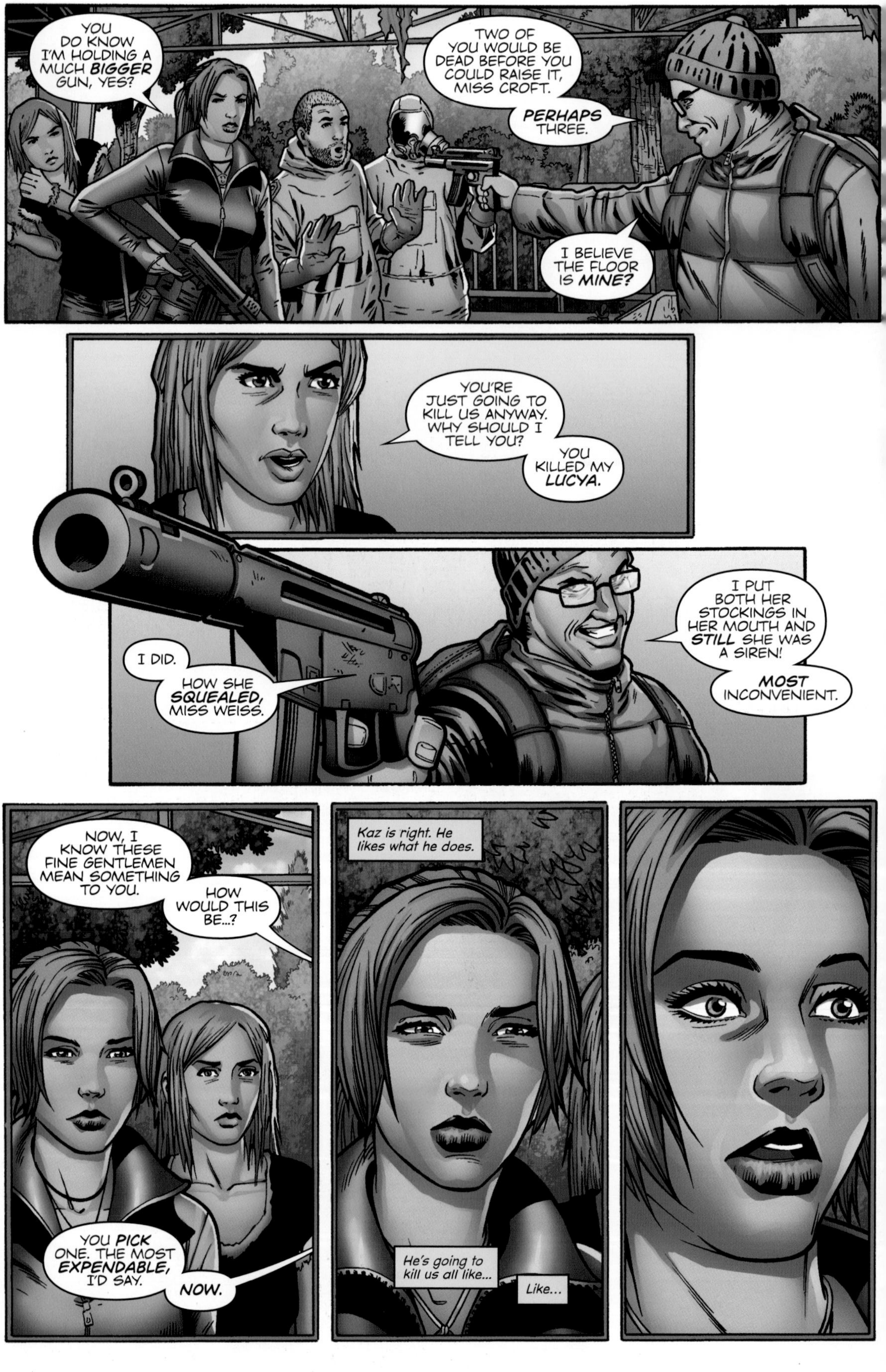
YOU DO KNOW I'M HOLDING A MUCH BIGGER GUN, YES?
TWO OF YOU WOULD BE DEAD BEFORE YOU COULD RAISE IT, MISS CROFT.
PERHAPS THREE.
I BELIEVE THE FLOOR IS MINE?
YOU'RE JUST GOING TO KILL US ANYWAY. WHY SHOULD I TELL YOU?
YOU KILLED MY LUCYA.
I DID.
HOW SHE SQUEALED, MISS WEISS.
I PUT BOTH HER STOCKINGS IN HER MOUTH AND STILL SHE WAS A SIREN!
MOST INCONVENIENT.
NOW, I KNOW THESE FINE GENTLEMEN MEAN SOMETHING TO YOU.
HOW WOULD THIS BE...?
YOU PICK ONE. THE MOST EXPENDABLE, I'D SAY.
NOW.
Kaz is right. He likes what he does.
He's going to kill us all like...
Like...

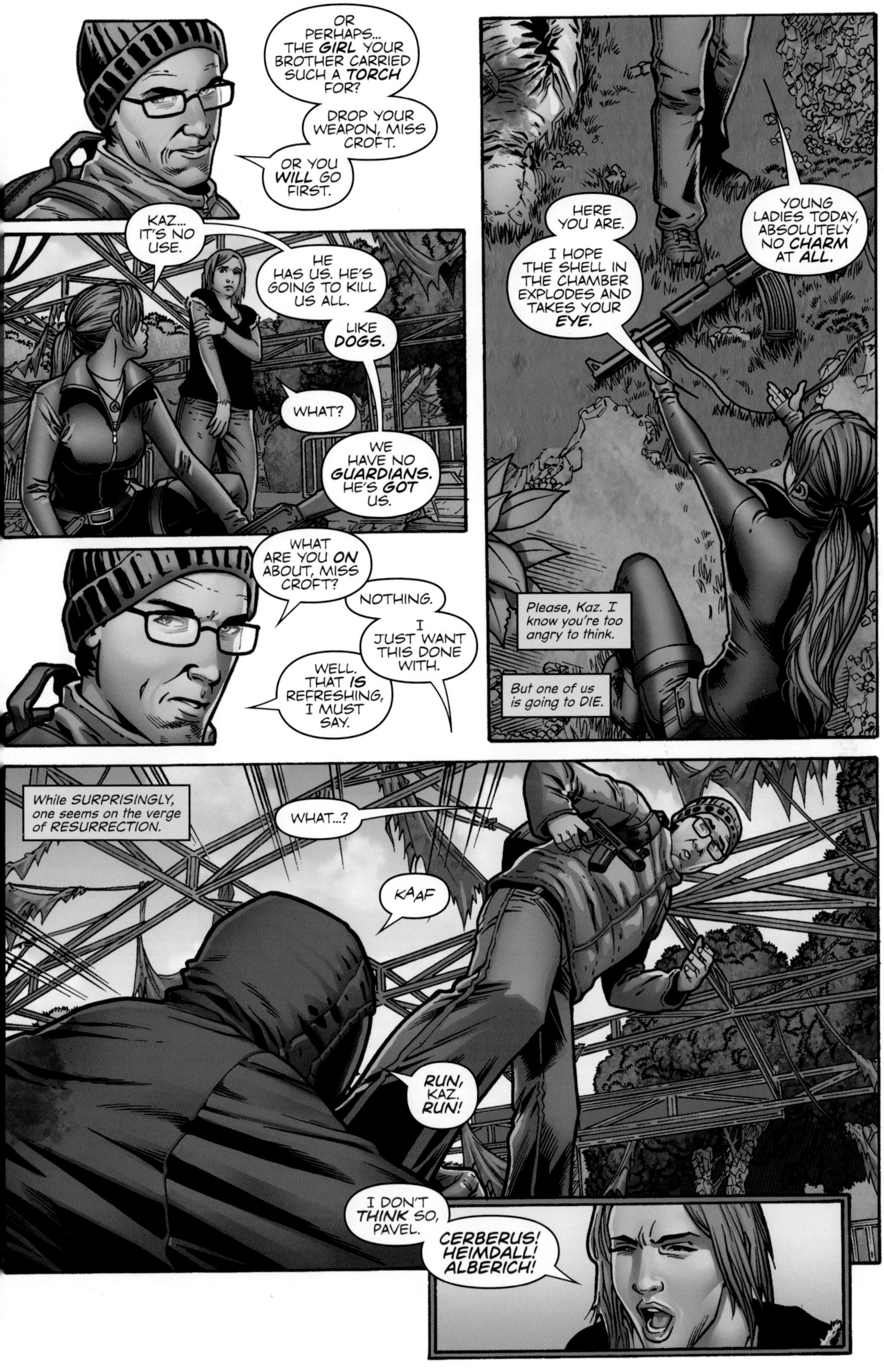
OR PERHAPS... THE GIRL YOUR BROTHER CARRIED SUCH A TORCH FOR?
DROP YOUR WEAPON, MISS CROFT.
OR YOU WILL GO FIRST.
KAZ... IT'S NO USE.
HE HAS US. HE'S GOING TO KILL US ALL.
LIKE DOGS.
WHAT?
WE HAVE NO GUARDIANS. HE'S GOT US.
WHAT ARE YOU ON ABOUT, MISS CROFT?
NOTHING.
I JUST WANT THIS DONE WITH.
WELL. THAT IS REFRESHING, I MUST SAY.
YOUNG LADIES TODAY, ABSOLUTELY NO CHARM AT ALL.
HERE YOU ARE.
I HOPE THE SHELL IN THE CHAMBER EXPLODES AND TAKES YOUR EYE.
Please, Kaz. I know you're too angry to think.
But one of us is going to DIE.
While SURPRISINGLY, one seems on the verge of RESURRECTION.
WHAT...?
KAAF
RUN, KAZ. RUN!
I DON'T THINK SO, PAVEL.
CERBERUS! HEIMDALL! ALBERICH!

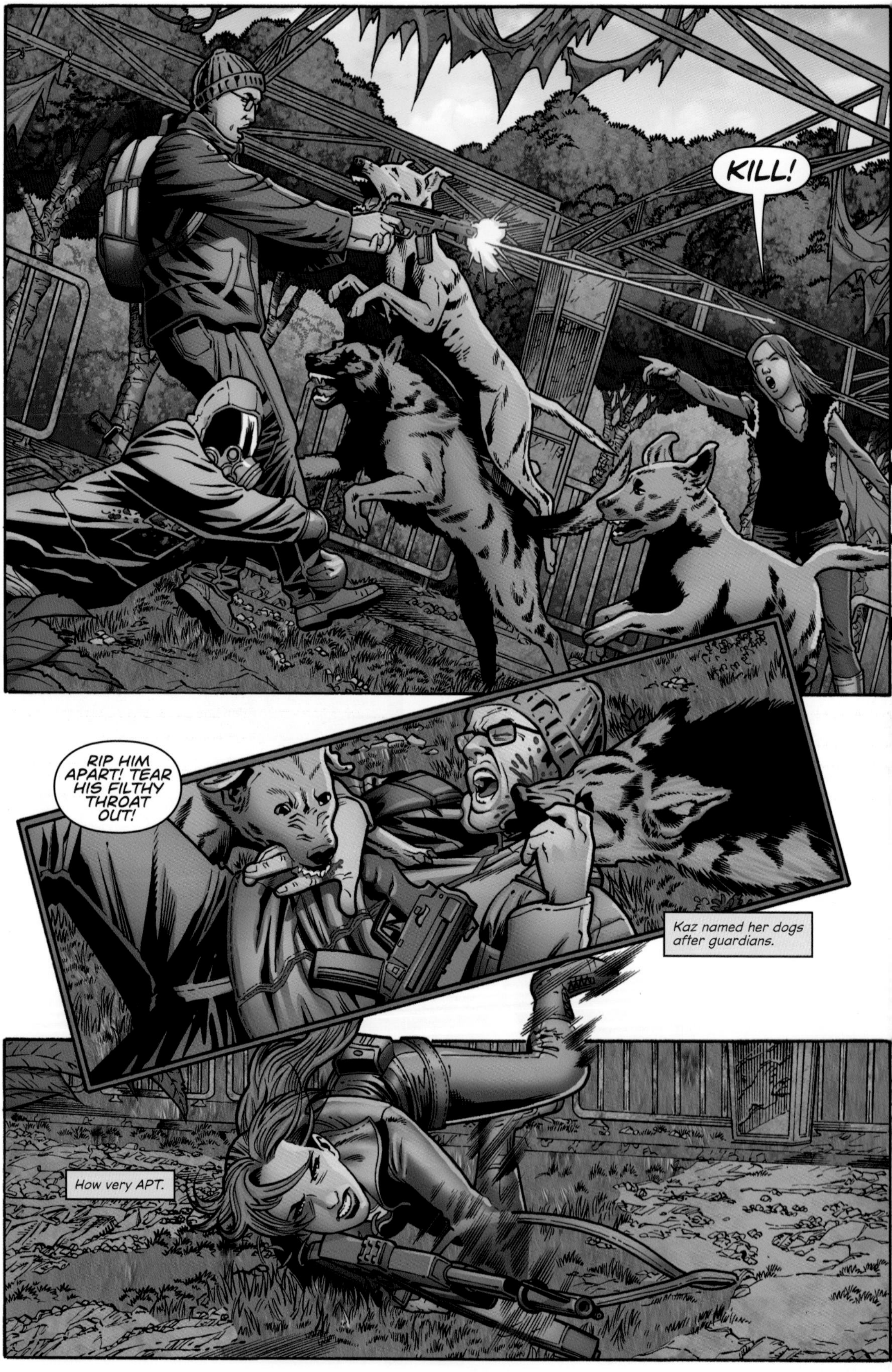
KILL!
RIP HIM APART! TEAR HIS FILTHY THROAT OUT!
Kaz named her dogs after guardians.
How very APT.

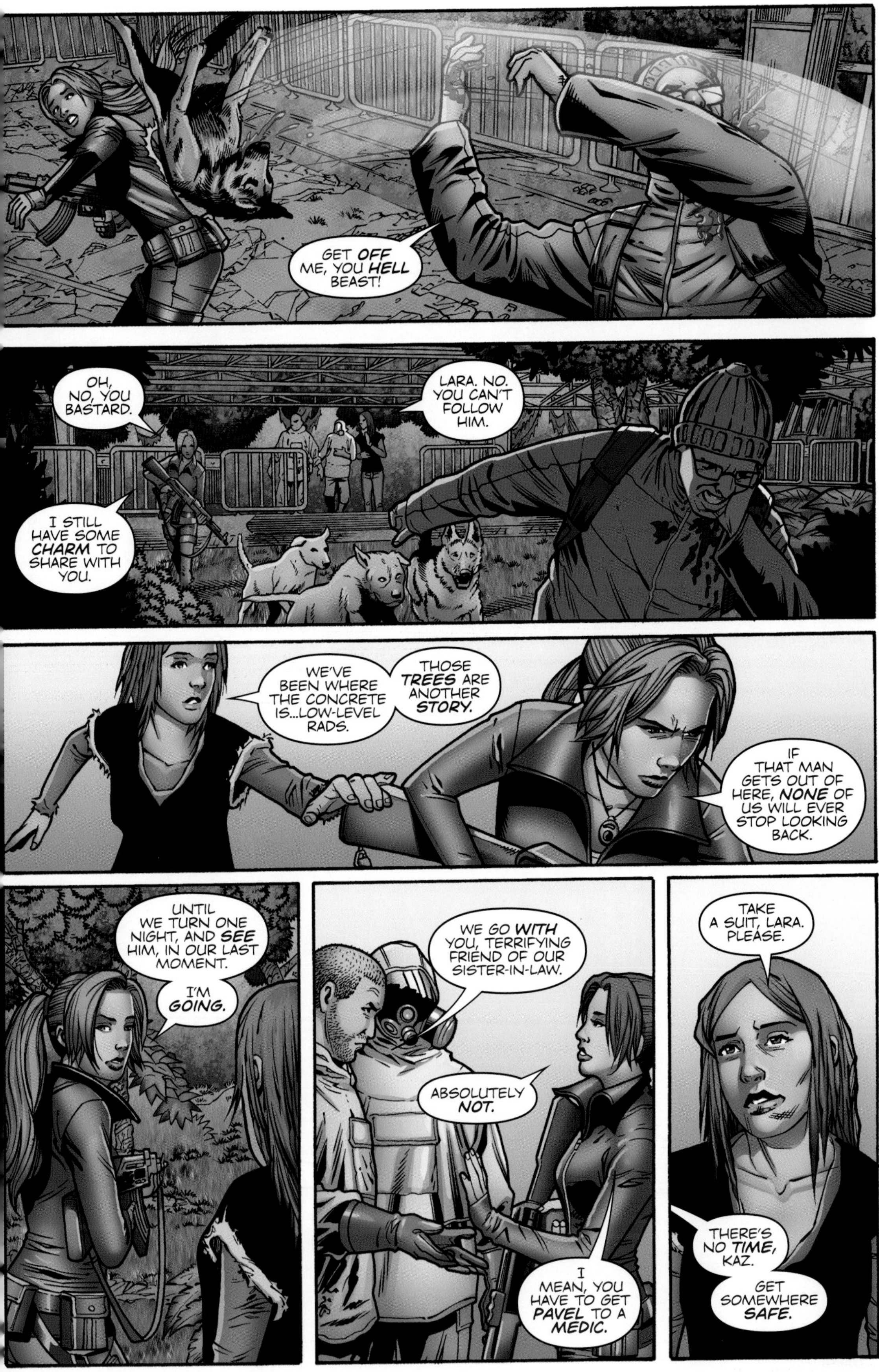
GET OFF ME, YOU HELL BEAST!
OH, NO, YOU BASTARD.
LARA. NO. YOU CAN'T FOLLOW HIM.
I STILL HAVE SOME CHARM TO SHARE WITH YOU.
WE'VE BEEN WHERE THE CONCRETE IS...LOW-LEVEL RADS.
THOSE TREES ARE ANOTHER STORY.
IF THAT MAN GETS OUT OF HERE, NONE OF US WILL EVER STOP LOOKING BACK.
UNTIL WE TURN ONE NIGHT, AND SEE HIM, IN OUR LAST MOMENT.
I'M GOING.
WE GO WITH YOU, TERRIFYING FRIEND OF OUR SISTER-IN-LAW.
ABSOLUTELY NOT.
I MEAN, YOU HAVE TO GET PAVEL TO A MEDIC.
TAKE A SUIT, LARA. PLEASE.
THERE'S NO TIME, KAZ.
GET SOMEWHERE SAFE.

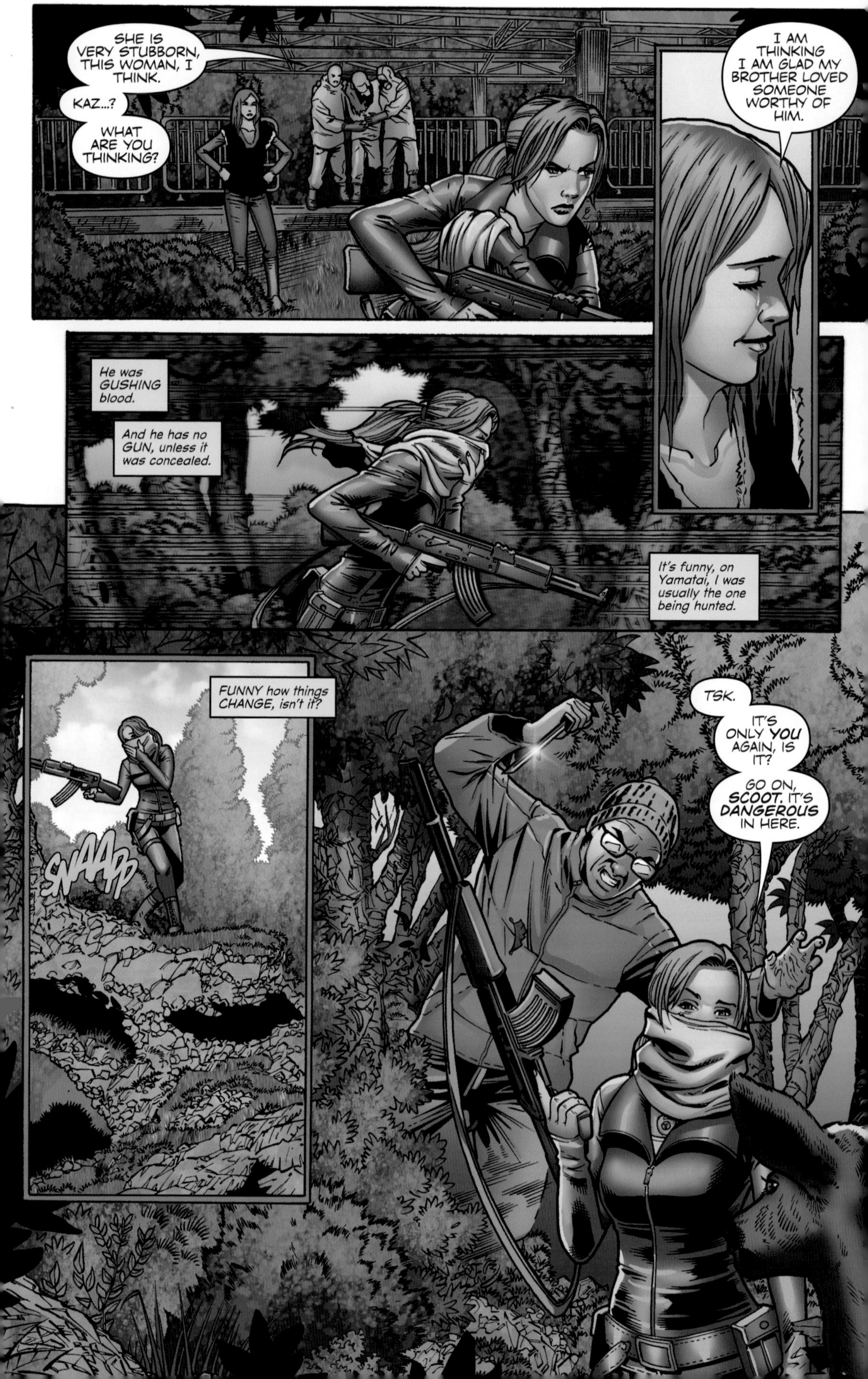

SHE IS VERY STUBBORN, THIS WOMAN, I THINK.
KAZ...?
WHAT ARE YOU THINKING?
I AM THINKING I AM GLAD MY BROTHER LOVED SOMEONE WORTHY OF HIM.
He was GUSHING blood.
And he has no GUN, unless it was concealed.
It's funny, on Yamatai, I was usually the one being hunted.
FUNNY how things CHANGE, isn't it?
SNAAPP
TSK.
IT'S ONLY YOU AGAIN, IS IT?
GO ON, SCOOT. IT'S DANGEROUS IN HERE.

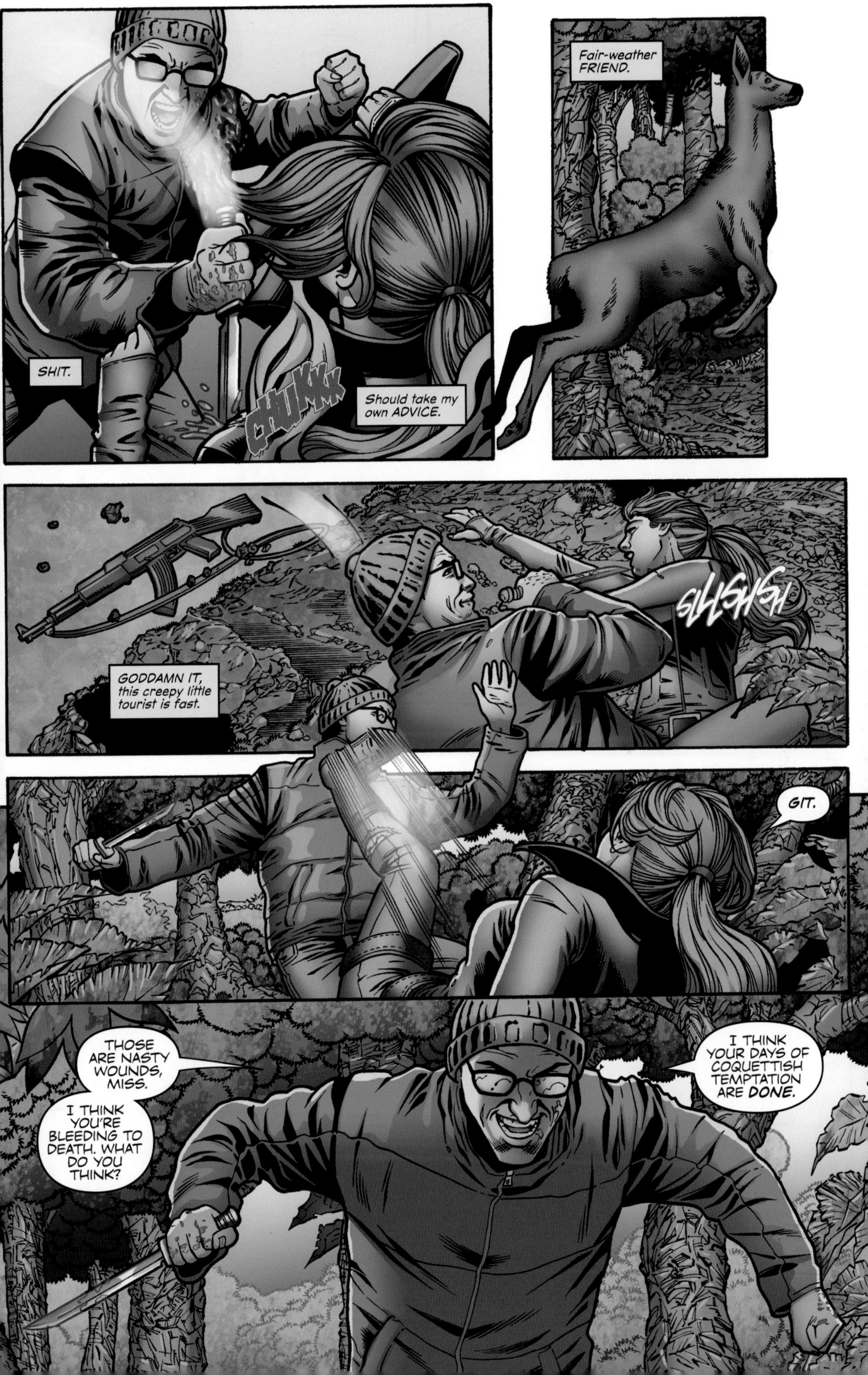
SHIT.
CHUKKK
Should take my own ADVICE.
Fair-weather FRIEND.
SLLLSHSH
GODDAMN IT, this creepy little tourist is fast.
GIT.
THOSE ARE NASTY WOUNDS, MISS.
I THINK YOU'RE BLEEDING TO DEATH. WHAT DO YOU THINK?
I THINK YOUR DAYS OF COQUETTISH TEMPTATION ARE DONE.

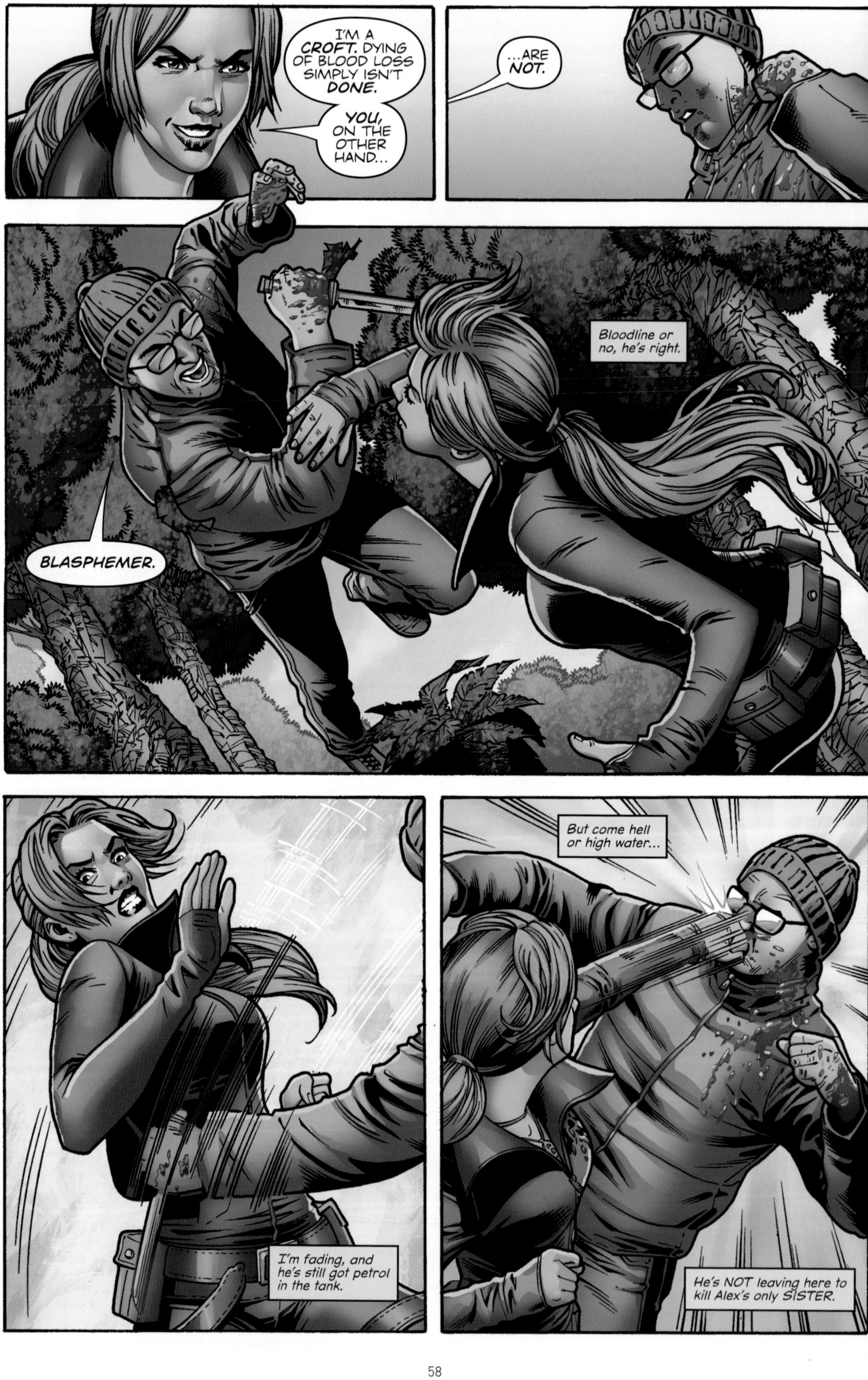

I'M A CROFT. DYING OF BLOOD LOSS SIMPLY ISN'T DONE.
YOU, ON THE OTHER HAND...
...ARE NOT.
Bloodline or no, he's right.
BLASPHEMER.
I'm fading, and he's still got petrol in the tank.
But come hell or high water...
He's NOT leaving here to kill Alex's only SISTER.

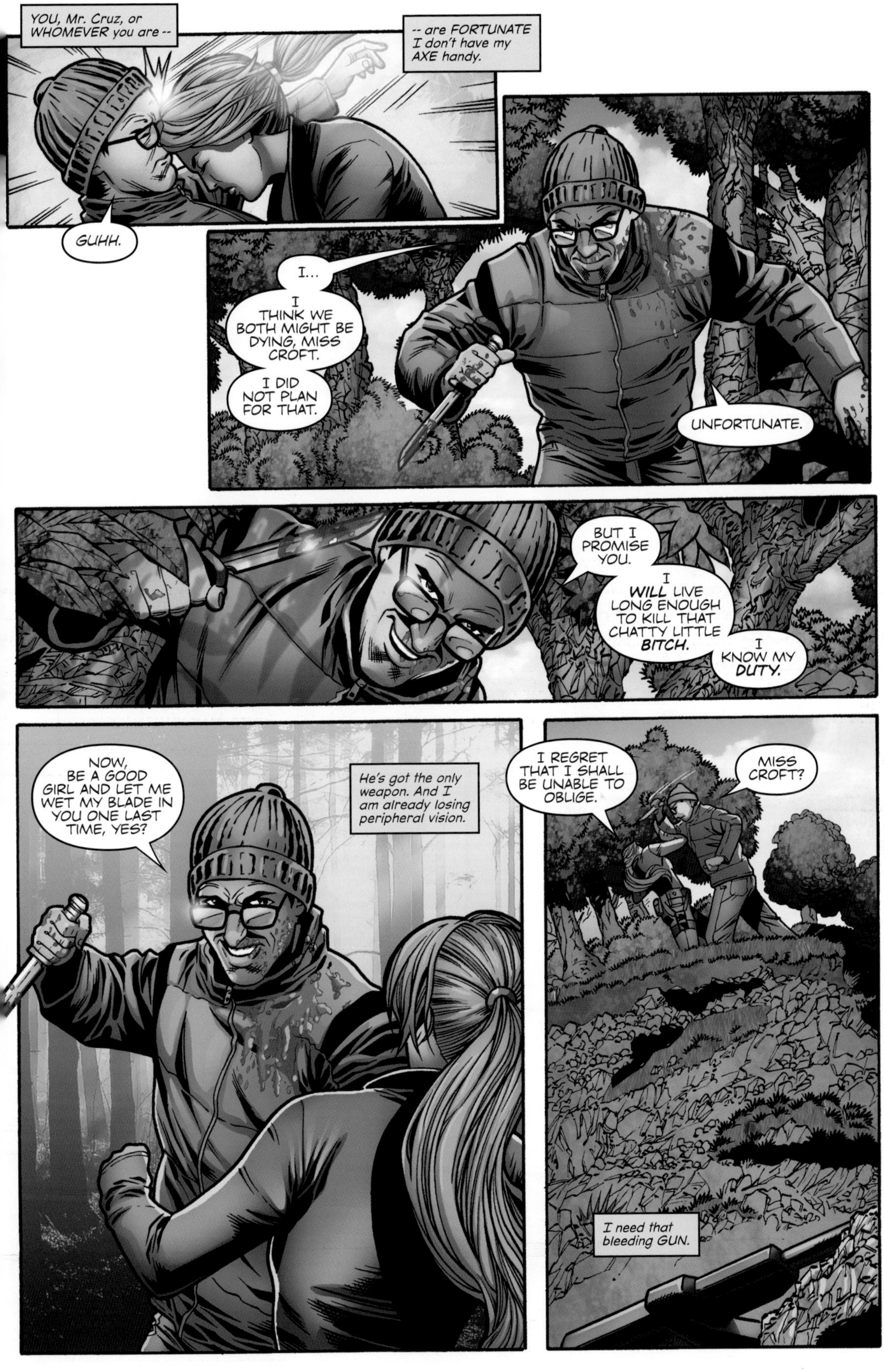
YOU, Mr. Cruz, or WHOMEVER you are --
-- are FORTUNATE I don't have my AXE handy.
GUHH.
I...
I THINK WE BOTH MIGHT BE DYING, MISS CROFT.
I DID NOT PLAN FOR THAT.
UNFORTUNATE.
BUT I PROMISE YOU.
I WILL LIVE LONG ENOUGH TO KILL THAT CHATTY LITTLE BITCH.
I KNOW MY DUTY.
NOW, BE A GOOD GIRL AND LET ME WET MY BLADE IN YOU ONE LAST TIME, YES?
He's got the only weapon. And I am already losing peripheral vision.
I REGRET THAT I SHALL BE UNABLE TO OBLIGE.
MISS CROFT?
I need that bleeding GUN.

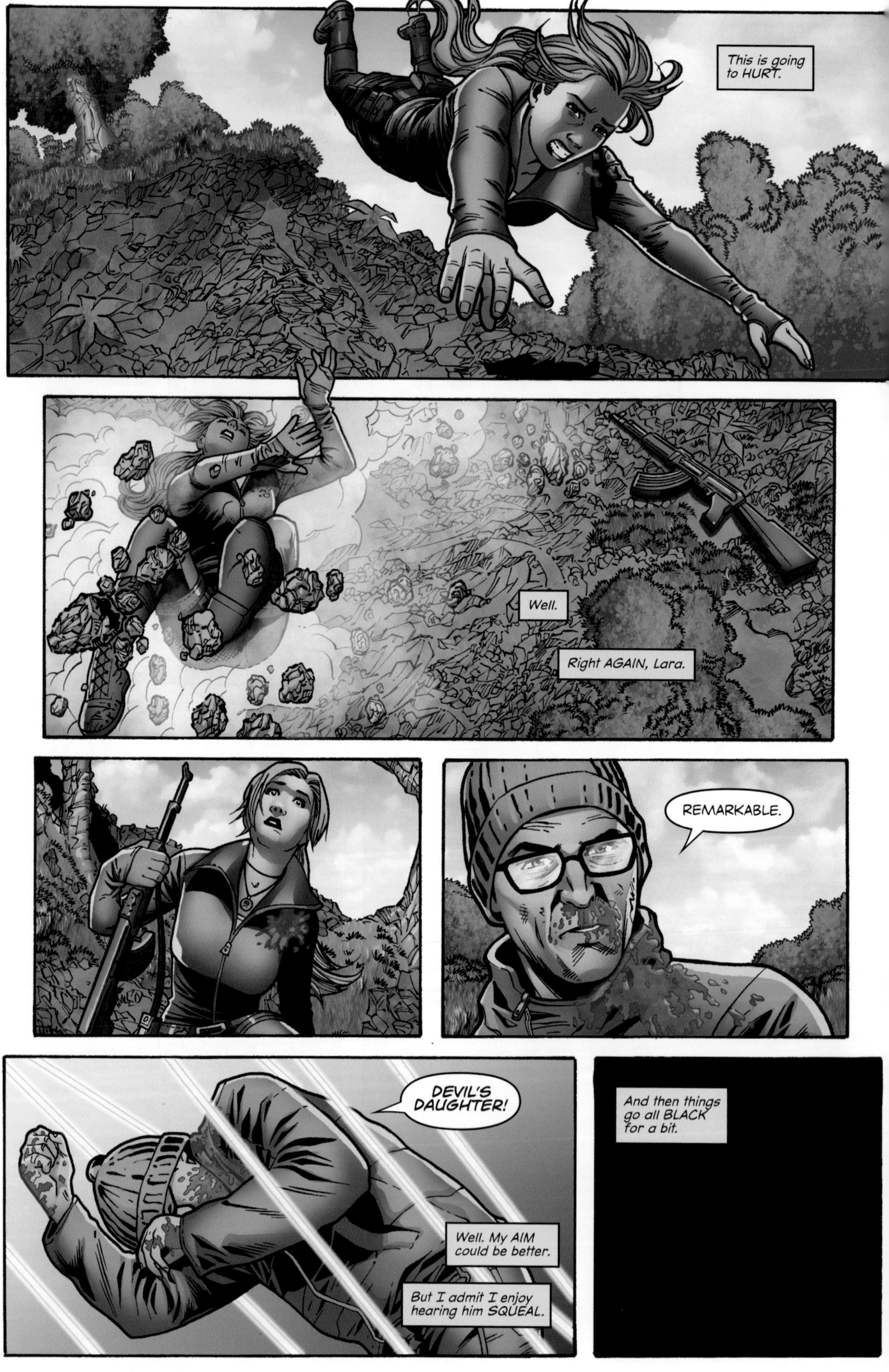
This is going to HURT.
Well.
Right AGAIN, Lara.
REMARKABLE.
DEVIL'S DAUGHTER!
Well. My AIM could be better.
But I admit I enjoy hearing him SQUEAL.
And then things go all BLACK for a bit.

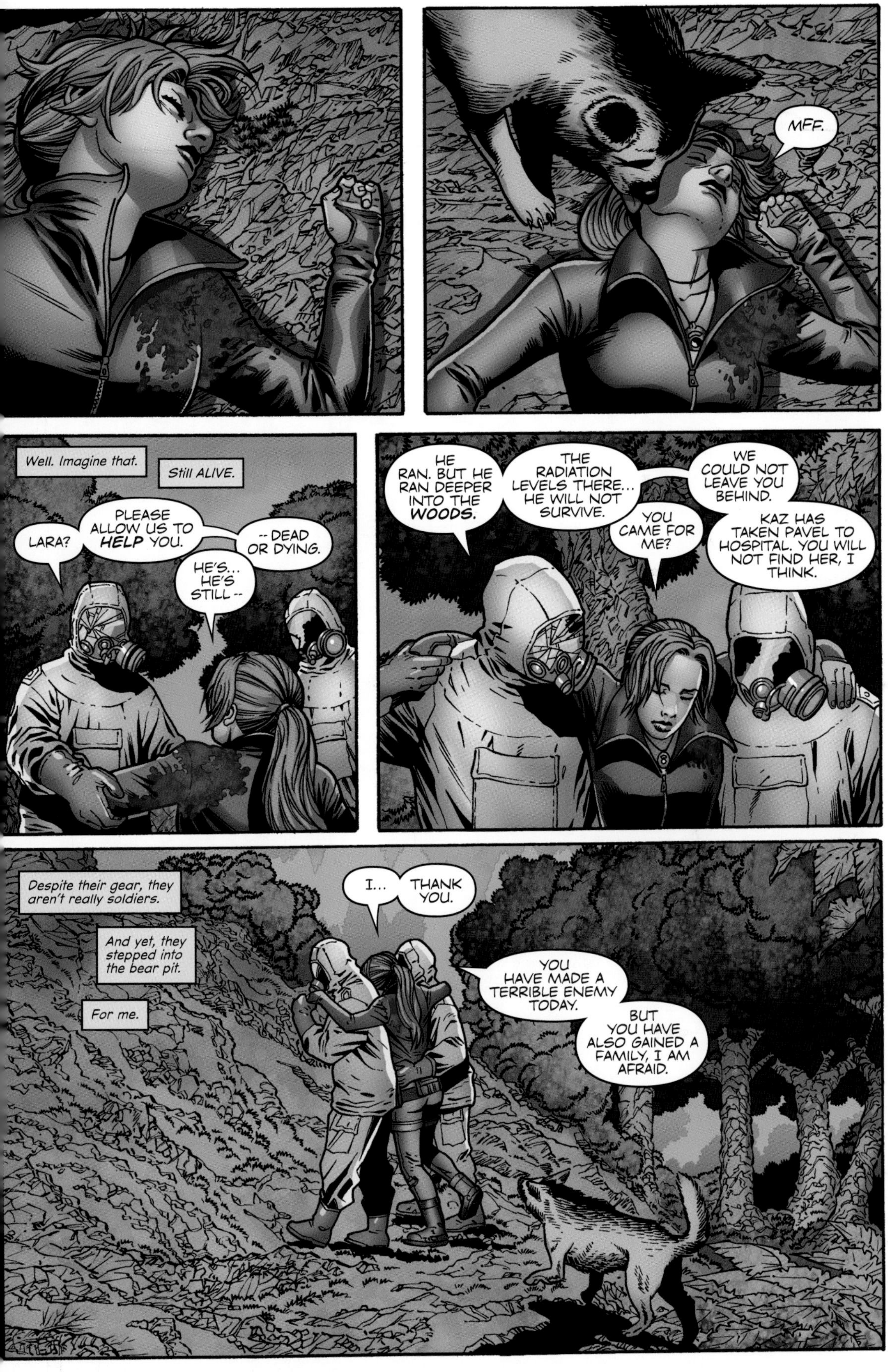
MFF.
Well. Imagine that.
Still ALIVE.
LARA?
PLEASE ALLOW US TO HELP YOU.
-- DEAD OR DYING.
HE'S... HE'S STILL --
HE RAN. BUT HE RAN DEEPER INTO THE WOODS.
THE RADIATION LEVELS THERE... HE WILL NOT SURVIVE.
WE COULD NOT LEAVE YOU BEHIND.
YOU CAME FOR ME?
KAZ HAS TAKEN PAVEL TO HOSPITAL. YOU WILL NOT FIND HER, I THINK.
Despite their gear, they aren't really soldiers.
I...
THANK YOU.
And yet, they stepped into the bear pit.
For me.
YOU HAVE MADE A TERRIBLE ENEMY TODAY.
BUT YOU HAVE ALSO GAINED A FAMILY, I AM AFRAID.

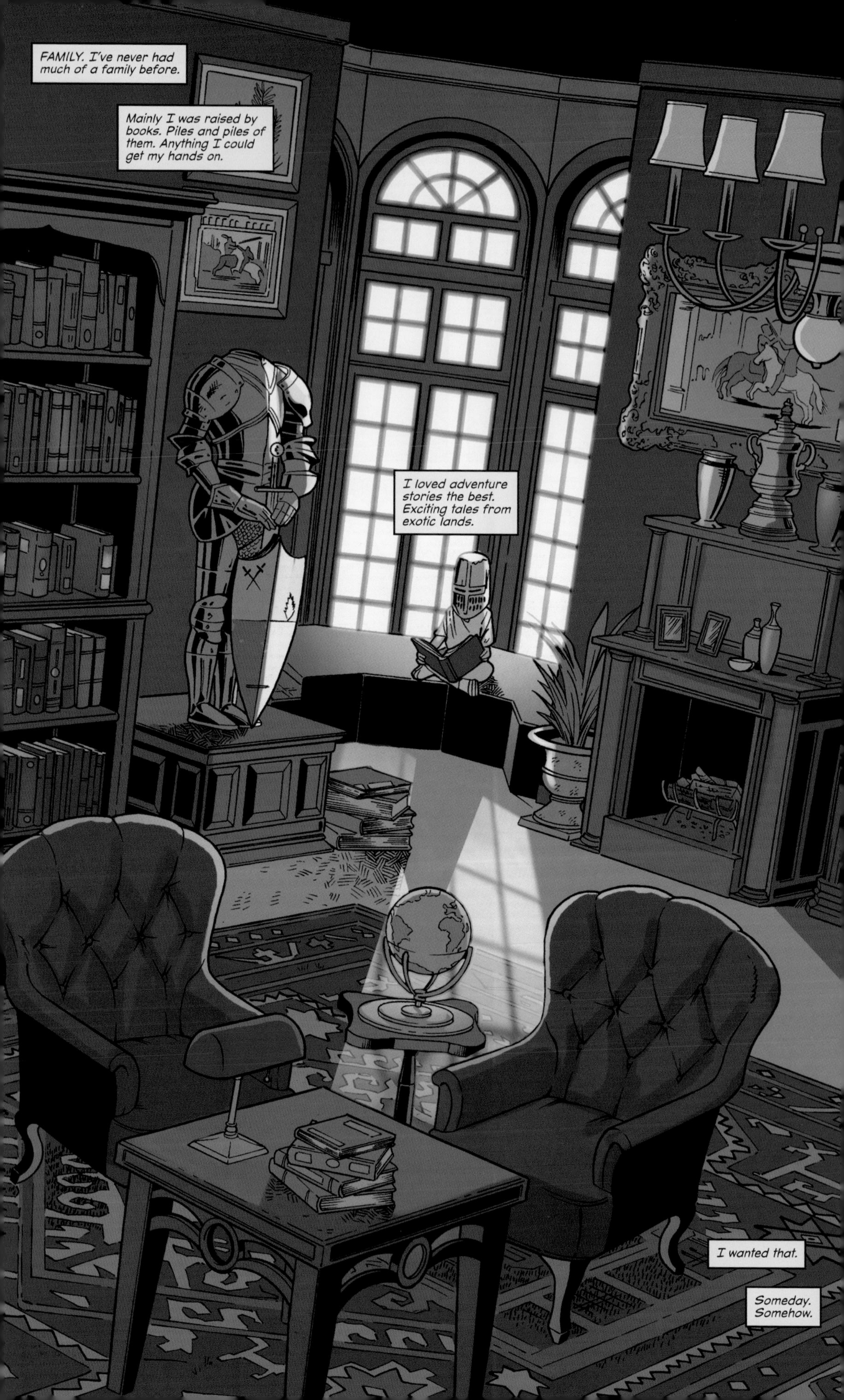
FAMILY. I've never had much of a family before.
Mainly I was raised by books. Piles and piles of them. Anything I could get my hands on.
I loved adventure stories the best. Exciting tales from exotic lands.
I wanted that.
Someday. Somehow.

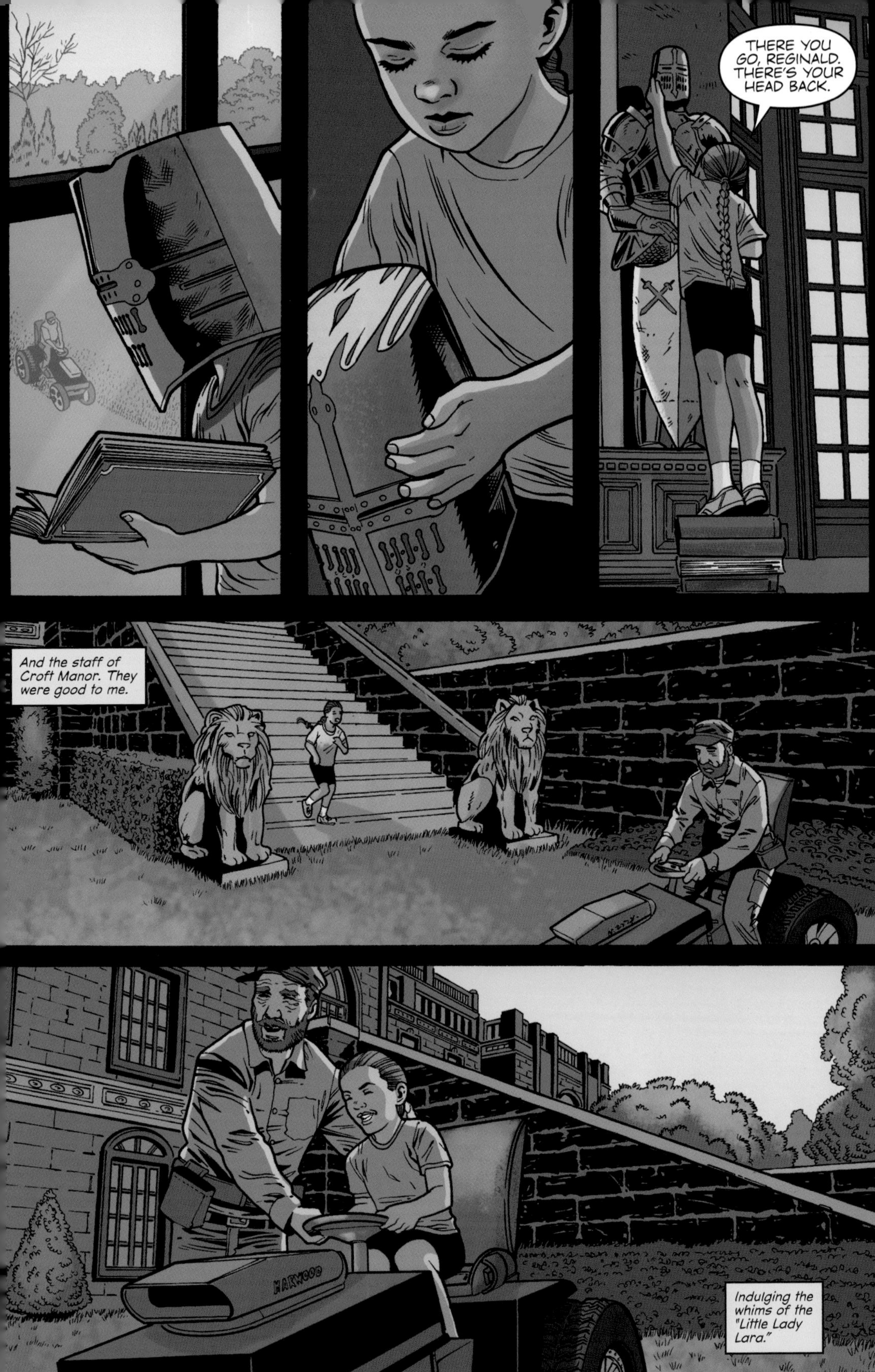
THERE YOU GO, REGINALD. THERE'S YOUR HEAD BACK.
And the staff of Croft Manor. They were good to me.
HARWOOD
Indulging the whims of the "Little Lady Lara."

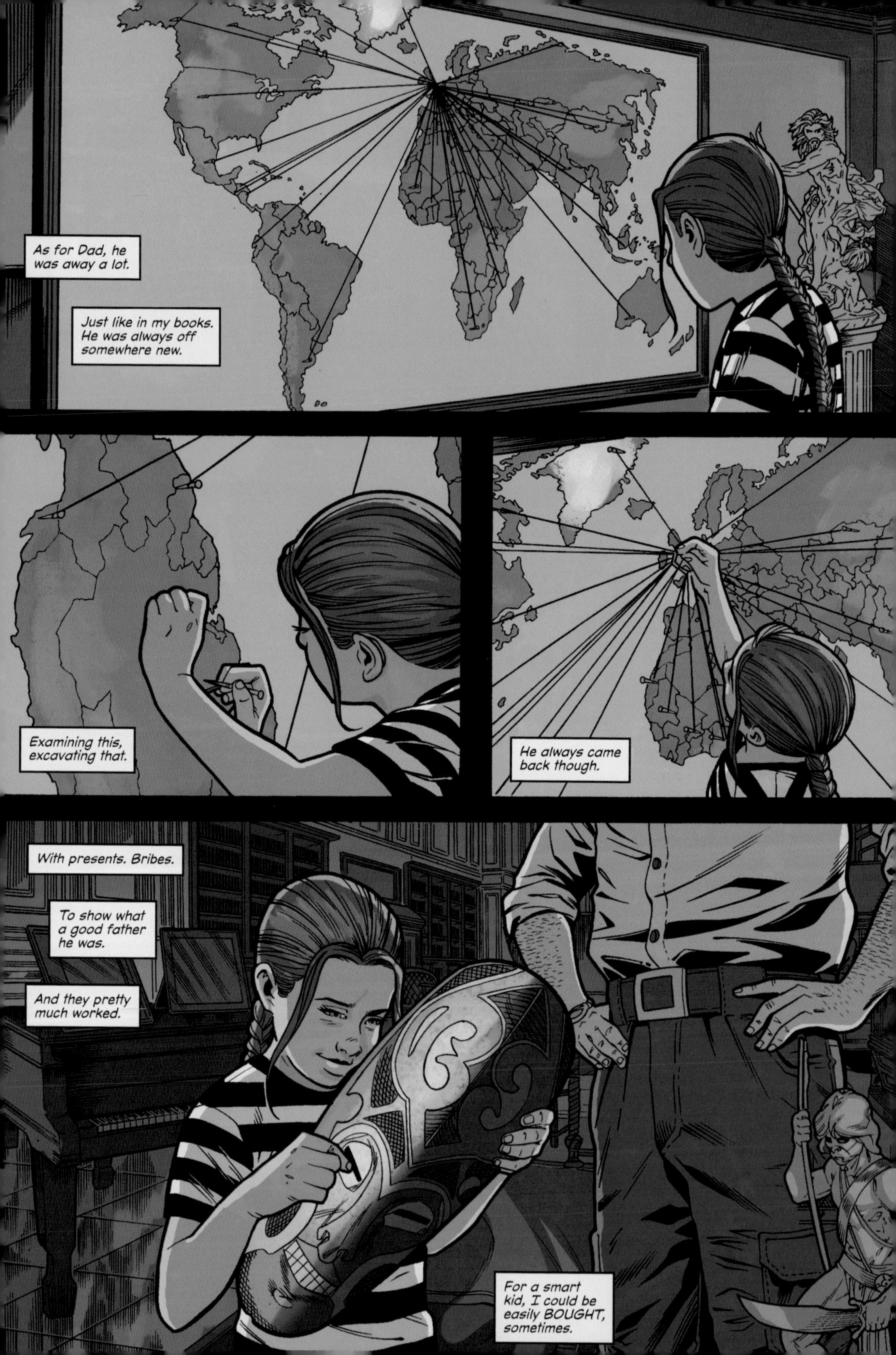
As for Dad, he was away a lot.
Just like in my books. He was always off somewhere new.
Examining this, excavating that.
He always came back though.
With presents. Bribes.
To show what a good father he was.
And they pretty much worked.
For a smart kid, I could be easily BOUGHT, sometimes.

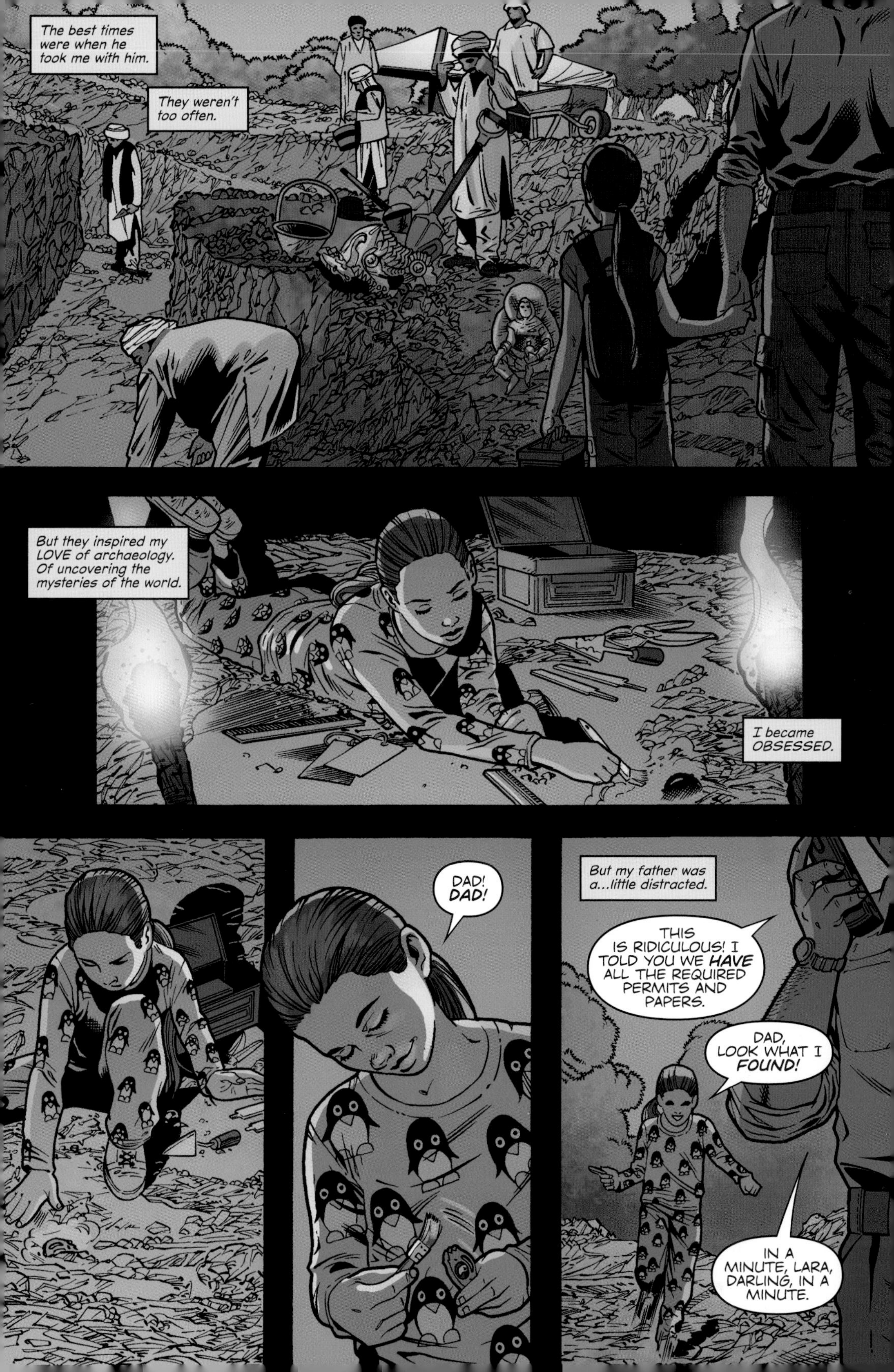
The best times were when he took me with him.
They weren't too often.
But they inspired my LOVE of archaeology. Of uncovering the mysteries of the world.
I became OBSESSED.
DAD! DAD!
But my father was a...little distracted.
THIS IS RIDICULOUS! I TOLD YOU WE HAVE ALL THE REQUIRED PERMITS AND PAPERS.
DAD, LOOK WHAT I FOUND!
IN A MINUTE, LARA, DARLING, IN A MINUTE.

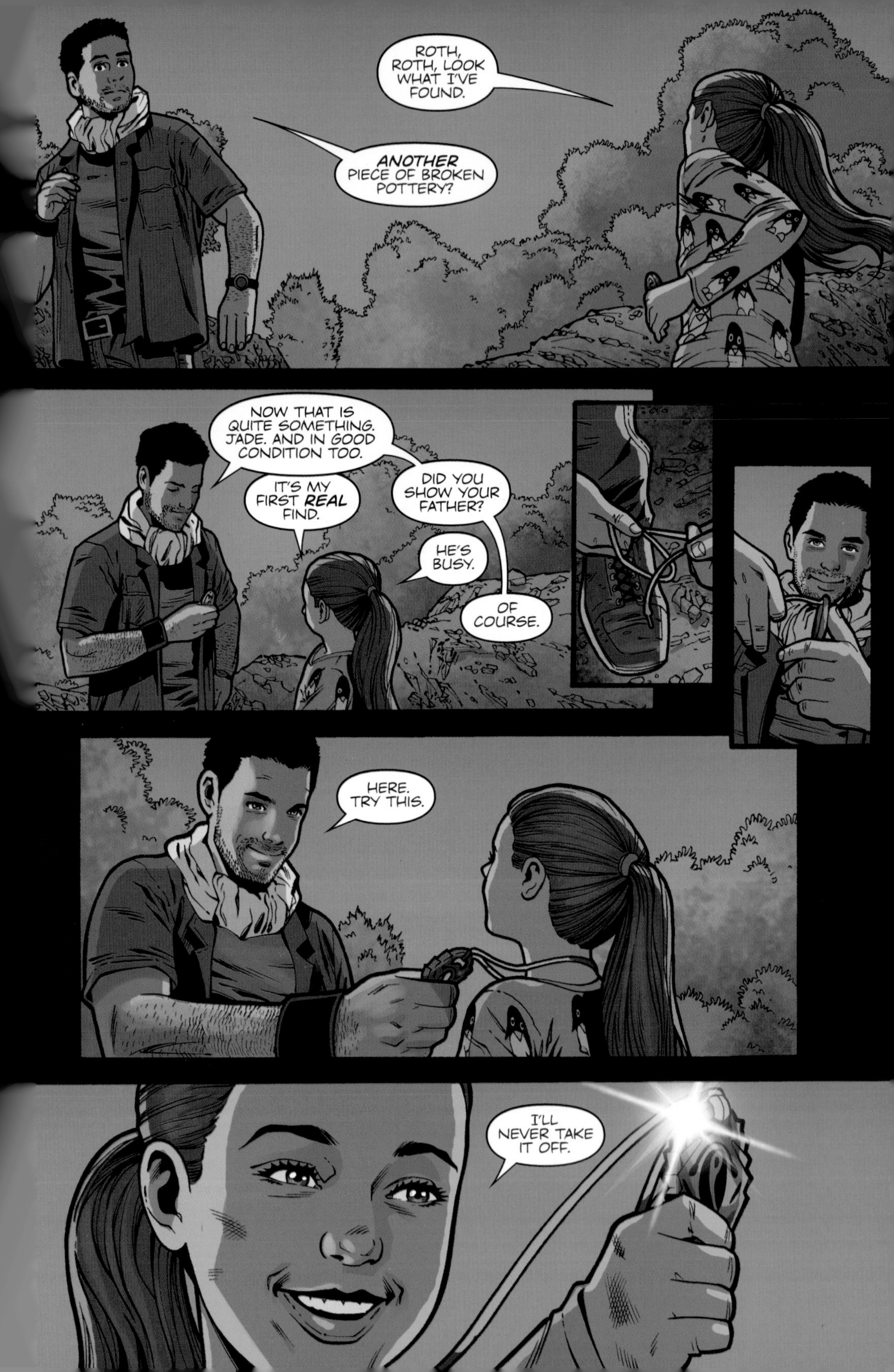

ROTH, ROTH, LOOK WHAT I'VE FOUND.
ANOTHER PIECE OF BROKEN POTTERY?
NOW THAT IS QUITE SOMETHING. JADE. AND IN GOOD CONDITION TOO.
IT'S MY FIRST ***REAL*** FIND.
DID YOU SHOW YOUR FATHER?
HE'S BUSY.
OF COURSE.
HERE. TRY THIS.
I'LL NEVER TAKE IT OFF.

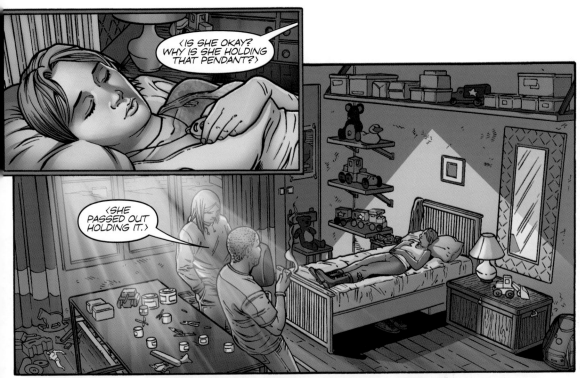

‹IS SHE OKAY? WHY IS SHE HOLDING THAT PENDANT?›

‹SHE PASSED OUT HOLDING IT.›

‹IDIOTS! JUST STANDING THERE LIKE THE LEMONS! CAN'T YOU SEE SHE'S AWAKE?!›

‹VIKTOR KIRILL! FILTHY HABIT!›

SORRY. THEY'RE OAFS, BUT MEAN WELL.

I HAVE TO GO. I HAVE TO FIND HIM.

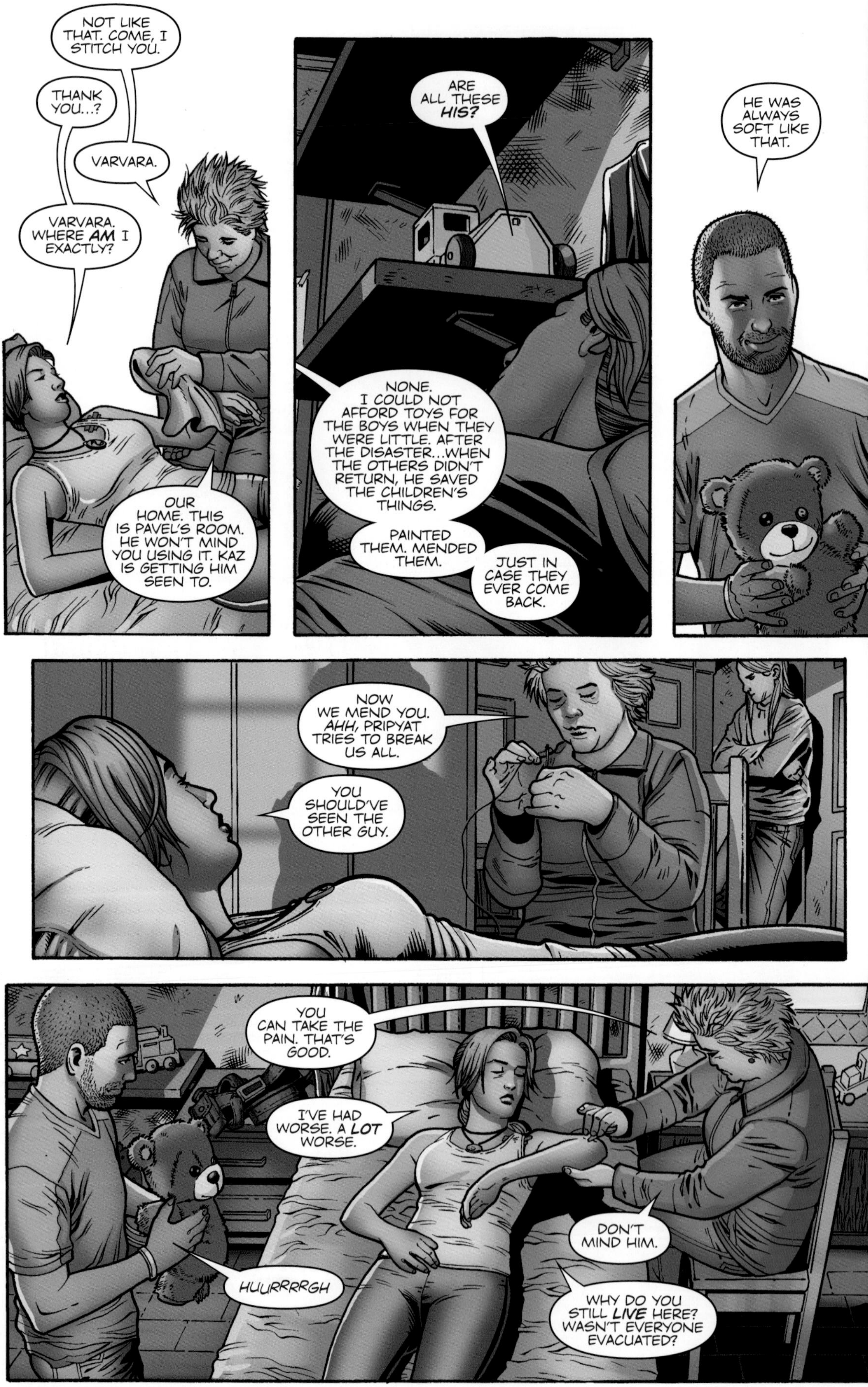

NOT LIKE THAT. COME, I STITCH YOU.
THANK YOU...?
VARVARA.
VARVARA. WHERE AM I EXACTLY?
OUR HOME. THIS IS PAVEL'S ROOM. HE WON'T MIND YOU USING IT. KAZ IS GETTING HIM SEEN TO.
ARE ALL THESE HIS?
NONE. I COULD NOT AFFORD TOYS FOR THE BOYS WHEN THEY WERE LITTLE. AFTER THE DISASTER...WHEN THE OTHERS DIDN'T RETURN, HE SAVED THE CHILDREN'S THINGS.
PAINTED THEM. MENDED THEM.
JUST IN CASE THEY EVER COME BACK.
HE WAS ALWAYS SOFT LIKE THAT.
NOW WE MEND YOU. AHH, PRIPYAT TRIES TO BREAK US ALL.
YOU SHOULD'VE SEEN THE OTHER GUY.
YOU CAN TAKE THE PAIN. THAT'S GOOD.
I'VE HAD WORSE. A LOT WORSE.
HUURRRRGH
DON'T MIND HIM.
WHY DO YOU STILL LIVE HERE? WASN'T EVERYONE EVACUATED?

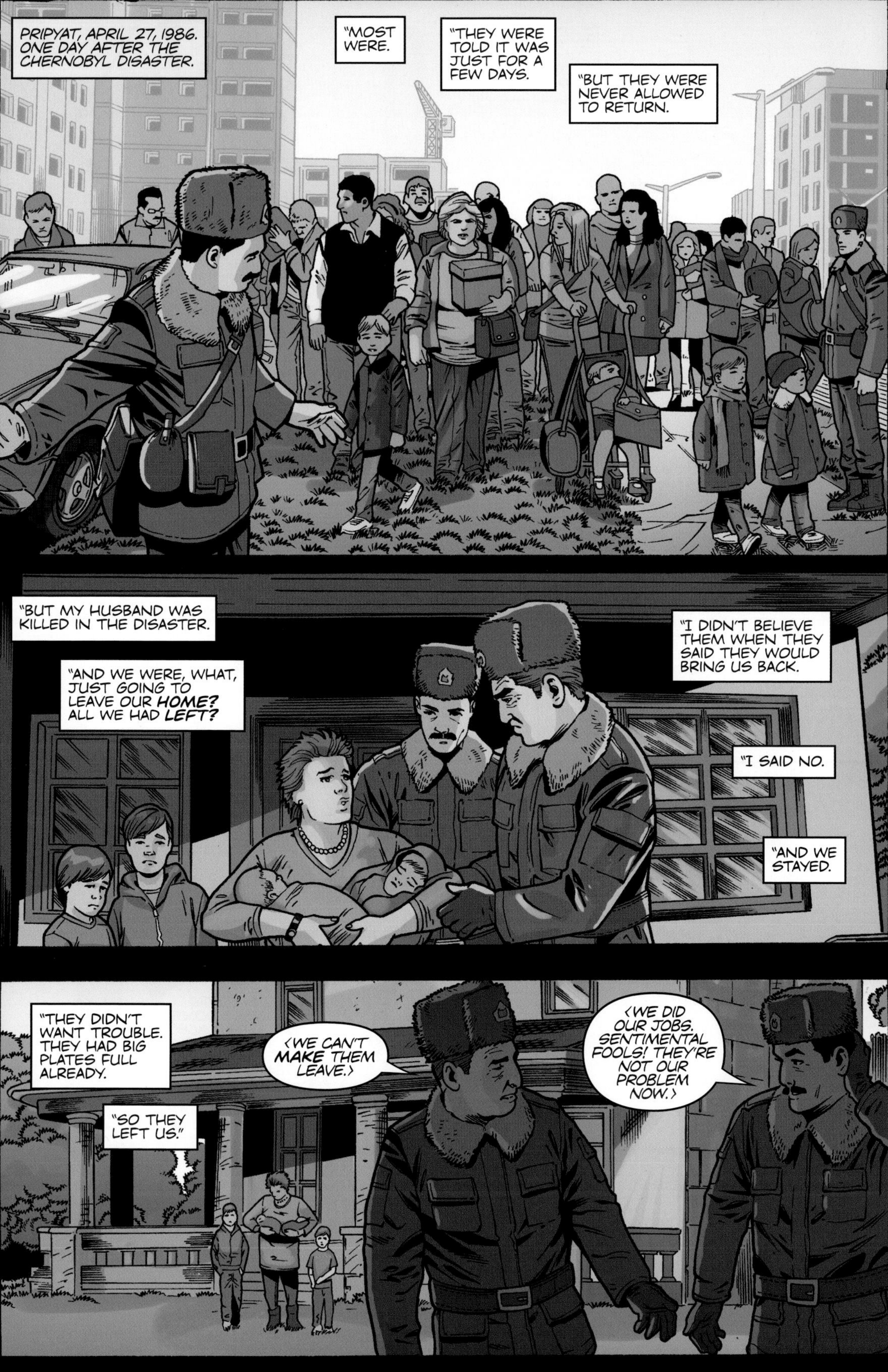
PRIPYAT, APRIL 27, 1986. ONE DAY AFTER THE CHERNOBYL DISASTER.
"MOST WERE.
"THEY WERE TOLD IT WAS JUST FOR A FEW DAYS.
"BUT THEY WERE NEVER ALLOWED TO RETURN.
"BUT MY HUSBAND WAS KILLED IN THE DISASTER.
"AND WE WERE, WHAT, JUST GOING TO LEAVE OUR **HOME?** ALL WE HAD **LEFT?**
"I DIDN'T BELIEVE THEM WHEN THEY SAID THEY WOULD BRING US BACK.
"I SAID NO.
"AND WE STAYED.
"THEY DIDN'T WANT TROUBLE. THEY HAD BIG PLATES FULL ALREADY.
"SO THEY LEFT US."
‹WE CAN'T **MAKE** THEM LEAVE.›
‹WE DID OUR JOBS. SENTIMENTAL FOOLS! THEY'RE NOT OUR PROBLEM NOW.›

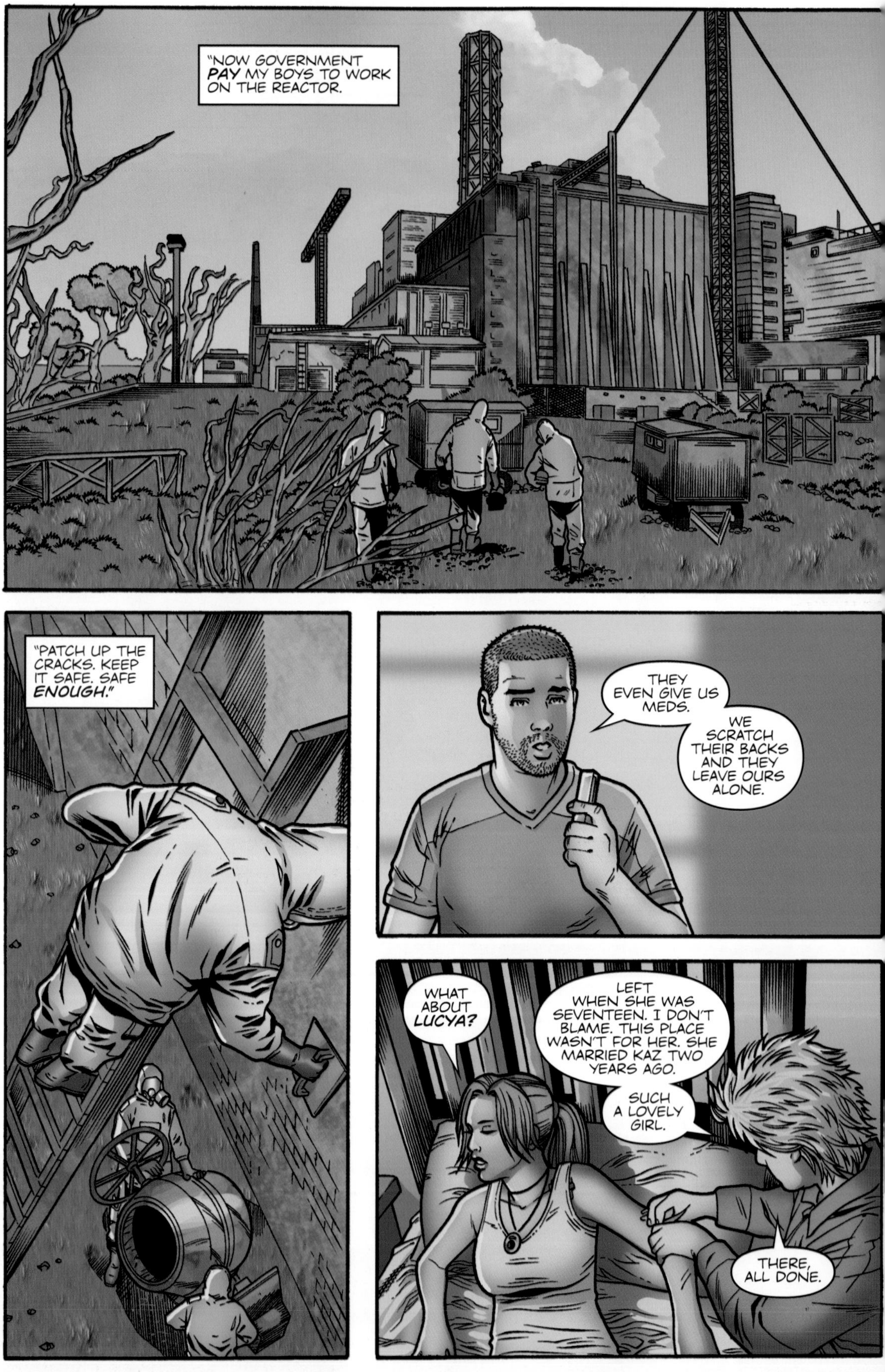
"NOW GOVERNMENT **PAY** MY BOYS TO WORK ON THE REACTOR.
"PATCH UP THE CRACKS. KEEP IT SAFE. SAFE **ENOUGH**."
THEY EVEN GIVE US MEDS.
WE SCRATCH THEIR BACKS AND THEY LEAVE OURS ALONE.
WHAT ABOUT **LUCYA?**
LEFT WHEN SHE WAS SEVENTEEN. I DON'T BLAME. THIS PLACE WASN'T FOR HER. SHE MARRIED KAZ TWO YEARS AGO.
SUCH A LOVELY GIRL.
THERE, ALL DONE.

THANK YOU, BUT I HAVE TO GO. CRUZ IS OUT THERE SOMEWHERE.

WHILST HE'S ALIVE KAZ WON'T BE SAFE.

NONE OF US WILL BE SAFE.

WHY DO YOU DO THIS? COME SO FAR FOR US?

A FAVOR TO A FRIEND. ALEX, KAZ'S BROTHER.

MUST HAVE BEEN QUITE A FRIEND.

HE WAS.

THWOCK THWOCK THWOCK

WHAT IS IT?

HELICOPTER. WE NEVER GET THOSE HERE. IT'S HEADING THIS WAY.

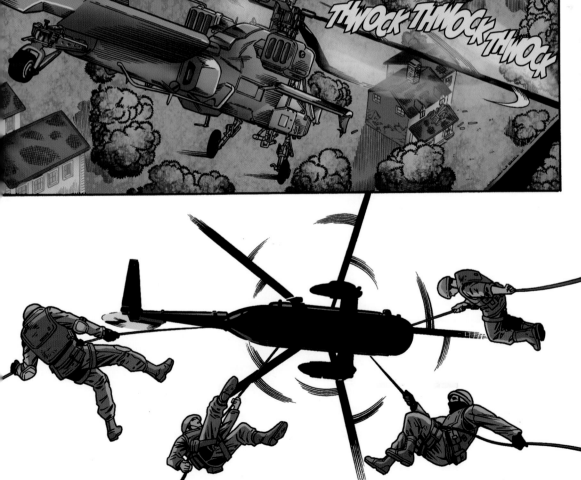

THWOCK THWOCK THWOCK

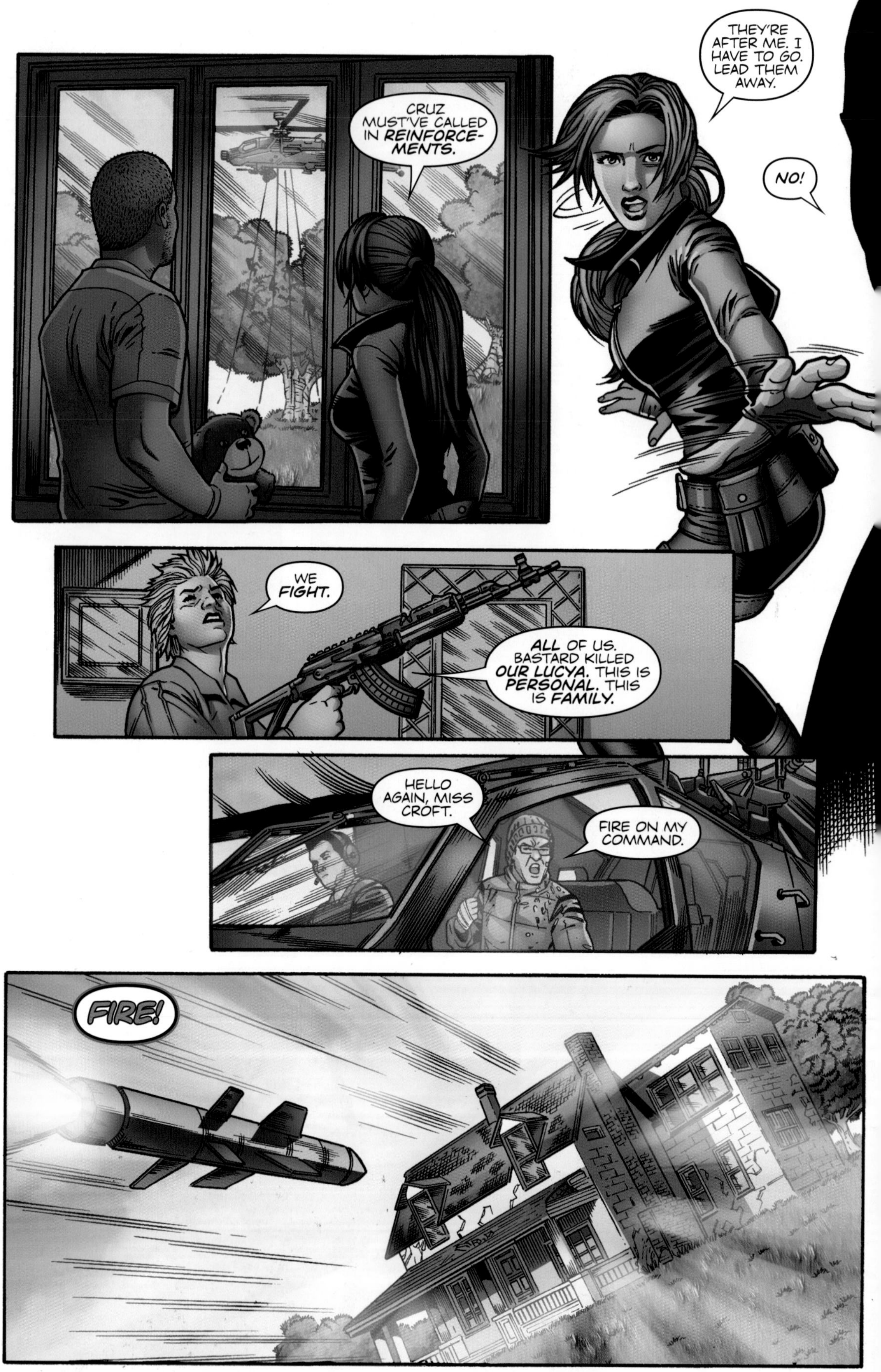
CRUZ MUST'VE CALLED IN REINFORCEMENTS.
THEY'RE AFTER ME. I HAVE TO GO. LEAD THEM AWAY.
NO!
WE FIGHT.
ALL OF US. BASTARD KILLED OUR LUCYA. THIS IS PERSONAL. THIS IS FAMILY.
HELLO AGAIN, MISS CROFT.
FIRE ON MY COMMAND.
FIRE!

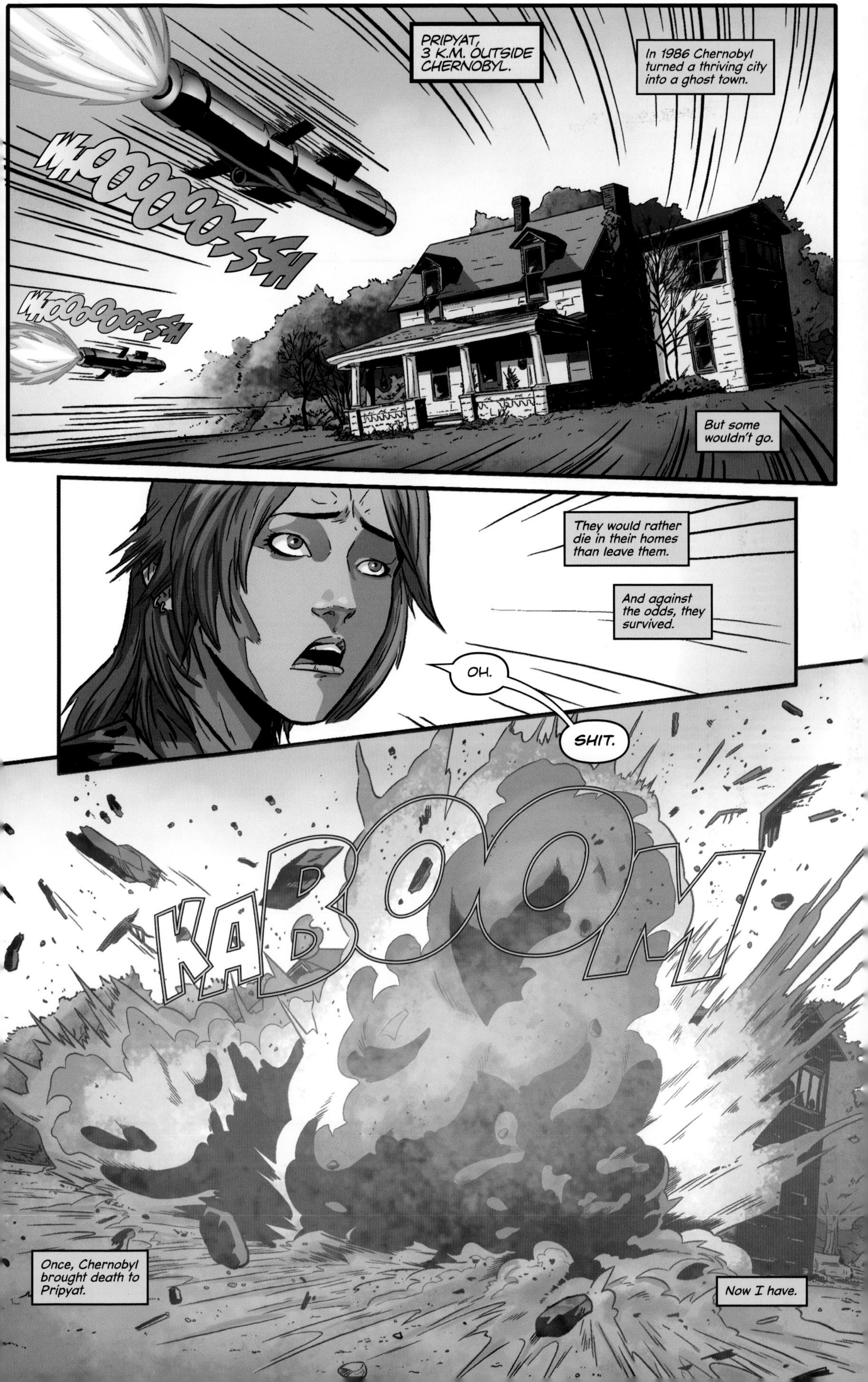
PRIPYAT, 3 K.M. OUTSIDE CHERNOBYL.
In 1986 Chernobyl turned a thriving city into a ghost town.
WHOOOOOOSSH
WHOOOOOOSSH
But some wouldn't go.
They would rather die in their homes than leave them.
And against the odds, they survived.
OH.
SHIT.
KABOOM
Once, Chernobyl brought death to Pripyat.
Now I have.

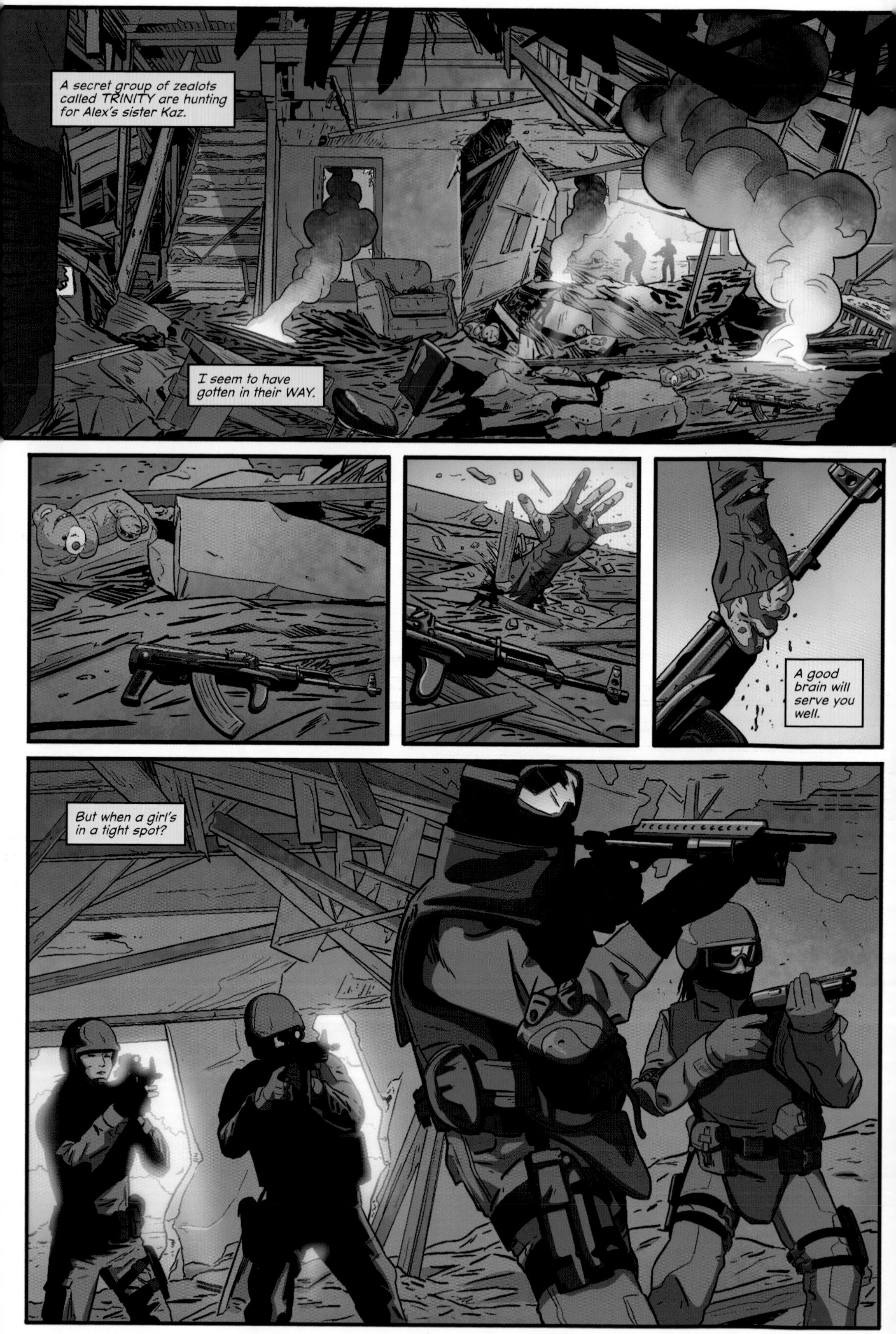
A secret group of zealots called TRINITY are hunting for Alex's sister Kaz.
I seem to have gotten in their WAY.
A good brain will serve you well.
But when a girl's in a tight spot?

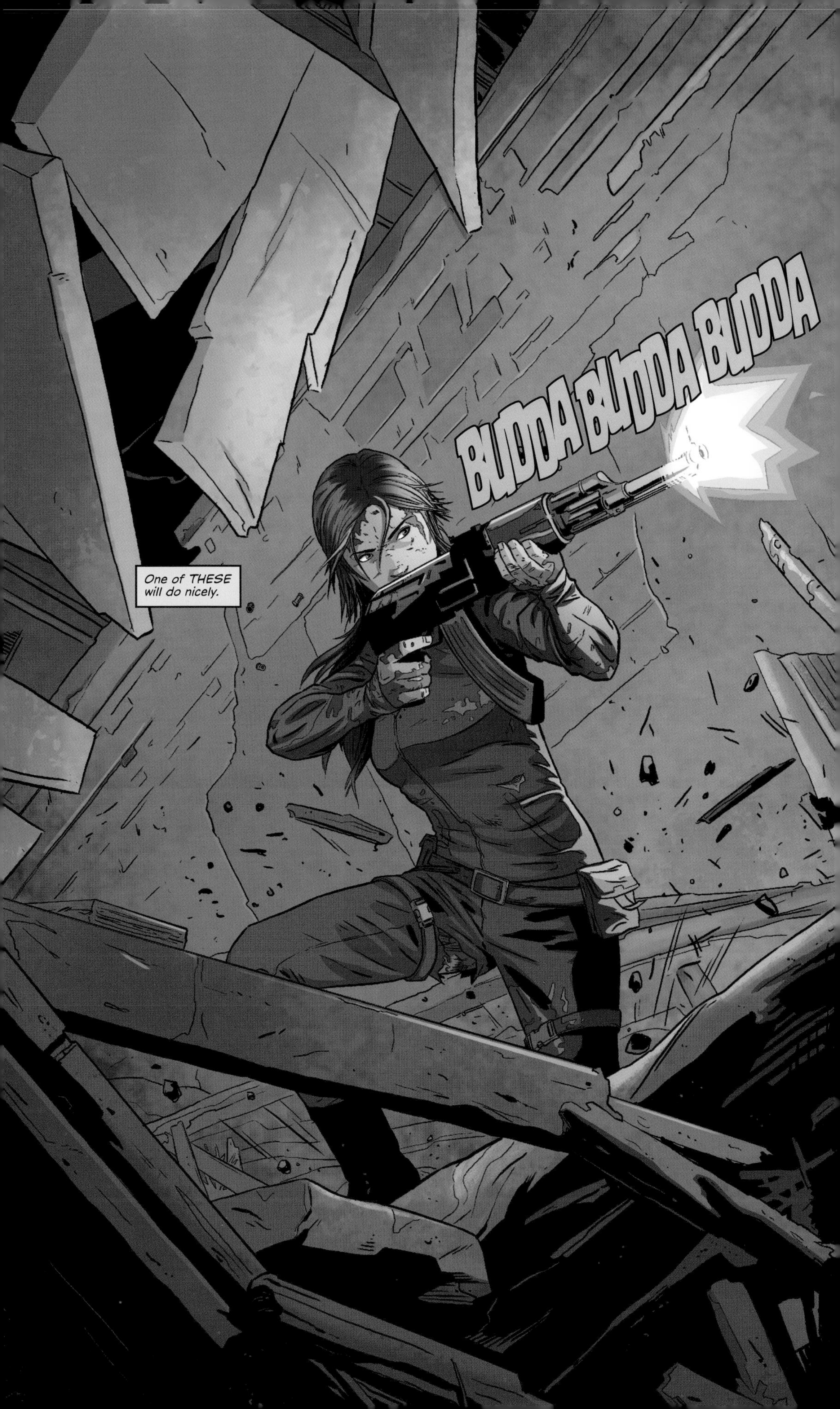
One of THESE will do nicely.
BUDDA BUDDA BUDDA

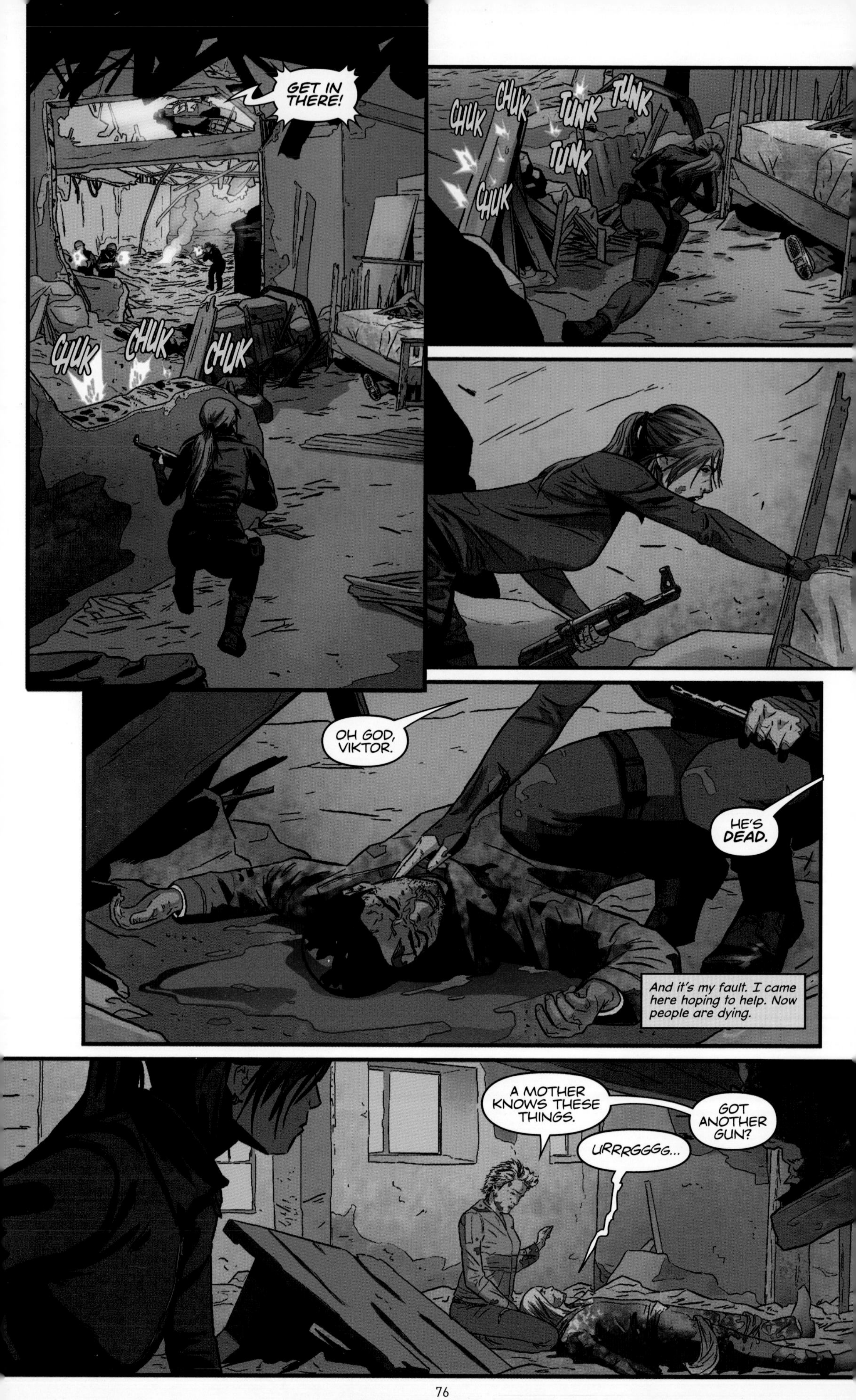
GET IN THERE!
CHUK
CHUK
CHUK
CHUK
CHUK
TUNK
TUNK
TUNK
CHUK
OH GOD, VIKTOR.
HE'S DEAD.
And it's my fault. I came here hoping to help. Now people are dying.
A MOTHER KNOWS THESE THINGS.
GOT ANOTHER GUN?
URRRGGGG...

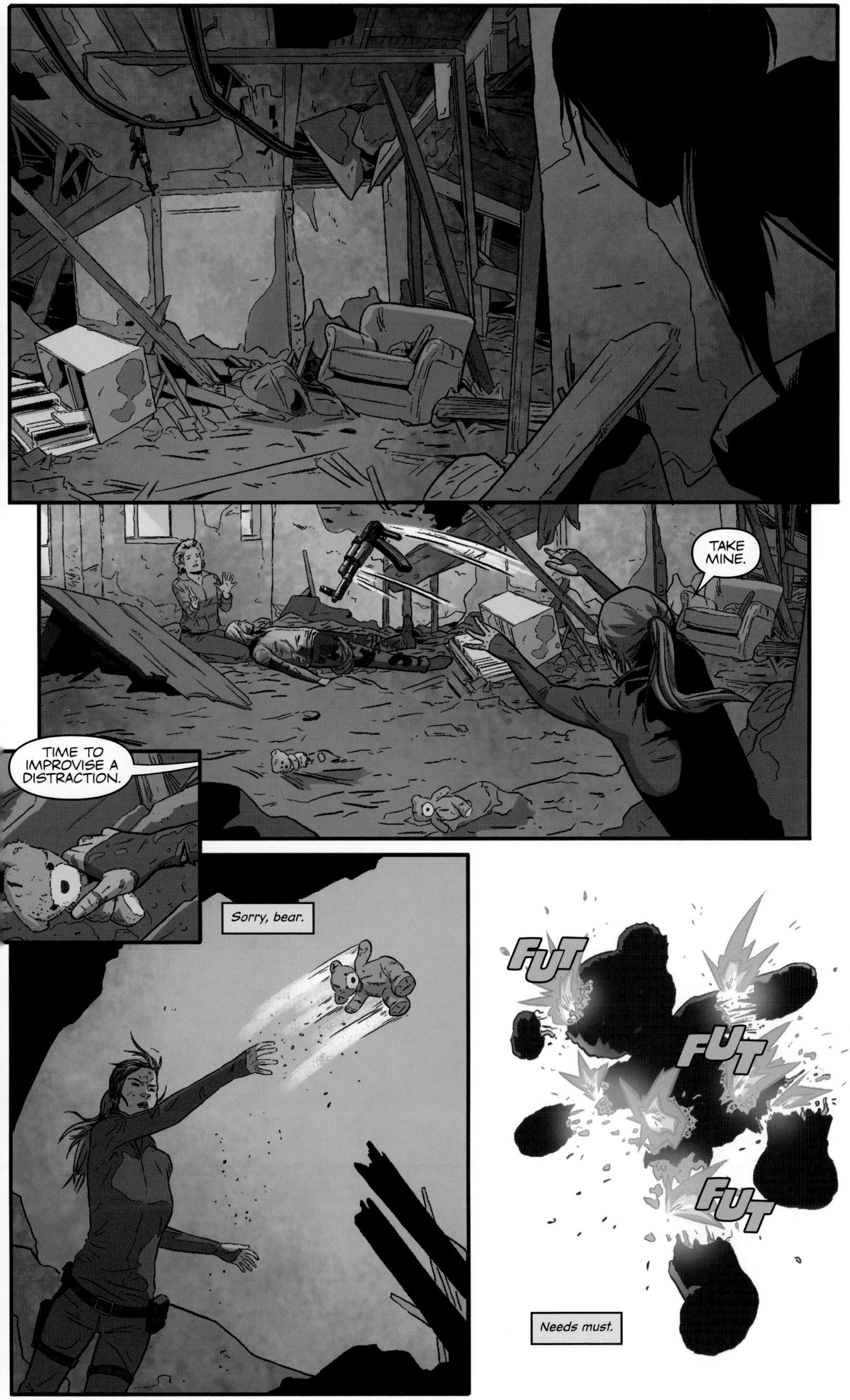
TAKE MINE.
TIME TO IMPROVISE A DISTRACTION.
Sorry, bear.
FUT
FUT
FUT
Needs must.

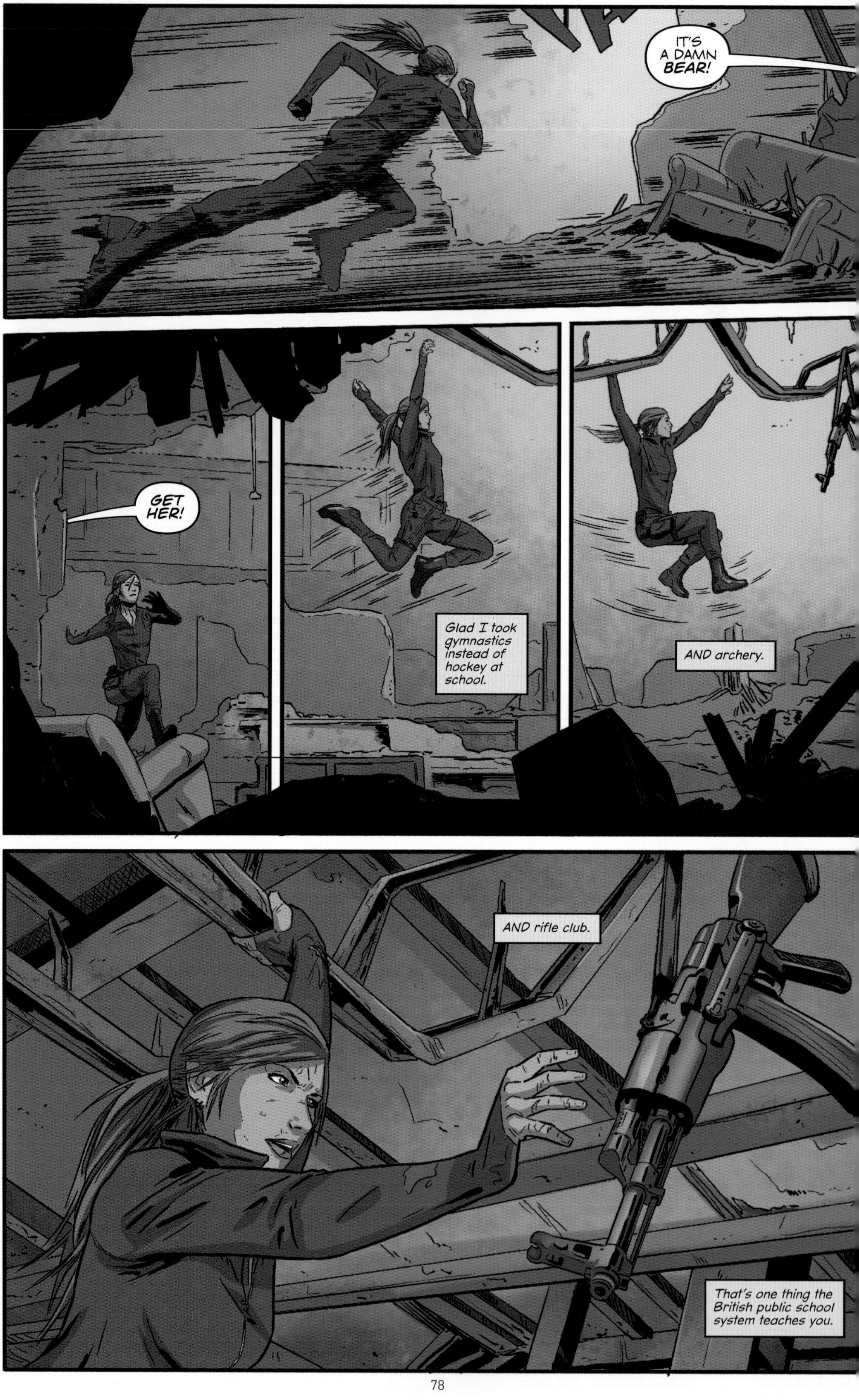
IT'S A DAMN BEAR!
GET HER!
Glad I took gymnastics instead of hockey at school.
AND archery.
AND rifle club.
That's one thing the British public school system teaches you.

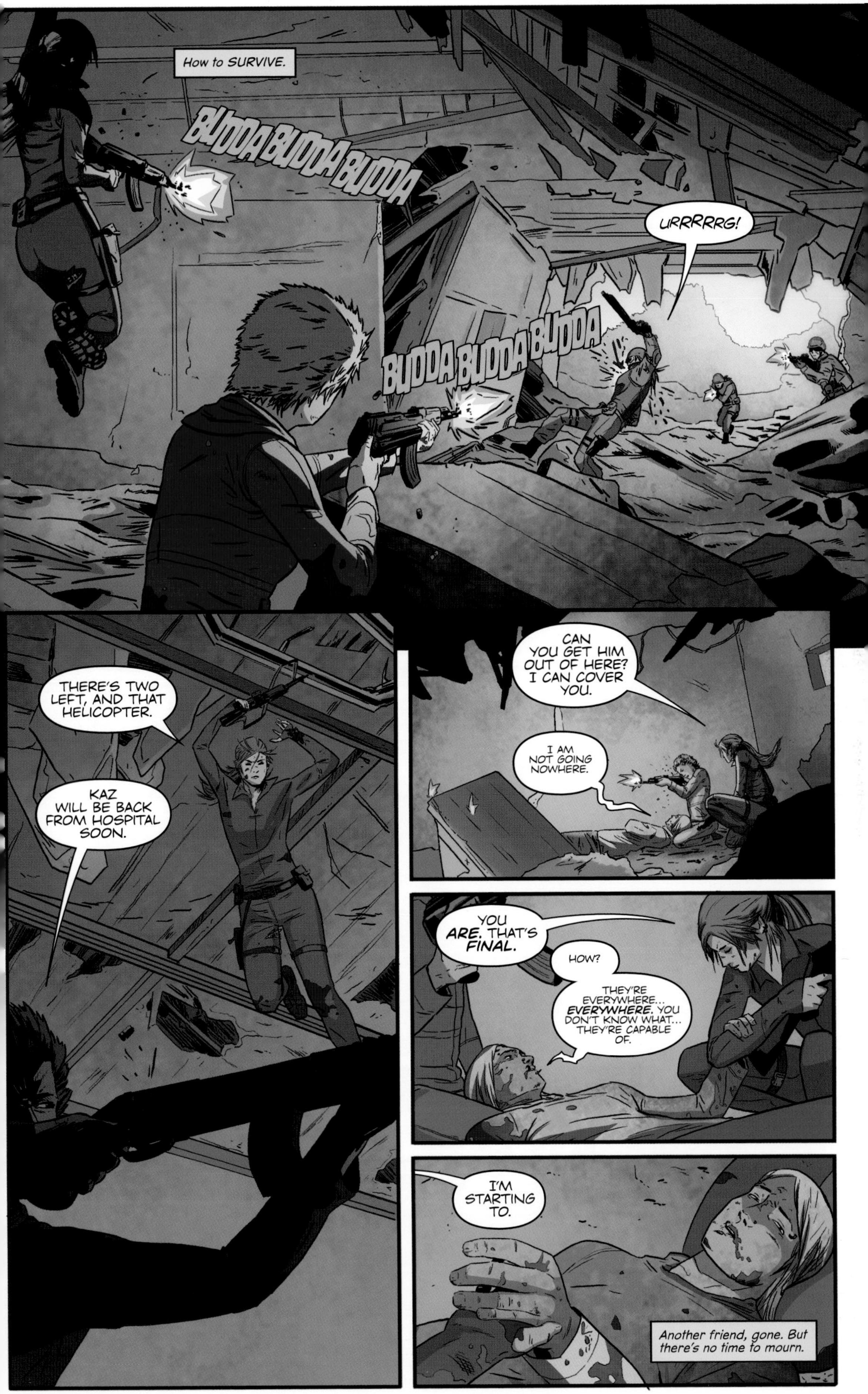
How to SURVIVE.
BUDDA BUDDA BUDDA
URRRRRG!
BUDDA BUDDA BUDDA
THERE'S TWO LEFT, AND THAT HELICOPTER.
KAZ WILL BE BACK FROM HOSPITAL SOON.
CAN YOU GET HIM OUT OF HERE? I CAN COVER YOU.
I AM NOT GOING NOWHERE.
YOU ARE. THAT'S FINAL.
HOW?
THEY'RE EVERYWHERE... EVERYWHERE. YOU DON'T KNOW WHAT... THEY'RE CAPABLE OF.
I'M STARTING TO.
Another friend, gone. But there's no time to mourn.

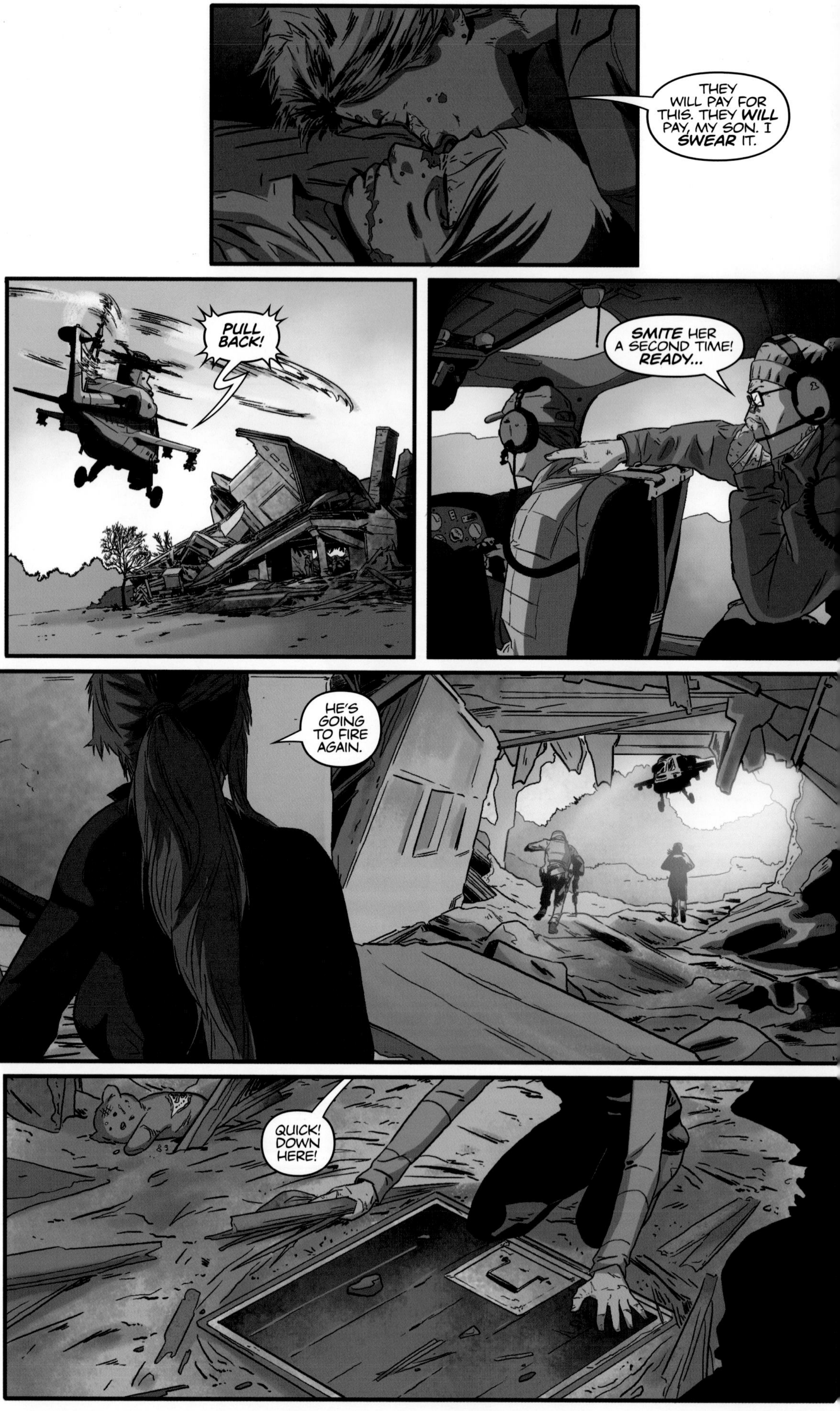
THEY WILL PAY FOR THIS. THEY **WILL** PAY, MY SON. I **SWEAR** IT.
PULL BACK!
SMITE HER A SECOND TIME! **READY...**
HE'S GOING TO FIRE AGAIN.
QUICK! DOWN HERE!

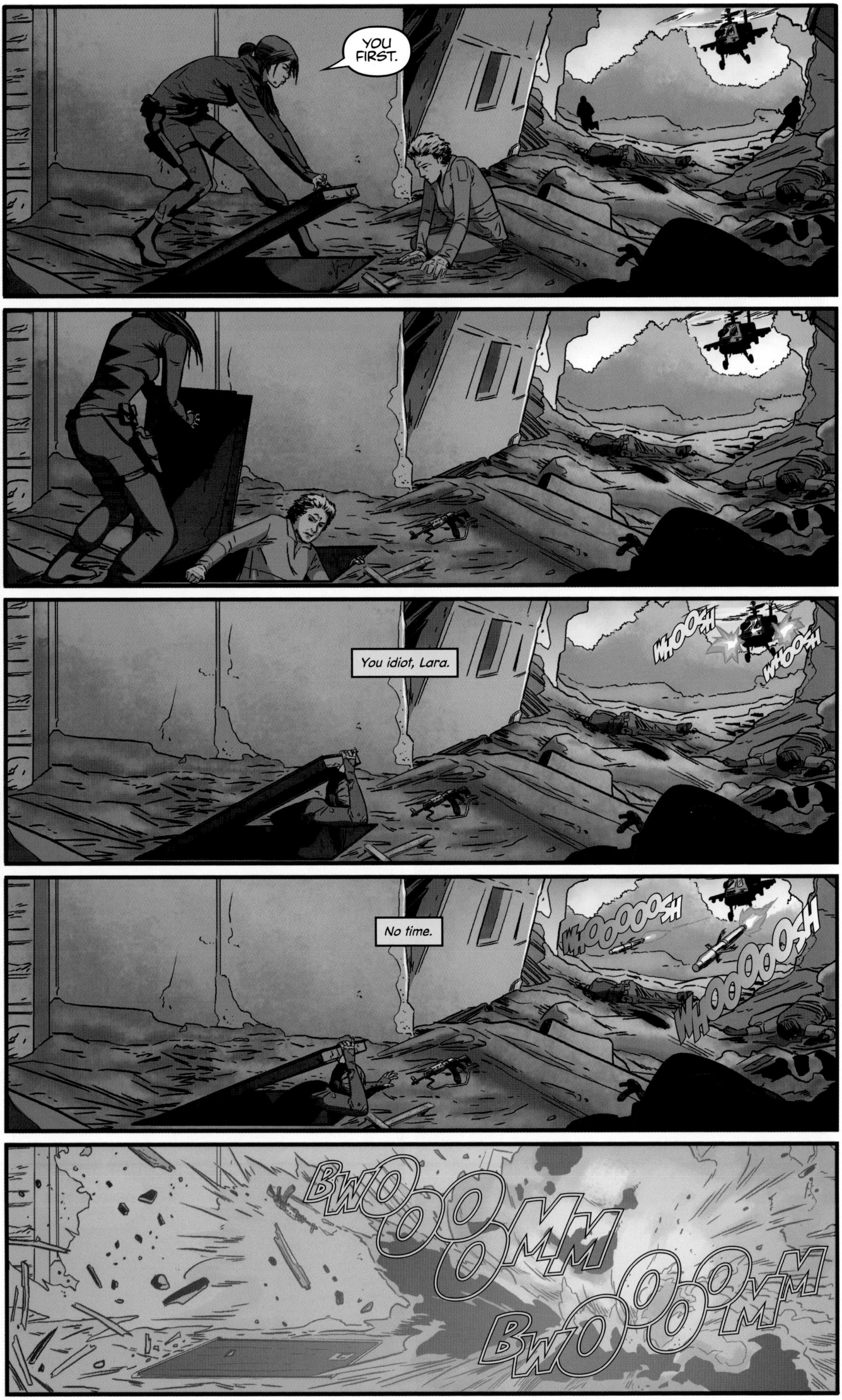
YOU FIRST.
You idiot, Lara.
WHOOSH
WHOOSH
No time.
WHOOOOOSH
WHOOOOOOSH
WHOOOOO
BWOOOOOMMM
BWOOOOOMMM

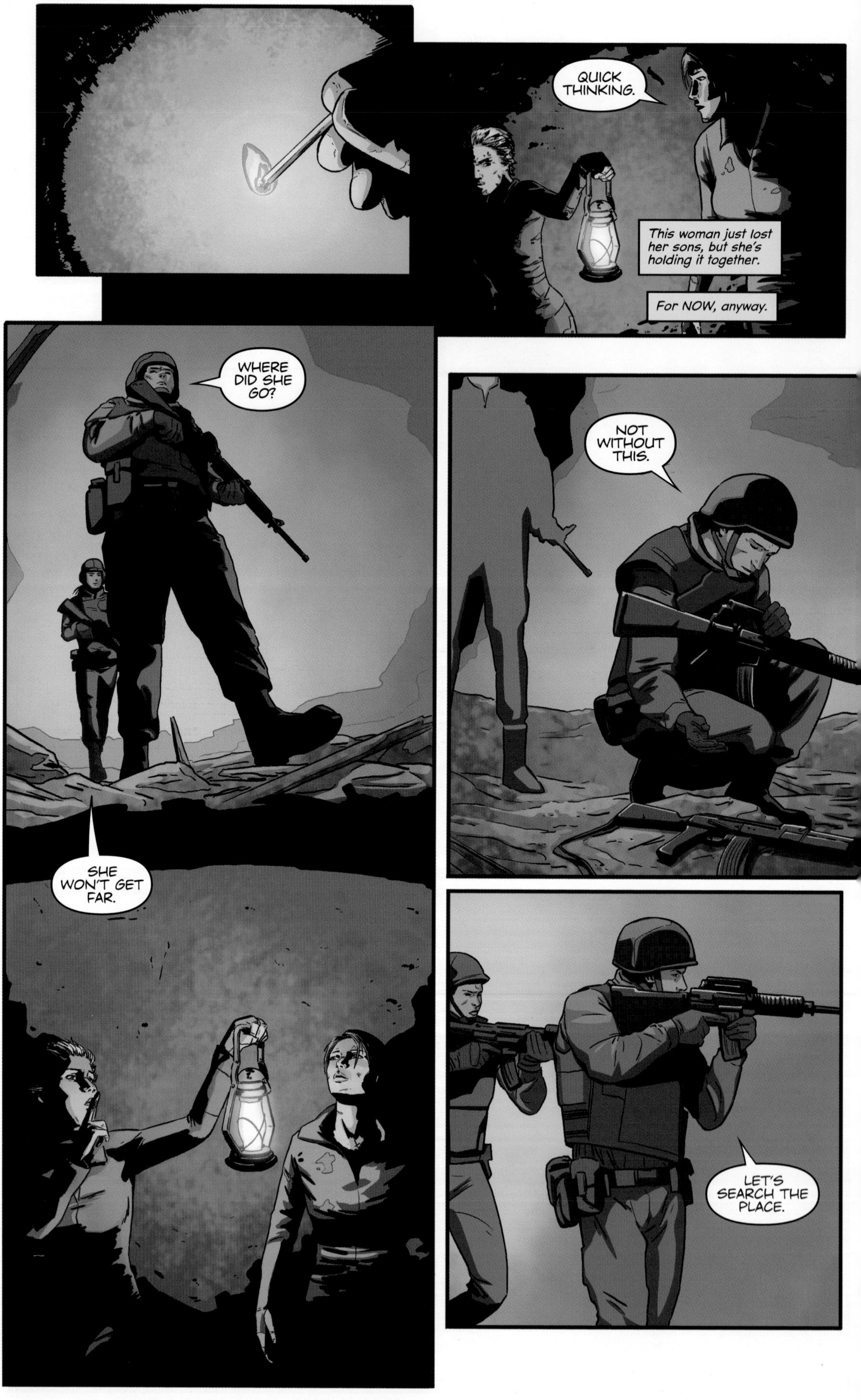
QUICK THINKING.
This woman just lost her sons, but she's holding it together.
For NOW, anyway.
WHERE DID SHE GO?
SHE WON'T GET FAR.
NOT WITHOUT THIS.
LET'S SEARCH THE PLACE.

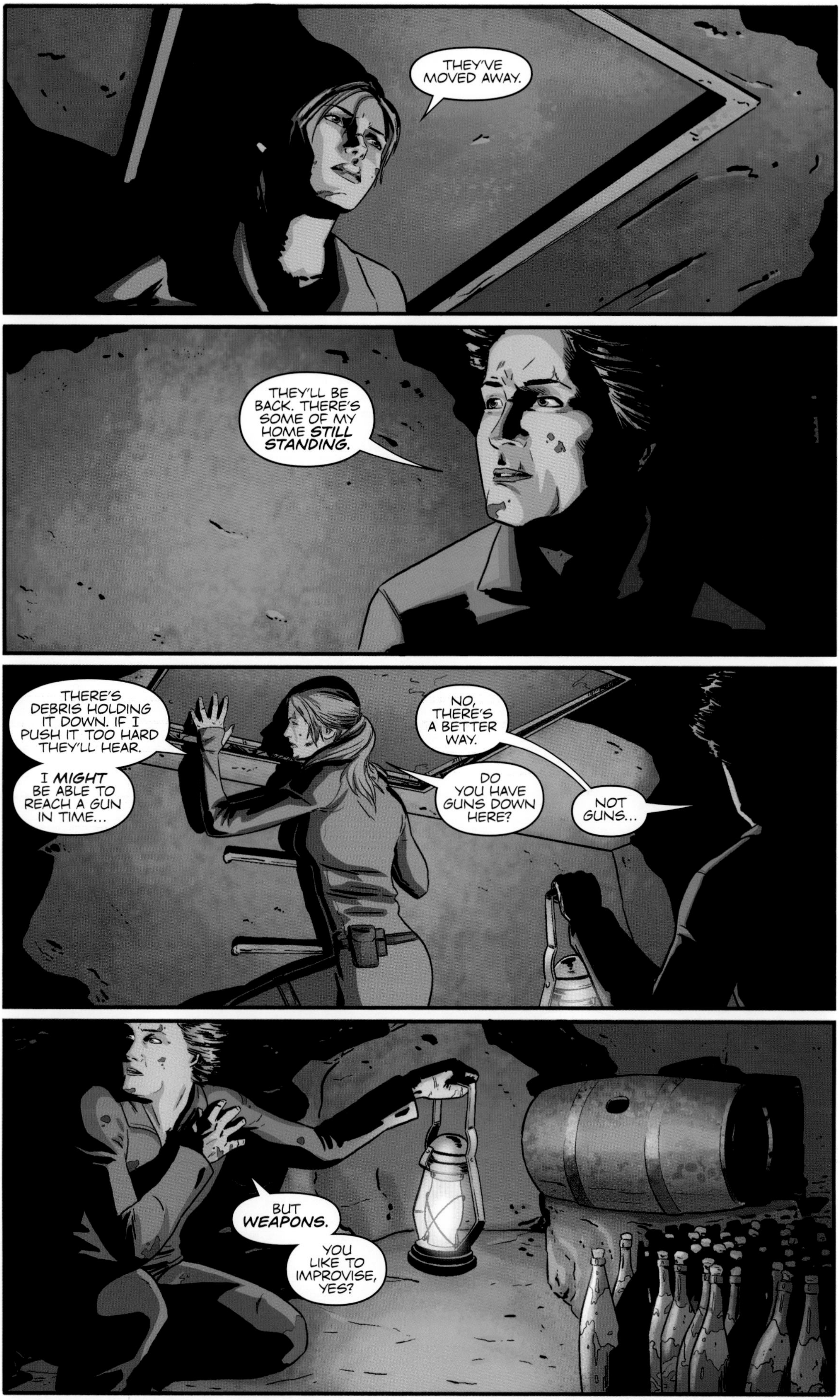
THEY'VE MOVED AWAY.
THEY'LL BE BACK. THERE'S SOME OF MY HOME **STILL STANDING.**
THERE'S DEBRIS HOLDING IT DOWN. IF I PUSH IT TOO HARD THEY'LL HEAR.
I ***MIGHT*** BE ABLE TO REACH A GUN IN TIME...
DO YOU HAVE GUNS DOWN HERE?
NO, THERE'S A BETTER WAY.
NOT GUNS...
BUT ***WEAPONS.***
YOU LIKE TO IMPROVISE, YES?

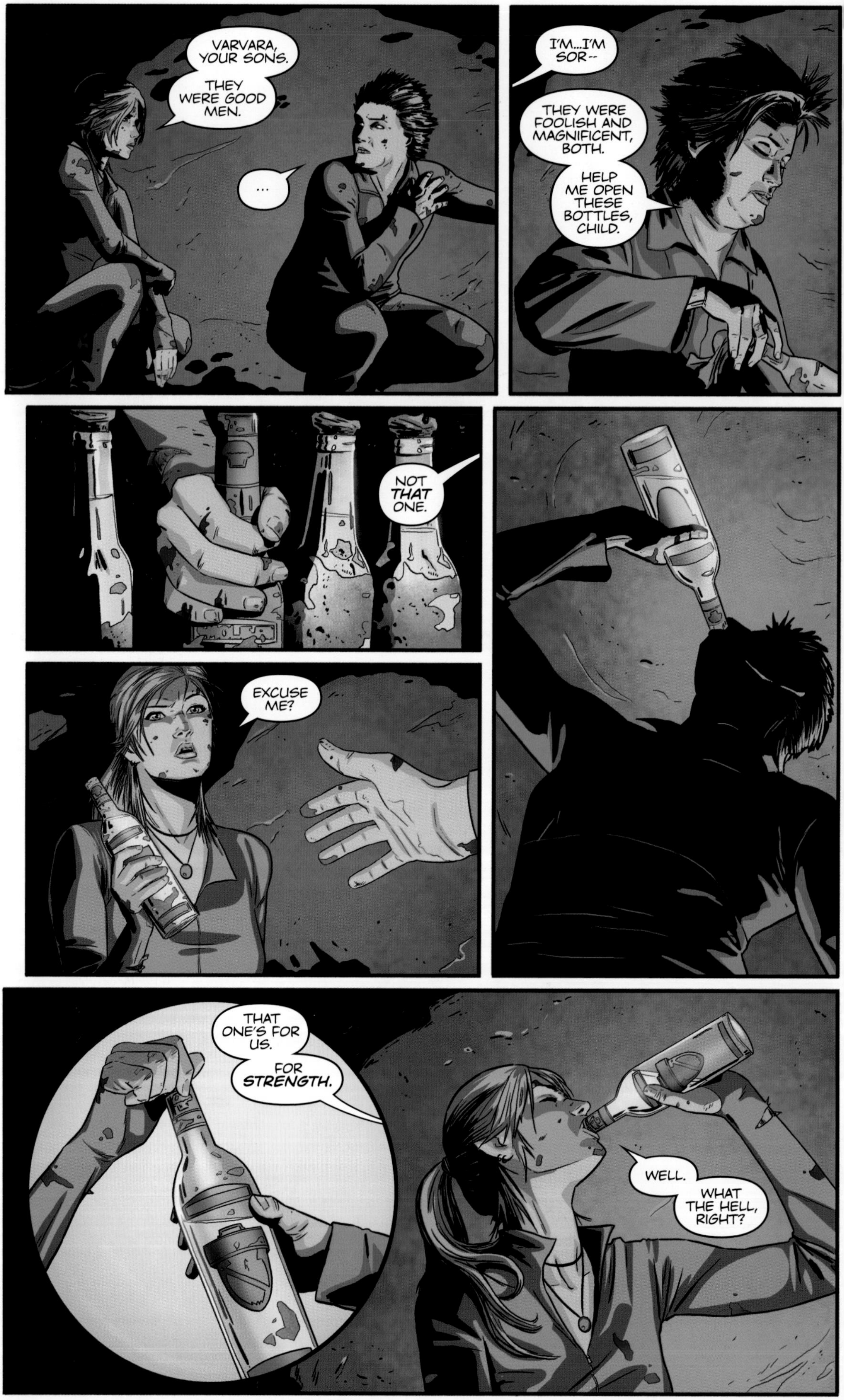
VARVARA, YOUR SONS.
THEY WERE GOOD MEN.
...
I'M...I'M SOR--
THEY WERE FOOLISH AND MAGNIFICENT, BOTH.
HELP ME OPEN THESE BOTTLES, CHILD.
NOT *THAT* ONE.
EXCUSE ME?
THAT ONE'S FOR US.
FOR **STRENGTH.**
WELL.
WHAT THE HELL, RIGHT?

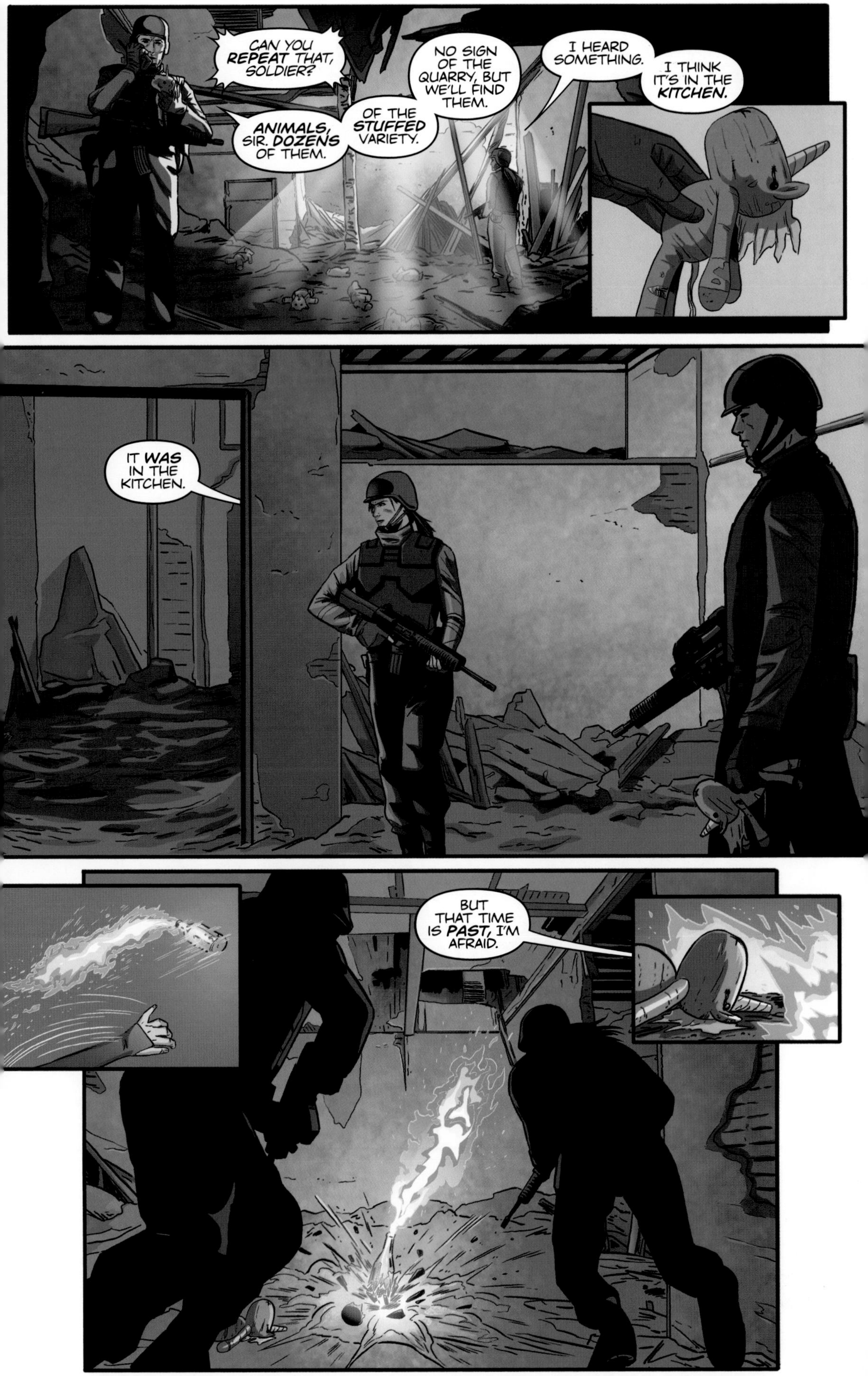
CAN YOU REPEAT THAT, SOLDIER?
ANIMALS, SIR. DOZENS OF THEM.
OF THE STUFFED VARIETY.
NO SIGN OF THE QUARRY, BUT WE'LL FIND THEM.
I HEARD SOMETHING.
I THINK IT'S IN THE KITCHEN.
IT WAS IN THE KITCHEN.
BUT THAT TIME IS PAST, I'M AFRAID.

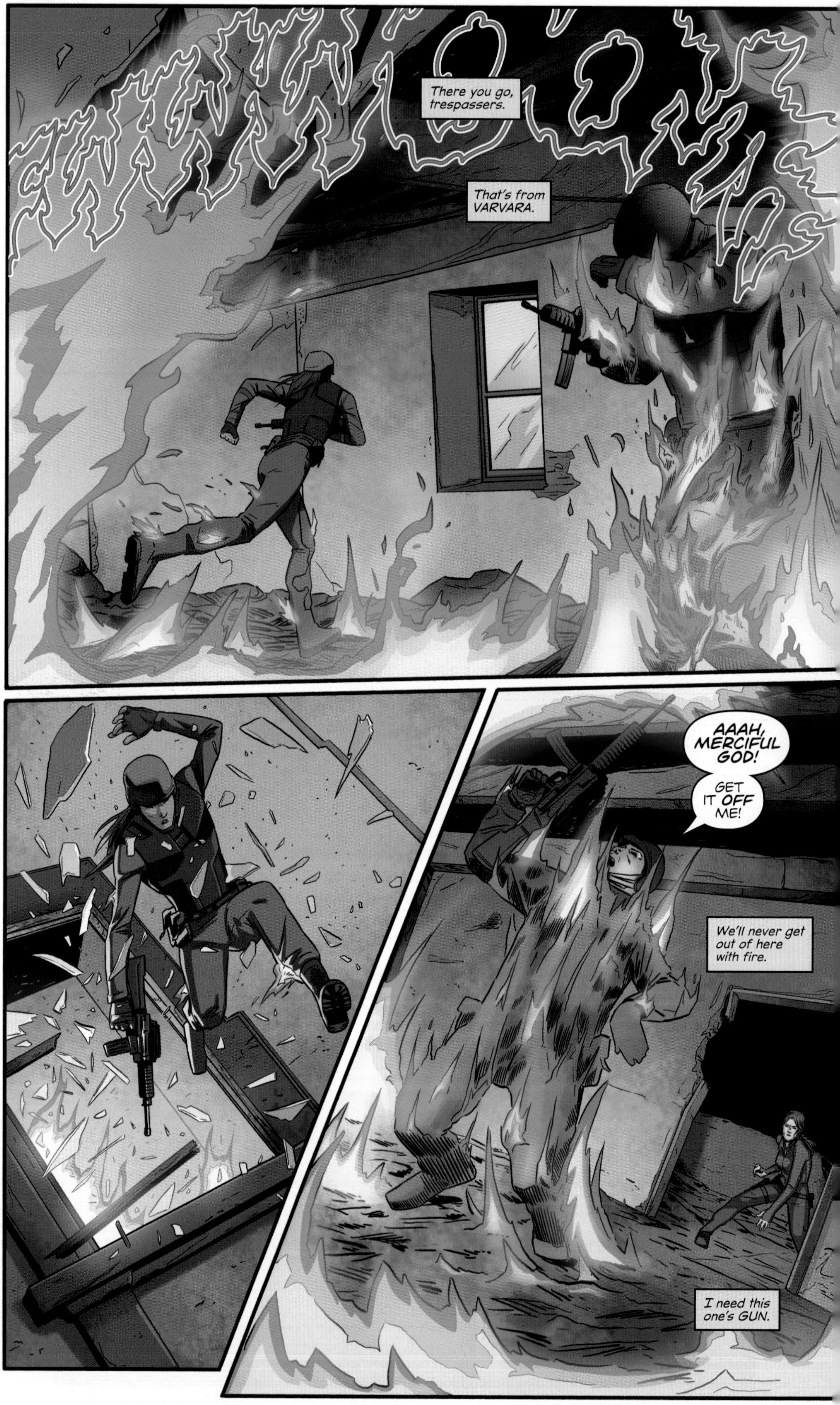
There you go, trespassers.
That's from VARVARA.
AAAH, MERCIFUL GOD!
GET IT OFF ME!
We'll never get out of here with fire.
I need this one's GUN.

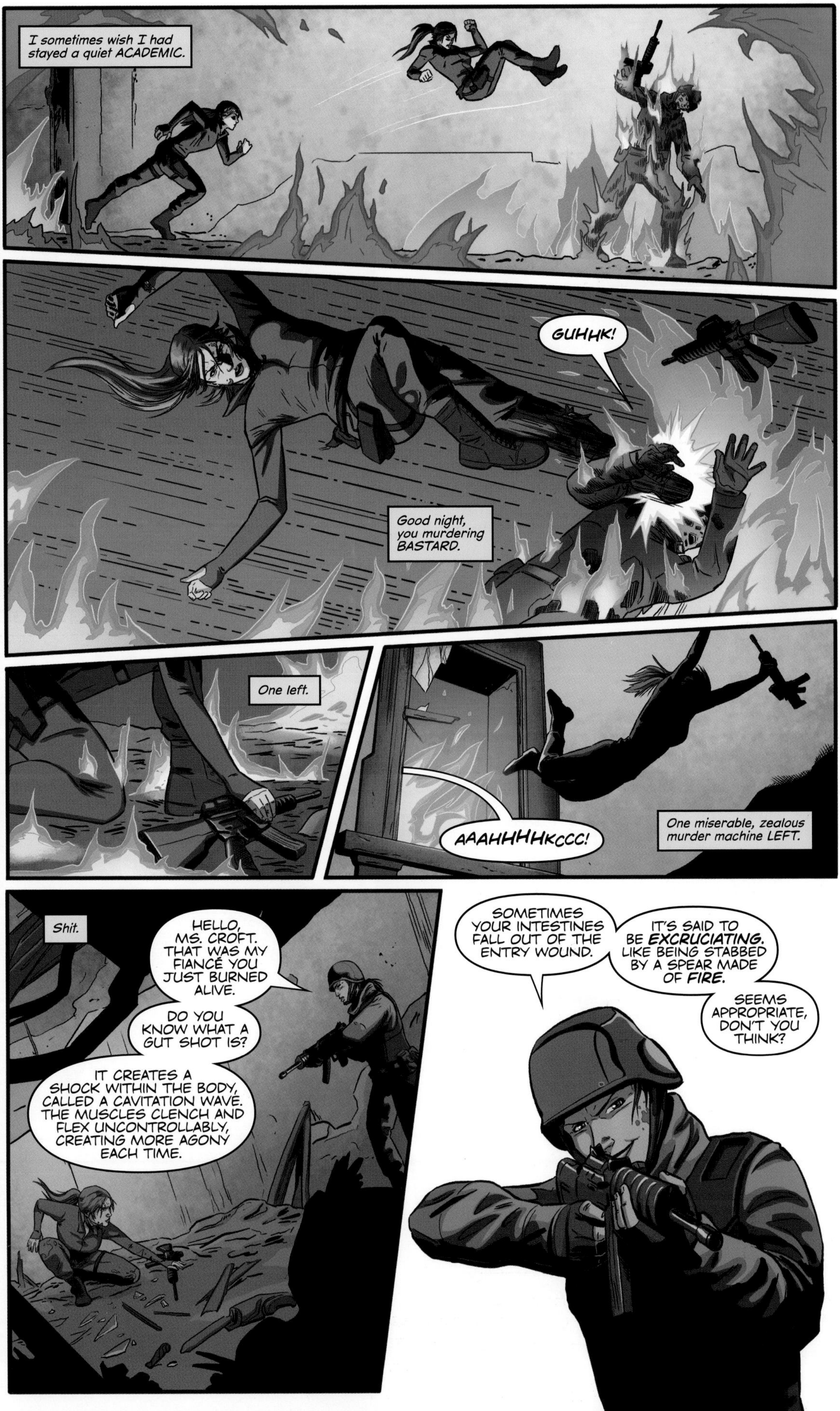

I sometimes wish I had stayed a quiet ACADEMIC.
GUHHK!
Good night, you murdering BASTARD.
One left.
AAAHHHHKCCC!
One miserable, zealous murder machine LEFT.
Shit.
HELLO, MS. CROFT. THAT WAS MY FIANCÉ YOU JUST BURNED ALIVE.
DO YOU KNOW WHAT A GUT SHOT IS?
IT CREATES A SHOCK WITHIN THE BODY, CALLED A CAVITATION WAVE. THE MUSCLES CLENCH AND FLEX UNCONTROLLABLY, CREATING MORE AGONY EACH TIME.
SOMETIMES YOUR INTESTINES FALL OUT OF THE ENTRY WOUND.
IT'S SAID TO BE EXCRUCIATING. LIKE BEING STABBED BY A SPEAR MADE OF FIRE.
SEEMS APPROPRIATE, DON'T YOU THINK?

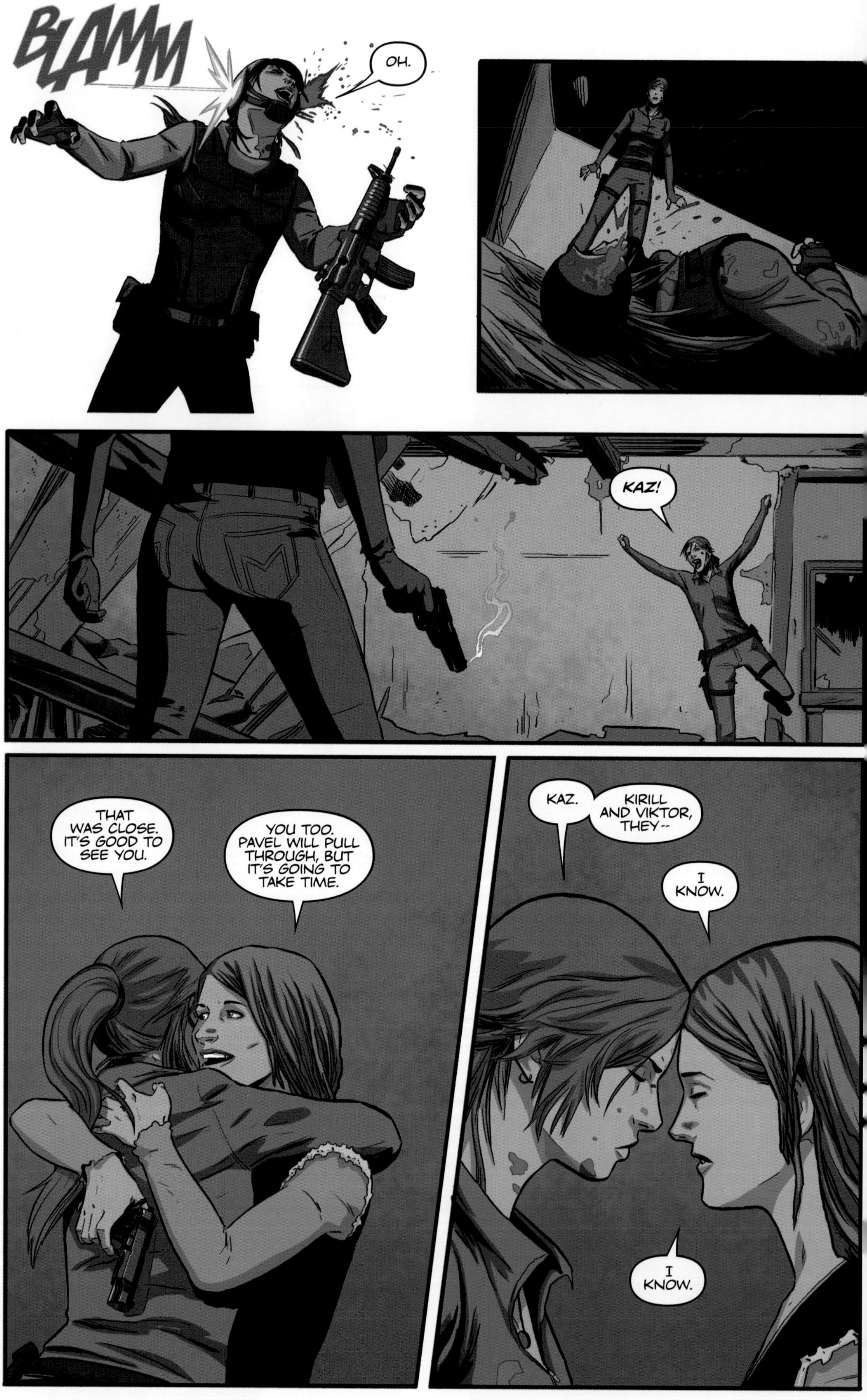
BLAMM
OH.
KAZ!
THAT WAS CLOSE. IT'S GOOD TO SEE YOU.
YOU TOO. PAVEL WILL PULL THROUGH, BUT IT'S GOING TO TAKE TIME.
KAZ.
KIRILL AND VIKTOR, THEY--
I KNOW.
I KNOW.

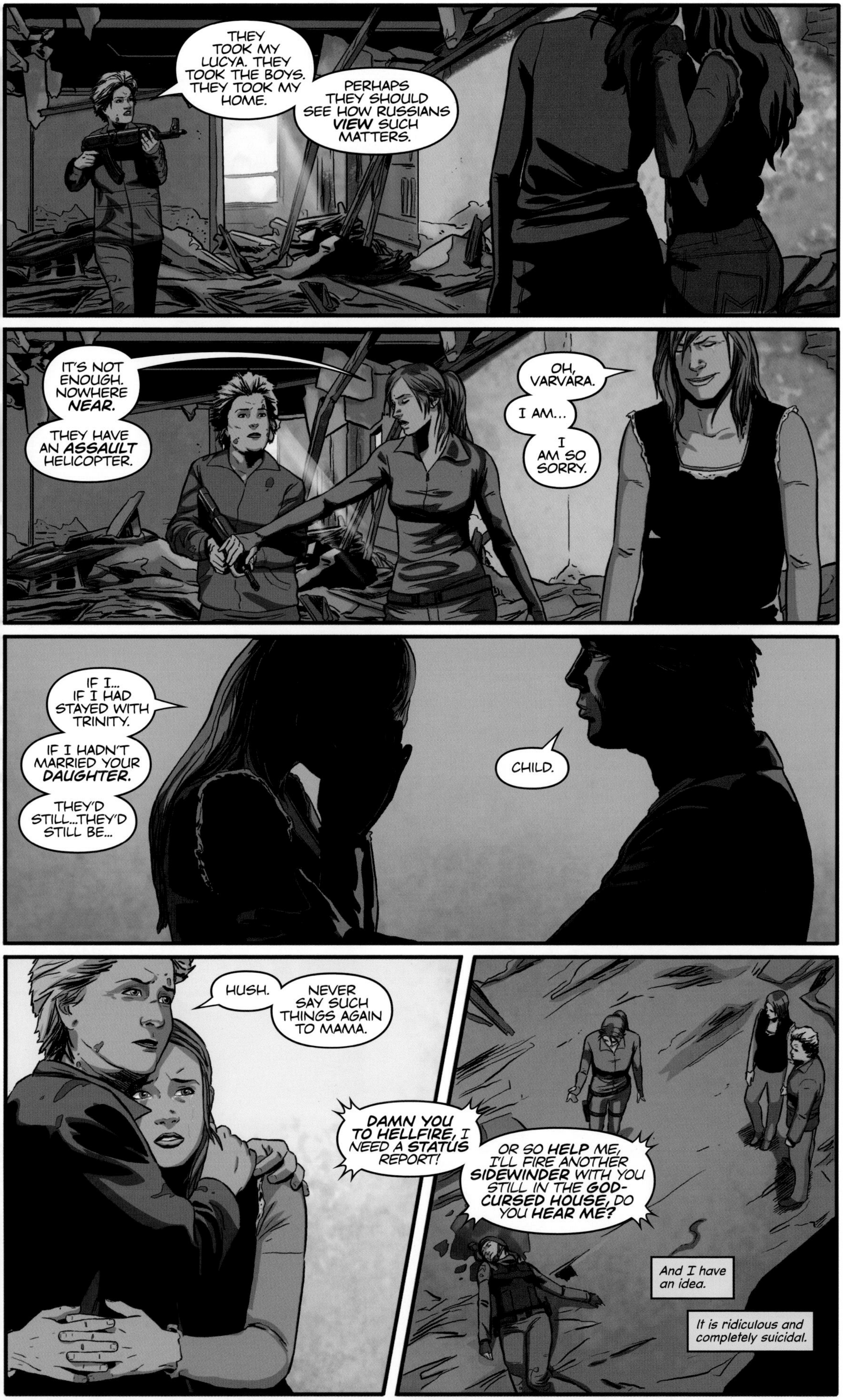
THEY TOOK MY LUCYA. THEY TOOK THE BOYS. THEY TOOK MY HOME.
PERHAPS THEY SHOULD SEE HOW RUSSIANS VIEW SUCH MATTERS.
IT'S NOT ENOUGH. NOWHERE NEAR.
THEY HAVE AN ASSAULT HELICOPTER.
OH, VARVARA.
I AM...
I AM SO SORRY.
IF I... IF I HAD STAYED WITH TRINITY.
IF I HADN'T MARRIED YOUR DAUGHTER.
THEY'D STILL...THEY'D STILL BE...
CHILD.
HUSH.
NEVER SAY SUCH THINGS AGAIN TO MAMA.
DAMN YOU TO HELLFIRE, I NEED A STATUS REPORT!
OR SO HELP ME, I'LL FIRE ANOTHER SIDEWINDER WITH YOU STILL IN THE GOD-CURSED HOUSE, DO YOU HEAR ME?
And I have an idea.
It is ridiculous and completely suicidal.

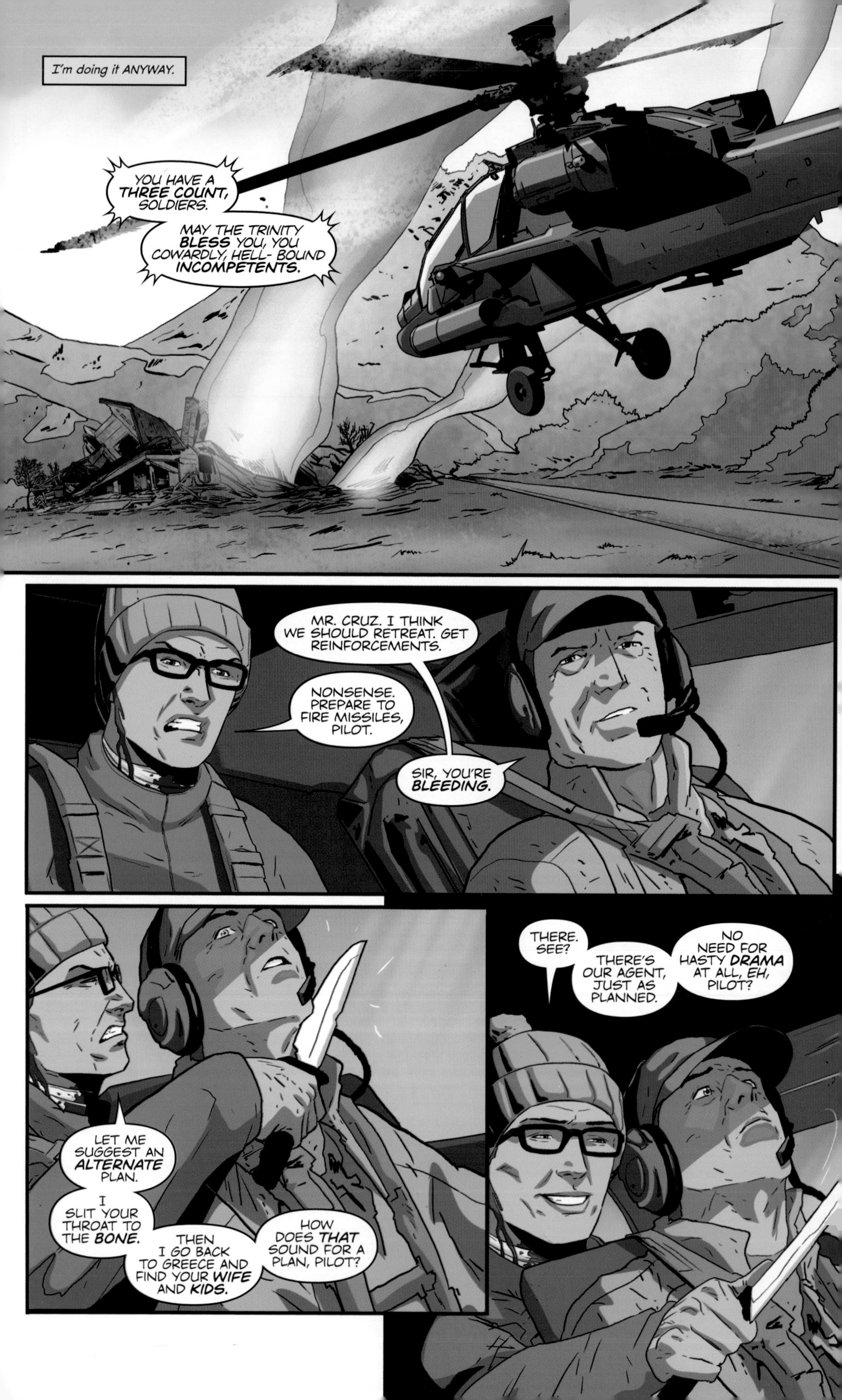
I'm doing it ANYWAY.
YOU HAVE A THREE COUNT, SOLDIERS.
MAY THE TRINITY BLESS YOU, YOU COWARDLY, HELL- BOUND INCOMPETENTS.
MR. CRUZ. I THINK WE SHOULD RETREAT. GET REINFORCEMENTS.
NONSENSE. PREPARE TO FIRE MISSILES, PILOT.
SIR, YOU'RE BLEEDING.
LET ME SUGGEST AN ALTERNATE PLAN.
I SLIT YOUR THROAT TO THE BONE.
THEN I GO BACK TO GREECE AND FIND YOUR WIFE AND KIDS.
HOW DOES THAT SOUND FOR A PLAN, PILOT?
THERE. SEE?
THERE'S OUR AGENT, JUST AS PLANNED.
NO NEED FOR HASTY DRAMA AT ALL, EH, PILOT?

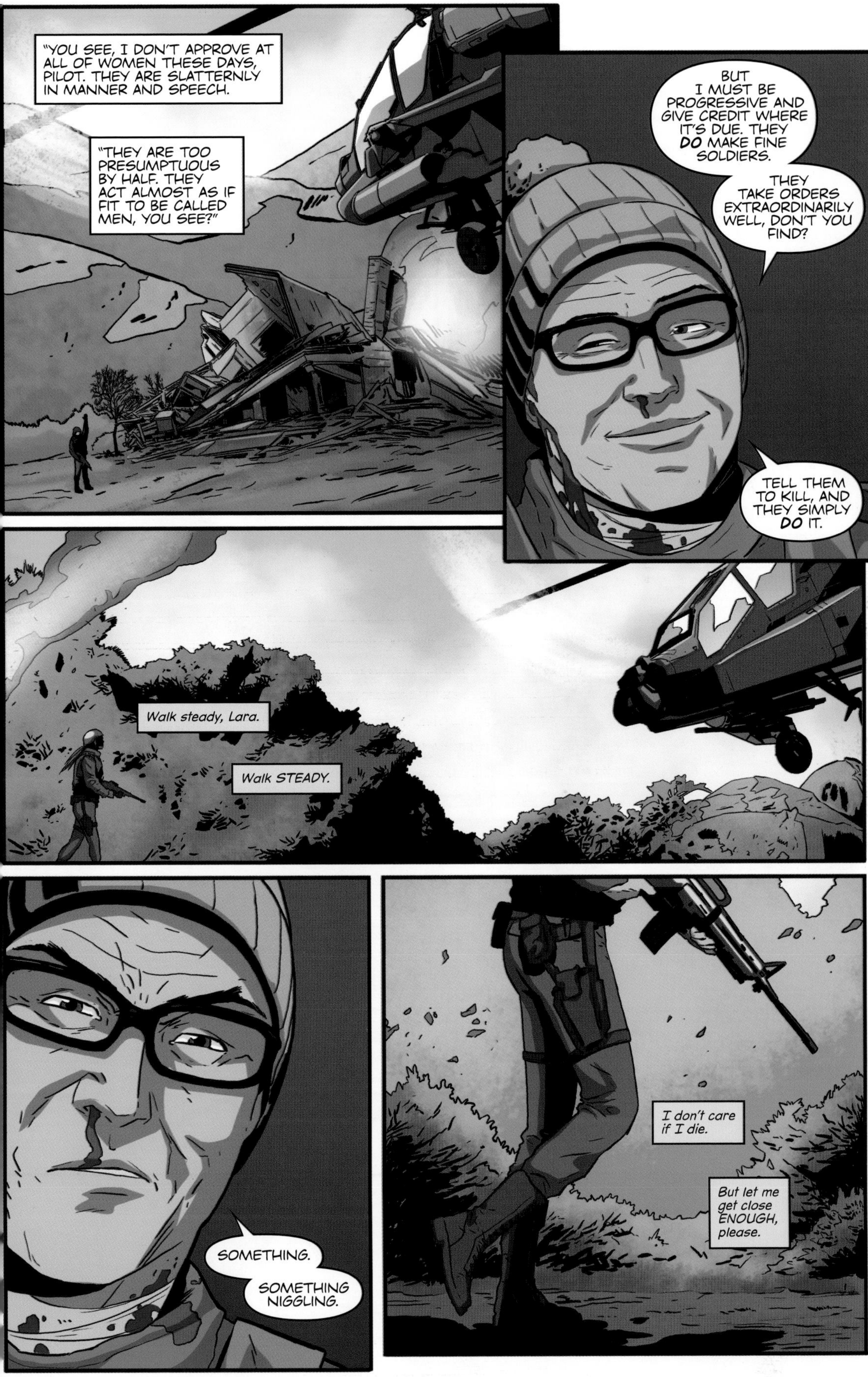
"YOU SEE, I DON'T APPROVE AT ALL OF WOMEN THESE DAYS, PILOT. THEY ARE SLATTERNLY IN MANNER AND SPEECH.
"THEY ARE TOO PRESUMPTUOUS BY HALF. THEY ACT ALMOST AS IF FIT TO BE CALLED MEN, YOU SEE?"
BUT I MUST BE PROGRESSIVE AND GIVE CREDIT WHERE IT'S DUE. THEY DO MAKE FINE SOLDIERS.
THEY TAKE ORDERS EXTRAORDINARILY WELL, DON'T YOU FIND?
TELL THEM TO KILL, AND THEY SIMPLY DO IT.
Walk steady, Lara.
Walk STEADY.
SOMETHING.
SOMETHING NIGGLING.
I don't care if I die.
But let me get close ENOUGH, please.

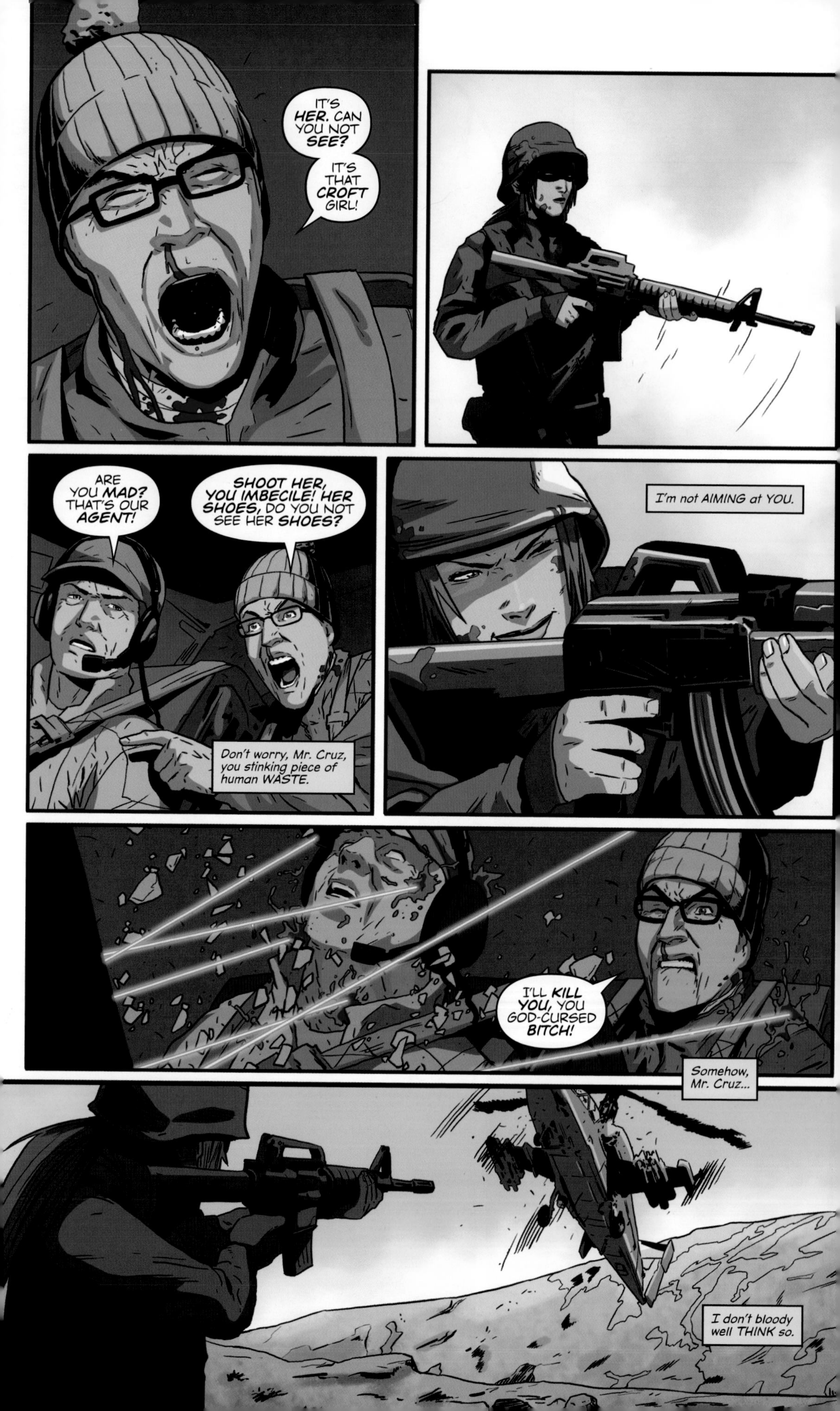
IT'S HER. CAN YOU NOT SEE?
IT'S THAT CROFT GIRL!
ARE YOU MAD? THAT'S OUR AGENT!
SHOOT HER, YOU IMBECILE! HER SHOES, DO YOU NOT SEE HER SHOES?
Don't worry, Mr. Cruz, you stinking piece of human WASTE.
I'm not AIMING at YOU.
I'LL KILL YOU, YOU GOD-CURSED BITCH!
Somehow, Mr. Cruz...
I don't bloody well THINK so.

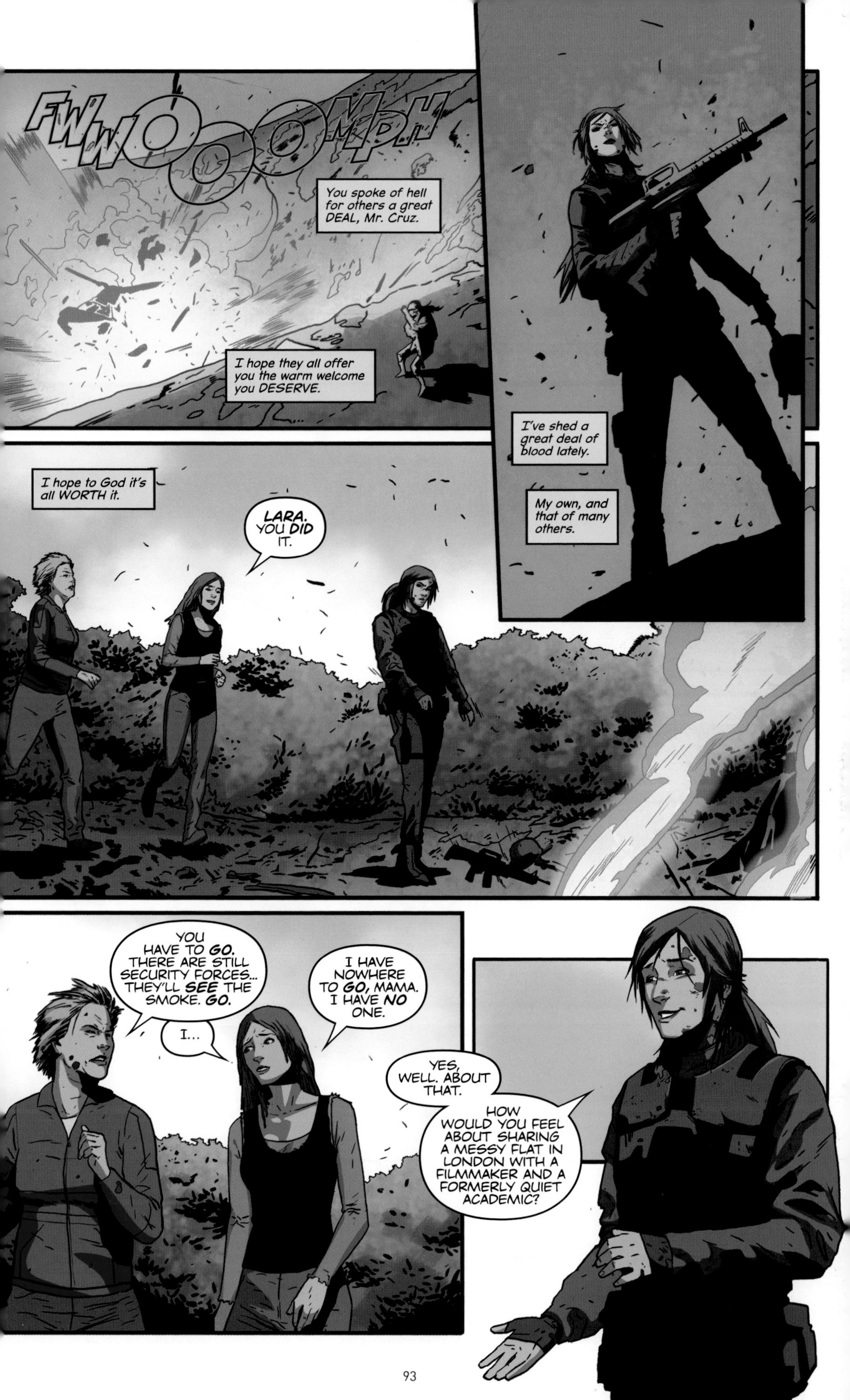
FWWOOOOMPH
You spoke of hell for others a great DEAL, Mr. Cruz.
I hope they all offer you the warm welcome you DESERVE.
I've shed a great deal of blood lately.
My own, and that of many others.
I hope to God it's all WORTH it.
LARA. YOU DID IT.
YOU HAVE TO GO. THERE ARE STILL SECURITY FORCES... THEY'LL SEE THE SMOKE. GO.
I...
I HAVE NOWHERE TO GO, MAMA. I HAVE NO ONE.
YES, WELL. ABOUT THAT.
HOW WOULD YOU FEEL ABOUT SHARING A MESSY FLAT IN LONDON WITH A FILMMAKER AND A FORMERLY QUIET ACADEMIC?

"ALTHOUGH I MAY HAVE SOME *EXPLAINING* TO DO TO *SAM*...

"BUT BEFORE WE GO...

"MAYBE WE CAN GO FIND THE REMAINS OF THAT *VODKA* AND PUT IT TO GOOD *USAGE.*

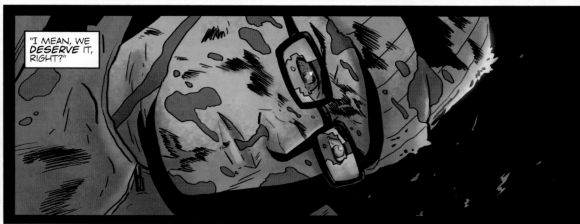

"I MEAN, WE *DESERVE* IT, RIGHT?"

Illustration by BRIAN HORTON

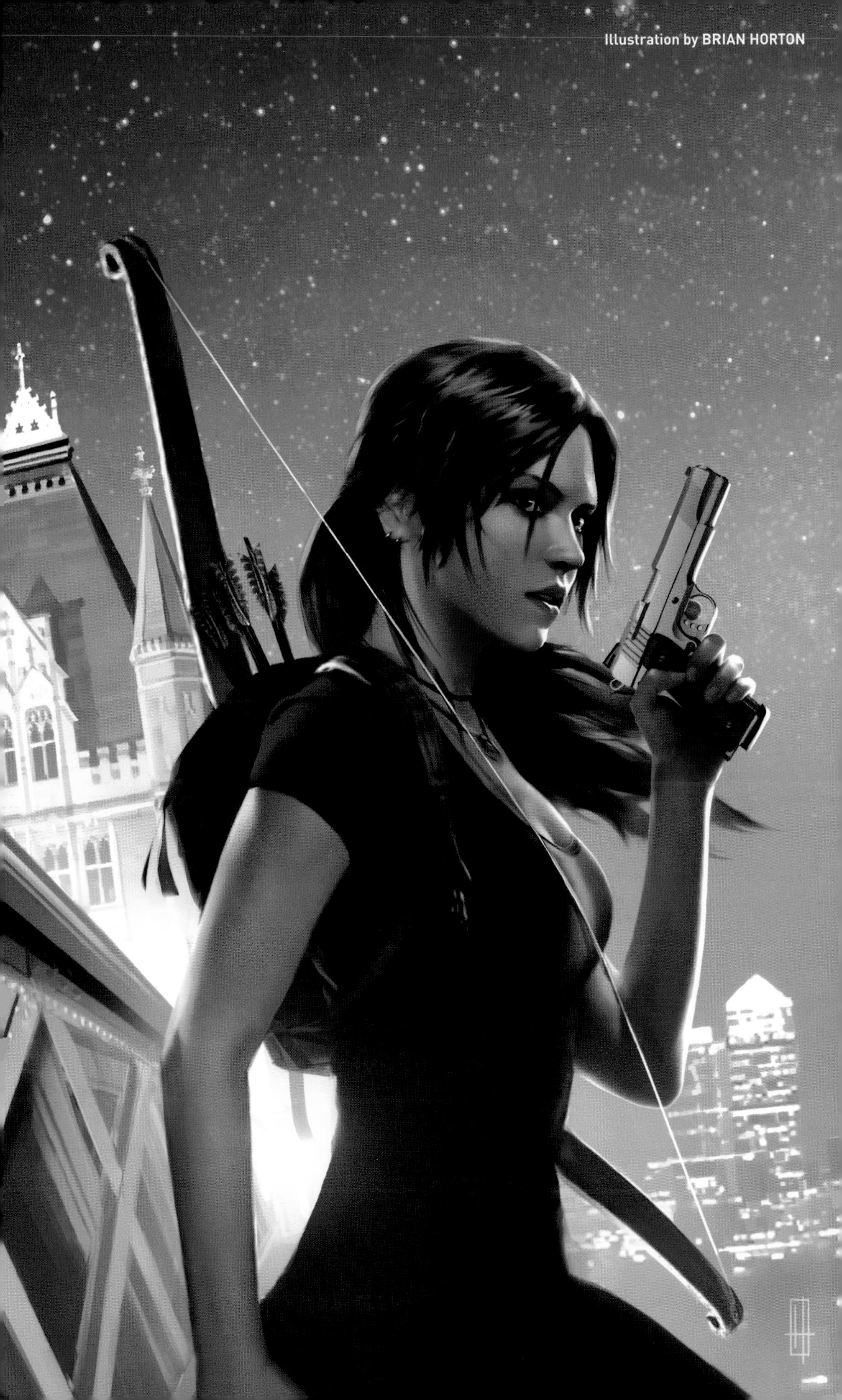

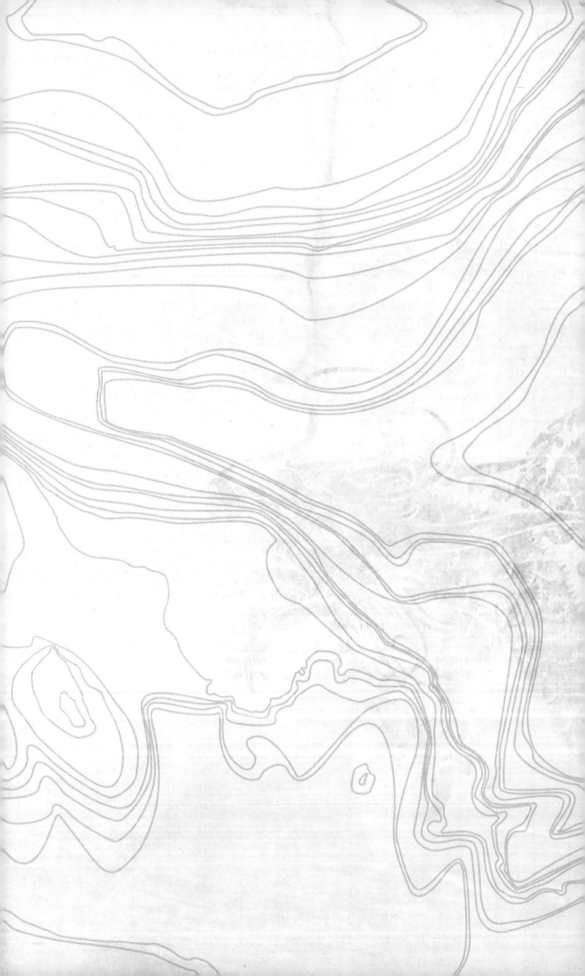

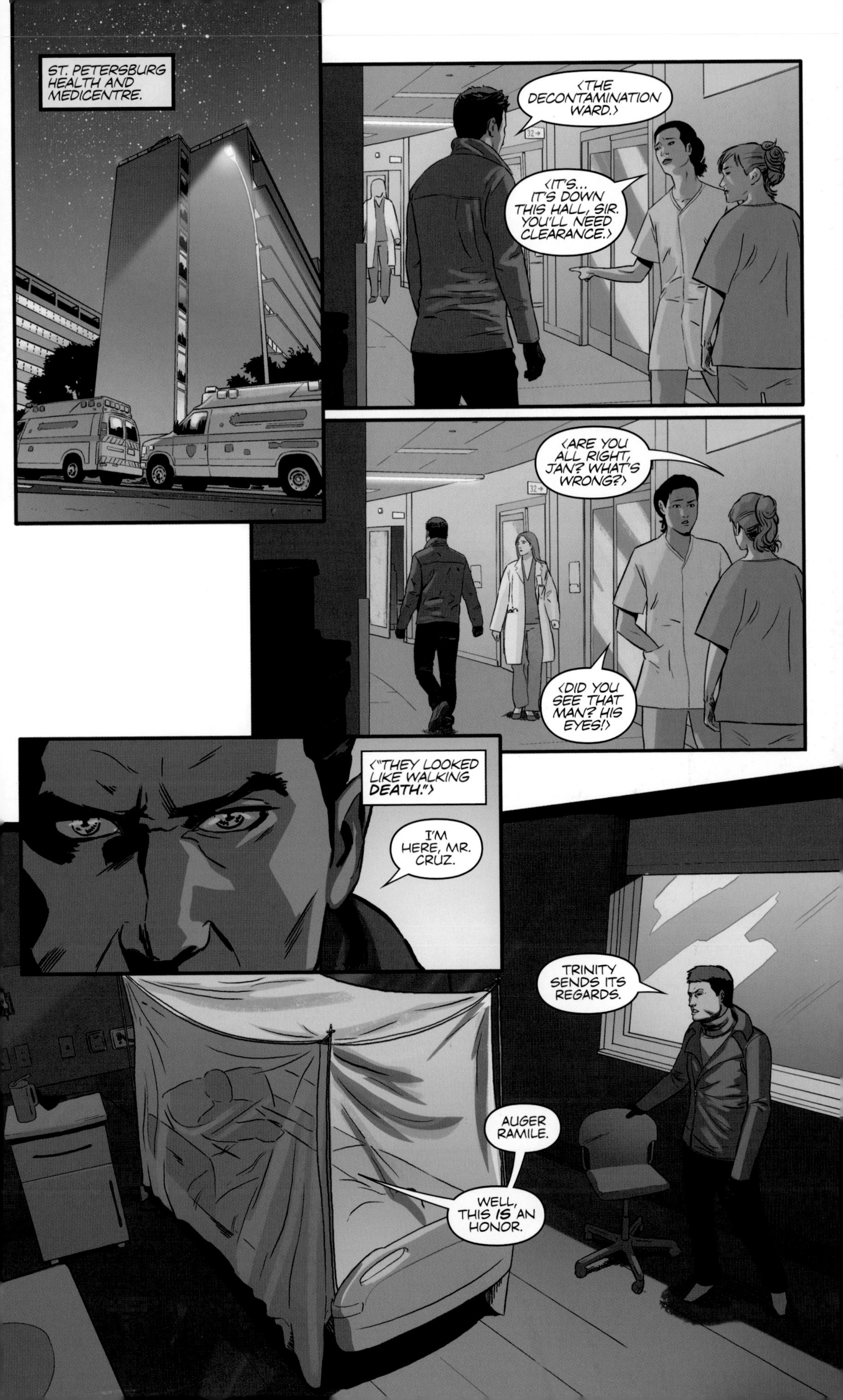
ST. PETERSBURG HEALTH AND MEDICENTRE.
<THE DECONTAMINATION WARD.>
<IT'S... IT'S DOWN THIS HALL, SIR. YOU'LL NEED CLEARANCE.>
<ARE YOU ALL RIGHT, JAN? WHAT'S WRONG?>
<DID YOU SEE THAT MAN? HIS EYES!>
<"THEY LOOKED LIKE WALKING DEATH.">
I'M HERE, MR. CRUZ.
TRINITY SENDS ITS REGARDS.
AUGER RAMILE.
WELL, THIS IS AN HONOR.

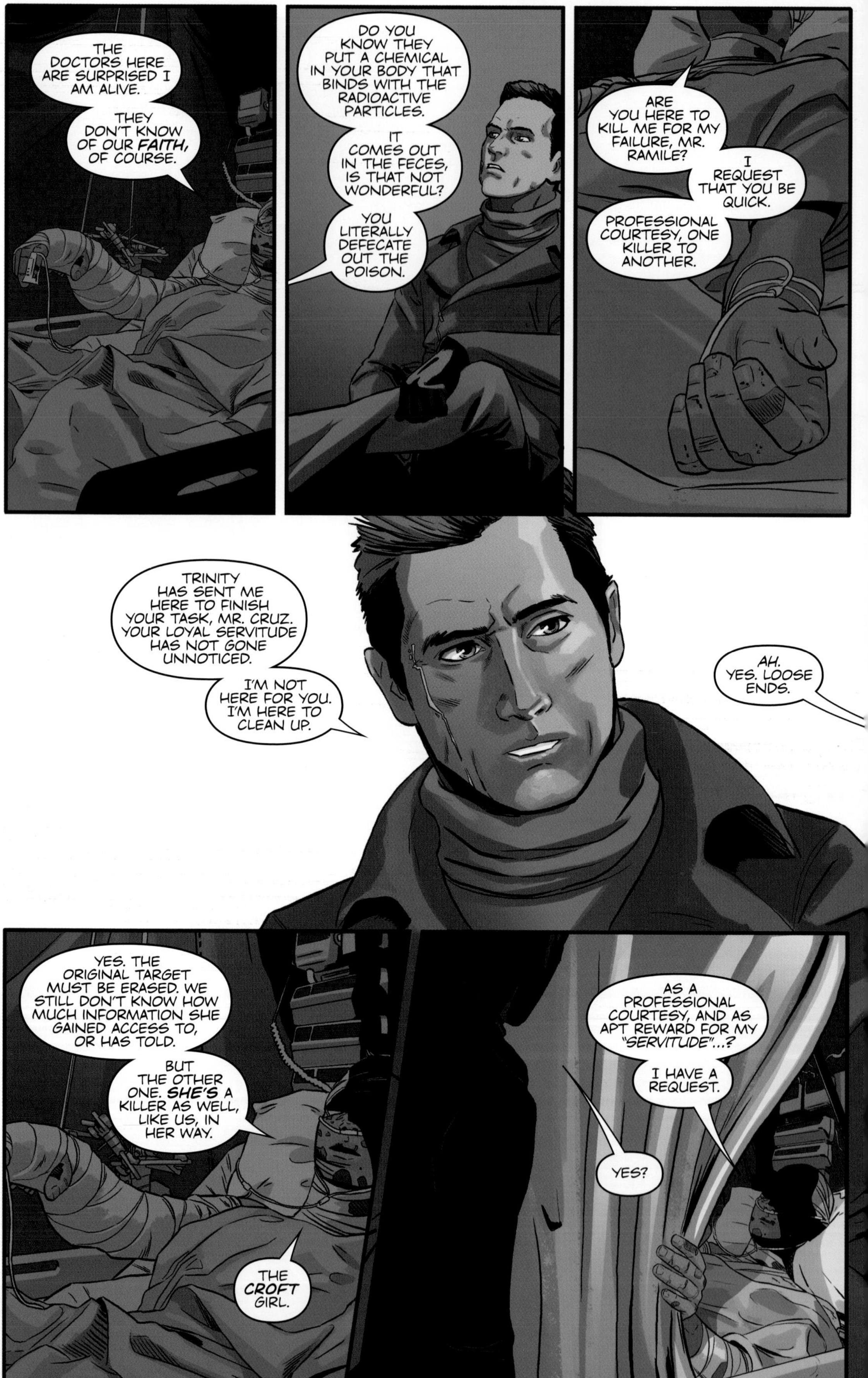
THE DOCTORS HERE ARE SURPRISED I AM ALIVE.
THEY DON'T KNOW OF OUR *FAITH,* OF COURSE.
DO YOU KNOW THEY PUT A CHEMICAL IN YOUR BODY THAT BINDS WITH THE RADIOACTIVE PARTICLES.
IT COMES OUT IN THE FECES, IS THAT NOT WONDERFUL?
YOU LITERALLY DEFECATE OUT THE POISON.
ARE YOU HERE TO KILL ME FOR MY FAILURE, MR. RAMILE?
I REQUEST THAT YOU BE QUICK.
PROFESSIONAL COURTESY, ONE KILLER TO ANOTHER.
TRINITY HAS SENT ME HERE TO FINISH YOUR TASK, MR. CRUZ. YOUR LOYAL SERVITUDE HAS NOT GONE UNNOTICED.
I'M NOT HERE FOR YOU. I'M HERE TO CLEAN UP.
AH. YES. LOOSE ENDS.
YES. THE ORIGINAL TARGET MUST BE ERASED. WE STILL DON'T KNOW HOW MUCH INFORMATION SHE GAINED ACCESS TO, OR HAS TOLD.
BUT THE OTHER ONE. *SHE'S* A KILLER AS WELL, LIKE US, IN HER WAY.
THE *CROFT* GIRL.
AS A PROFESSIONAL COURTESY, AND AS APT REWARD FOR MY "*SERVITUDE*"...?
I HAVE A REQUEST.
YES?

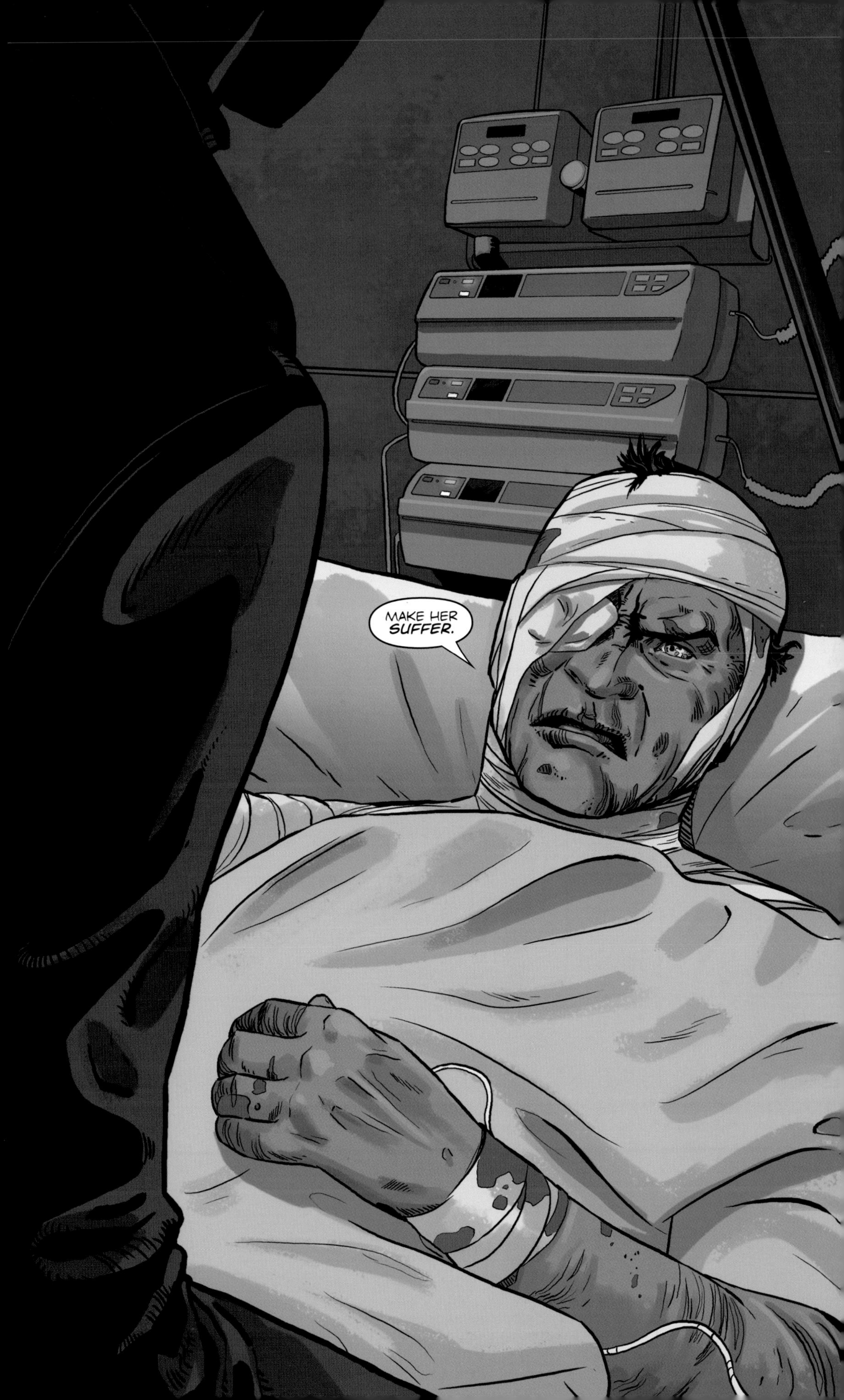
MAKE HER SUFFER.

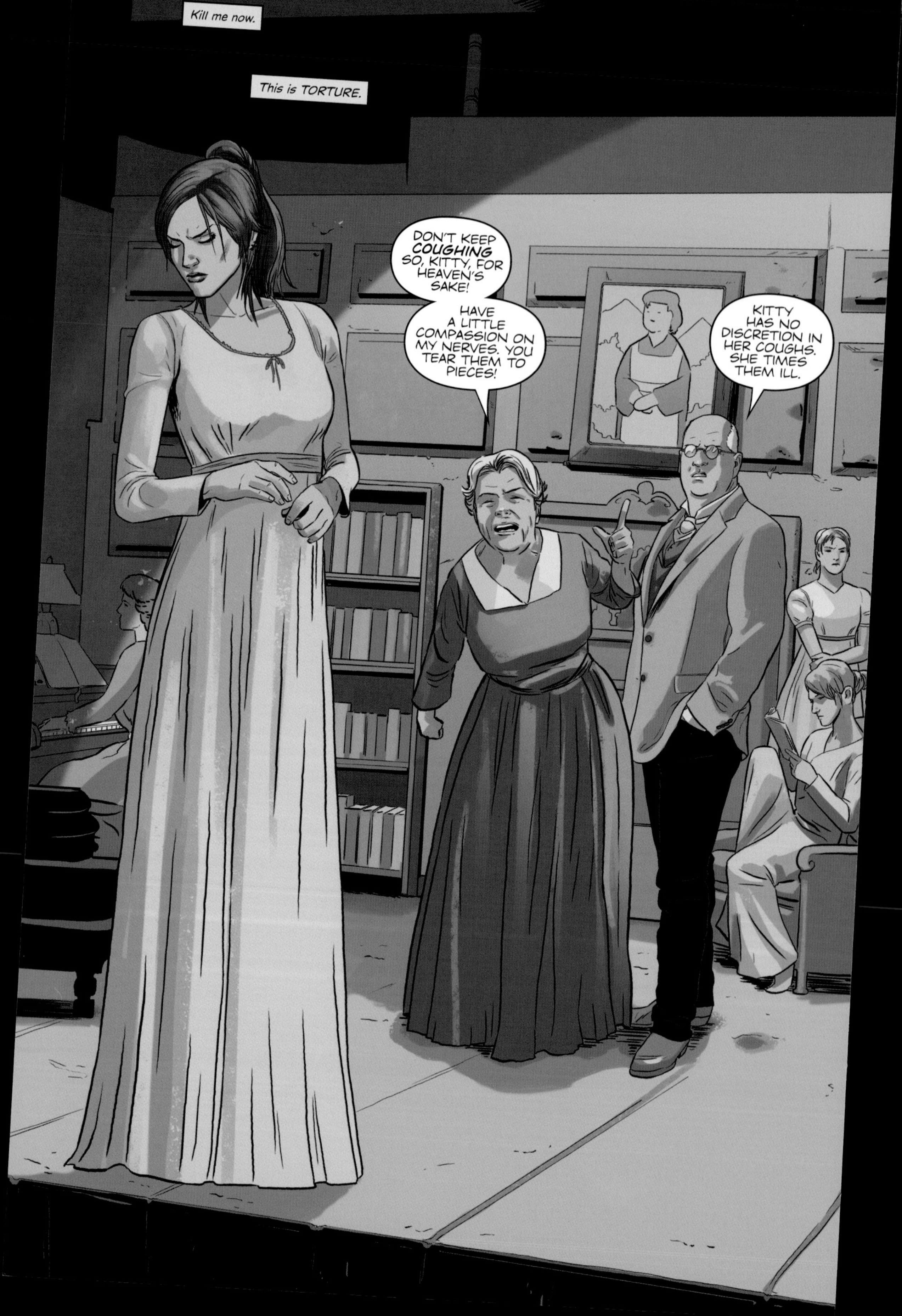
Kill me now.
This is TORTURE.
DON'T KEEP COUGHING SO, KITTY, FOR HEAVEN'S SAKE!
HAVE A LITTLE COMPASSION ON MY NERVES. YOU TEAR THEM TO PIECES!
KITTY HAS NO DISCRETION IN HER COUGHS. SHE TIMES THEM ILL.

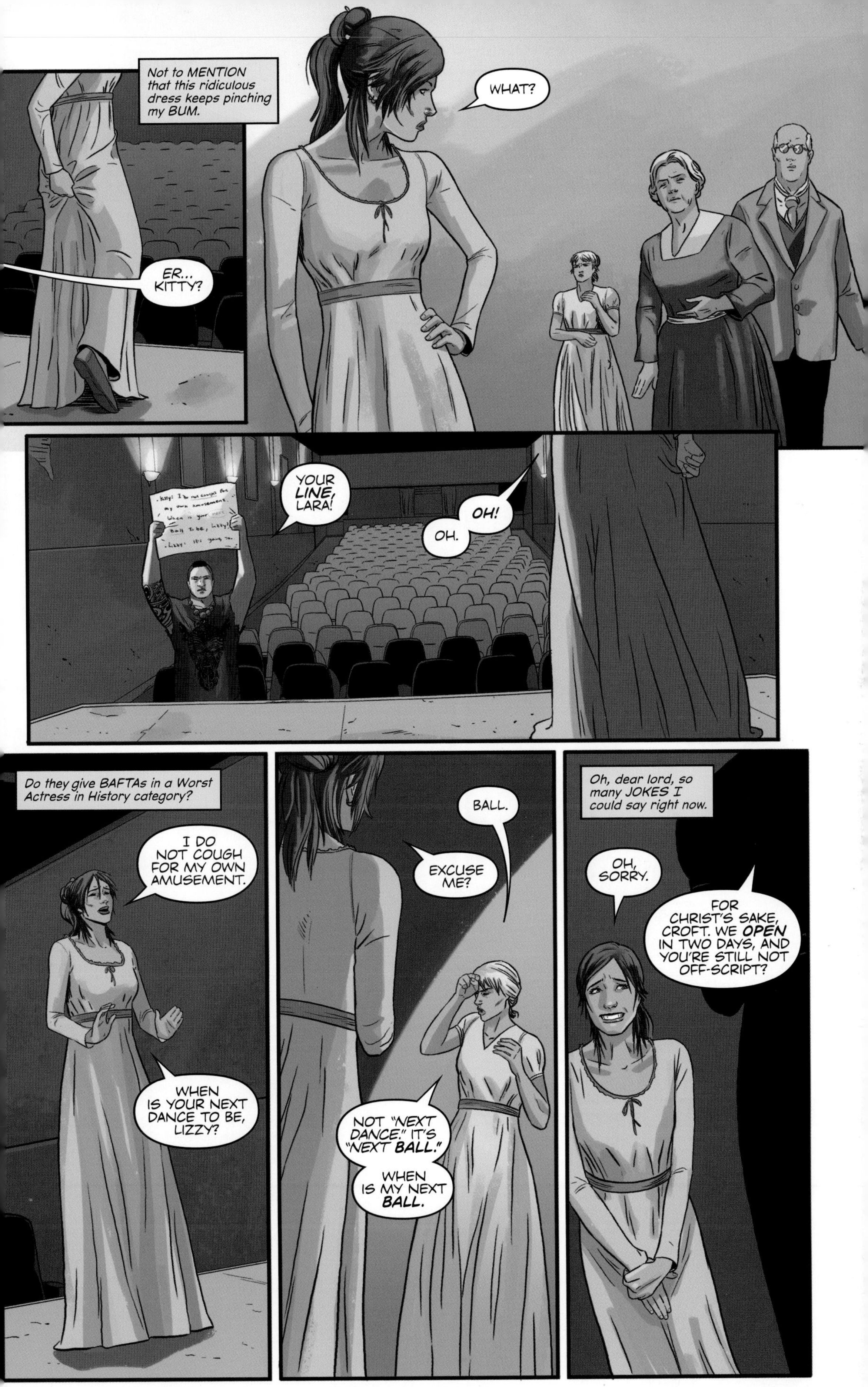
Not to MENTION that this ridiculous dress keeps pinching my BUM.
ER... KITTY?
WHAT?
YOUR LINE, LARA!
OH.
OH!
Do they give BAFTAs in a Worst Actress in History category?
I DO NOT COUGH FOR MY OWN AMUSEMENT.
WHEN IS YOUR NEXT DANCE TO BE, LIZZY?
BALL.
EXCUSE ME?
NOT "NEXT DANCE." IT'S "NEXT BALL."
WHEN IS MY NEXT BALL.
Oh, dear lord, so many JOKES I could say right now.
OH, SORRY.
FOR CHRIST'S SAKE, CROFT. WE OPEN IN TWO DAYS, AND YOU'RE STILL NOT OFF-SCRIPT?

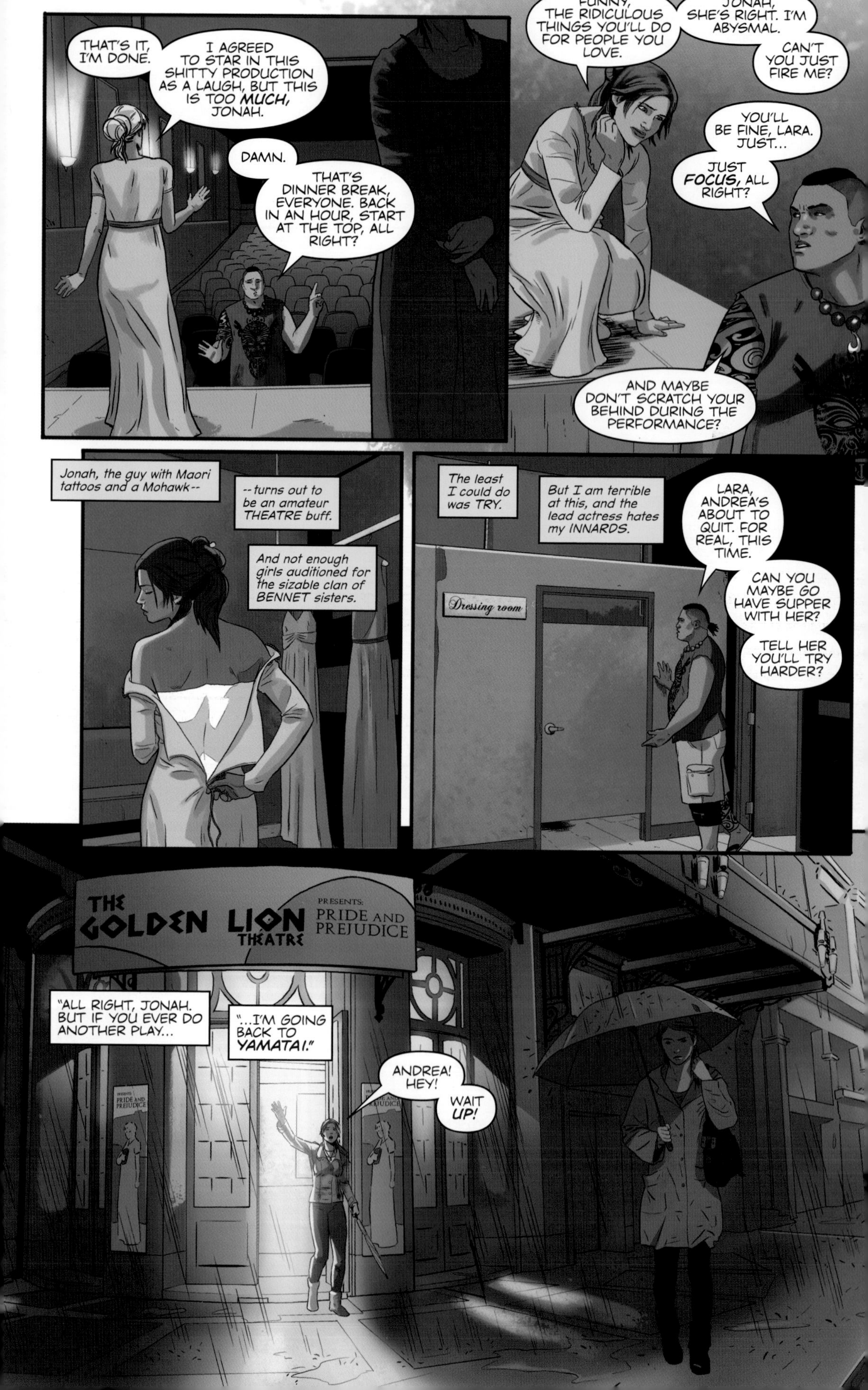
THAT'S IT, I'M DONE.
I AGREED TO STAR IN THIS SHITTY PRODUCTION AS A LAUGH, BUT THIS IS TOO *MUCH,* JONAH.
DAMN.
THAT'S DINNER BREAK, EVERYONE. BACK IN AN HOUR, START AT THE TOP, ALL RIGHT?
FUNNY, THE RIDICULOUS THINGS YOU'LL DO FOR PEOPLE YOU LOVE.
JONAH, SHE'S RIGHT. I'M ABYSMAL.
CAN'T YOU JUST FIRE ME?
YOU'LL BE FINE, LARA. JUST...
JUST *FOCUS,* ALL RIGHT?
AND MAYBE DON'T SCRATCH YOUR BEHIND DURING THE PERFORMANCE?
Jonah, the guy with Maori tattoos and a Mohawk--
--turns out to be an amateur THEATRE buff.
And not enough girls auditioned for the sizable clan of BENNET sisters.
The least I could do was TRY.
But I am terrible at this, and the lead actress hates my INNARDS.
Dressing room
LARA, ANDREA'S ABOUT TO QUIT. FOR REAL, THIS TIME.
CAN YOU MAYBE GO HAVE SUPPER WITH HER?
TELL HER YOU'LL TRY HARDER?
THE GOLDEN LION THEATRE
PRESENTS: PRIDE AND PREJUDICE
"ALL RIGHT, JONAH. BUT IF YOU EVER DO ANOTHER PLAY...
"...I'M GOING BACK TO *YAMATAI.*"
PRIDE AND PREJUDICE
ANDREA! HEY!
WAIT *UP!*

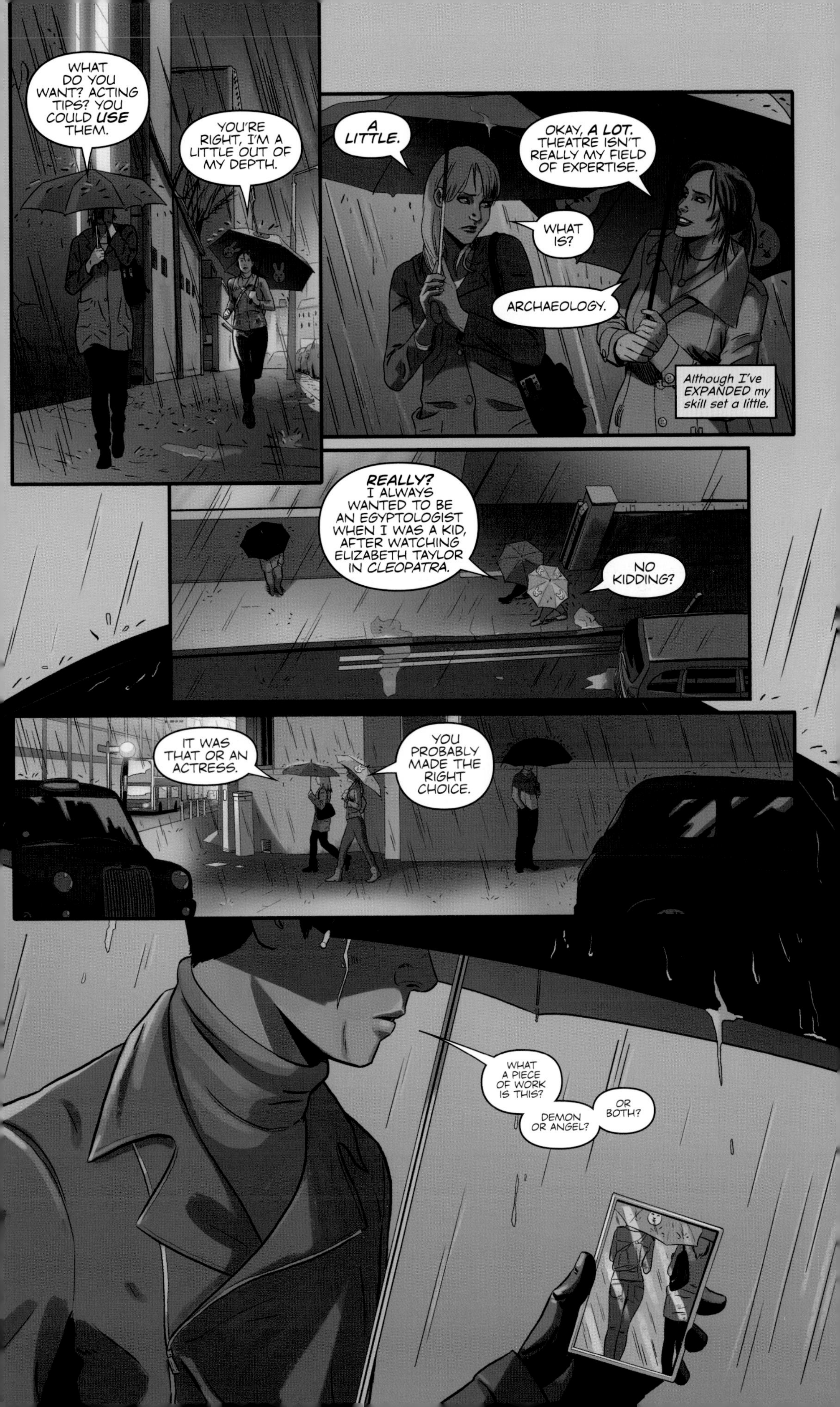
WHAT DO YOU WANT? ACTING TIPS? YOU COULD USE THEM.
YOU'RE RIGHT, I'M A LITTLE OUT OF MY DEPTH.
A LITTLE.
OKAY, A LOT. THEATRE ISN'T REALLY MY FIELD OF EXPERTISE.
WHAT IS?
ARCHAEOLOGY.
Although I've EXPANDED my skill set a little.
REALLY? I ALWAYS WANTED TO BE AN EGYPTOLOGIST WHEN I WAS A KID, AFTER WATCHING ELIZABETH TAYLOR IN CLEOPATRA.
NO KIDDING?
IT WAS THAT OR AN ACTRESS.
YOU PROBABLY MADE THE RIGHT CHOICE.
WHAT A PIECE OF WORK IS THIS?
DEMON OR ANGEL?
OR BOTH?

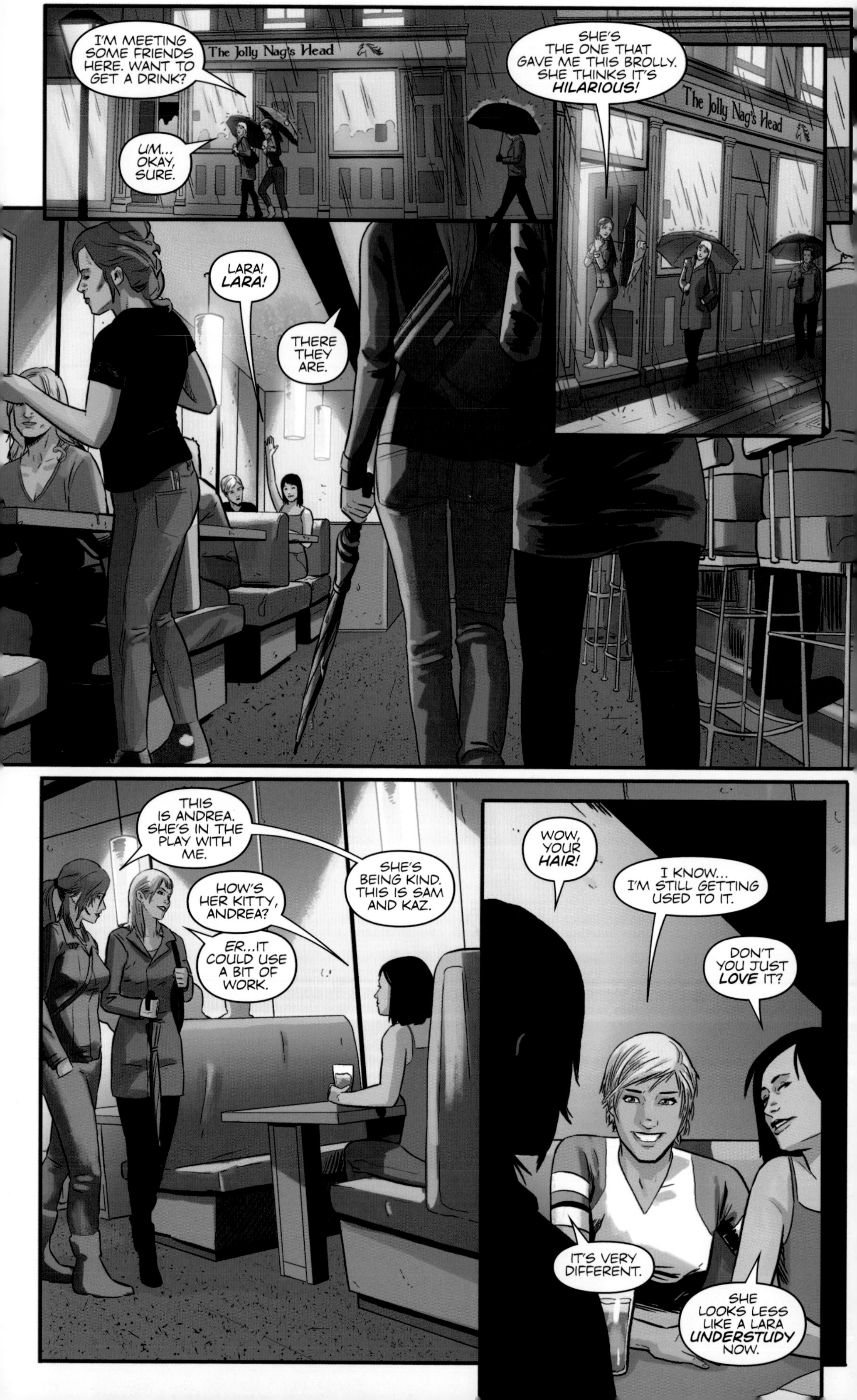

The Jolly Nag's Head
I'M MEETING SOME FRIENDS HERE. WANT TO GET A DRINK?
UM... OKAY, SURE.
SHE'S THE ONE THAT GAVE ME THIS BROLLY. SHE THINKS IT'S HILARIOUS!
The Jolly Nag's Head
LARA! LARA!
THERE THEY ARE.
THIS IS ANDREA. SHE'S IN THE PLAY WITH ME.
HOW'S HER KITTY, ANDREA?
ER...IT COULD USE A BIT OF WORK.
SHE'S BEING KIND. THIS IS SAM AND KAZ.
WOW, YOUR HAIR!
I KNOW... I'M STILL GETTING USED TO IT.
DON'T YOU JUST LOVE IT?
IT'S VERY DIFFERENT.
SHE LOOKS LESS LIKE A LARA UNDERSTUDY NOW.

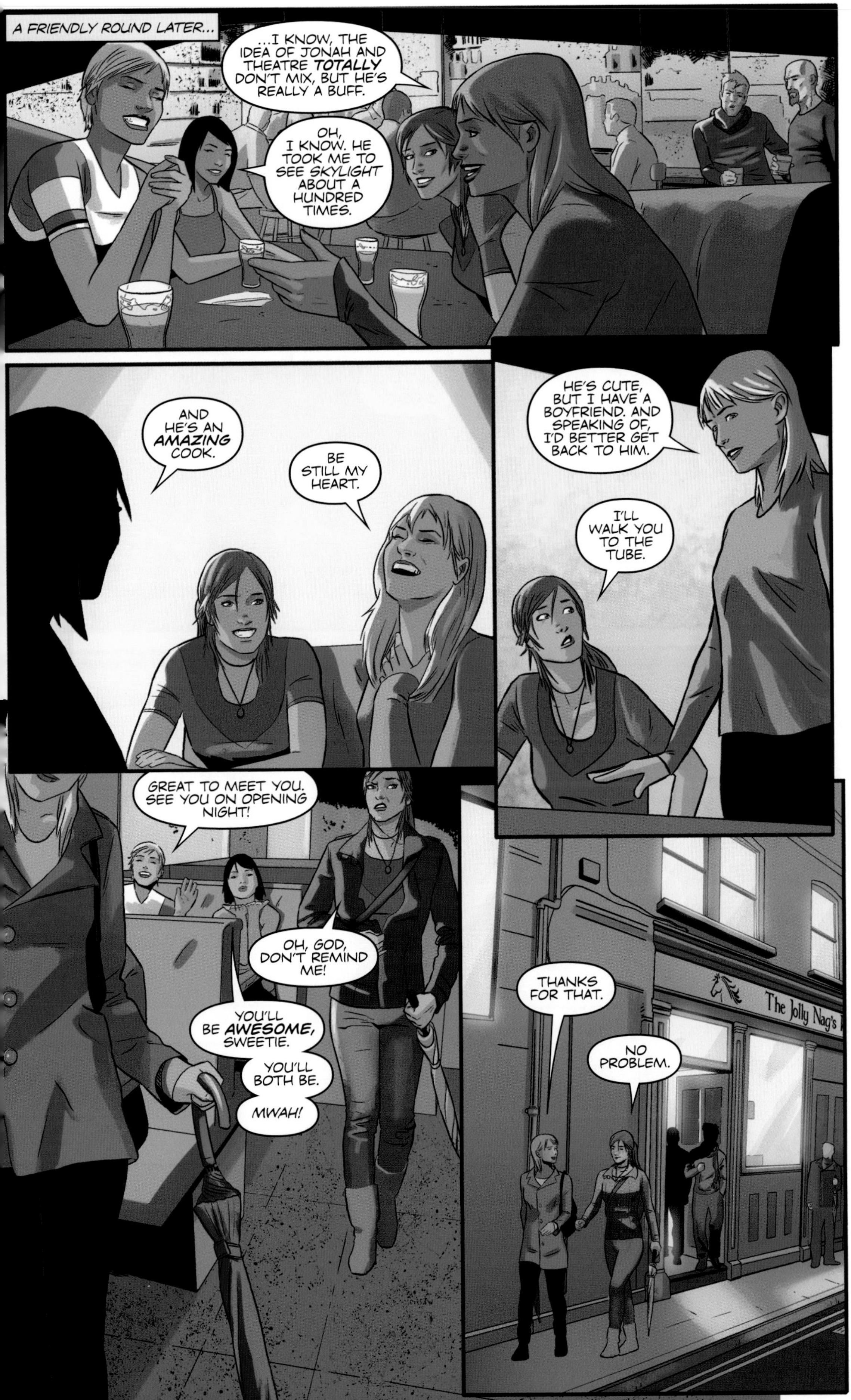
A FRIENDLY ROUND LATER...
...I KNOW, THE IDEA OF JONAH AND THEATRE TOTALLY DON'T MIX, BUT HE'S REALLY A BUFF.
OH, I KNOW. HE TOOK ME TO SEE SKYLIGHT ABOUT A HUNDRED TIMES.
AND HE'S AN AMAZING COOK.
BE STILL MY HEART.
HE'S CUTE, BUT I HAVE A BOYFRIEND. AND SPEAKING OF, I'D BETTER GET BACK TO HIM.
I'LL WALK YOU TO THE TUBE.
GREAT TO MEET YOU. SEE YOU ON OPENING NIGHT!
OH, GOD, DON'T REMIND ME!
YOU'LL BE AWESOME, SWEETIE.
YOU'LL BOTH BE.
MWAH!
THANKS FOR THAT.
NO PROBLEM.
The Jolly Nag's

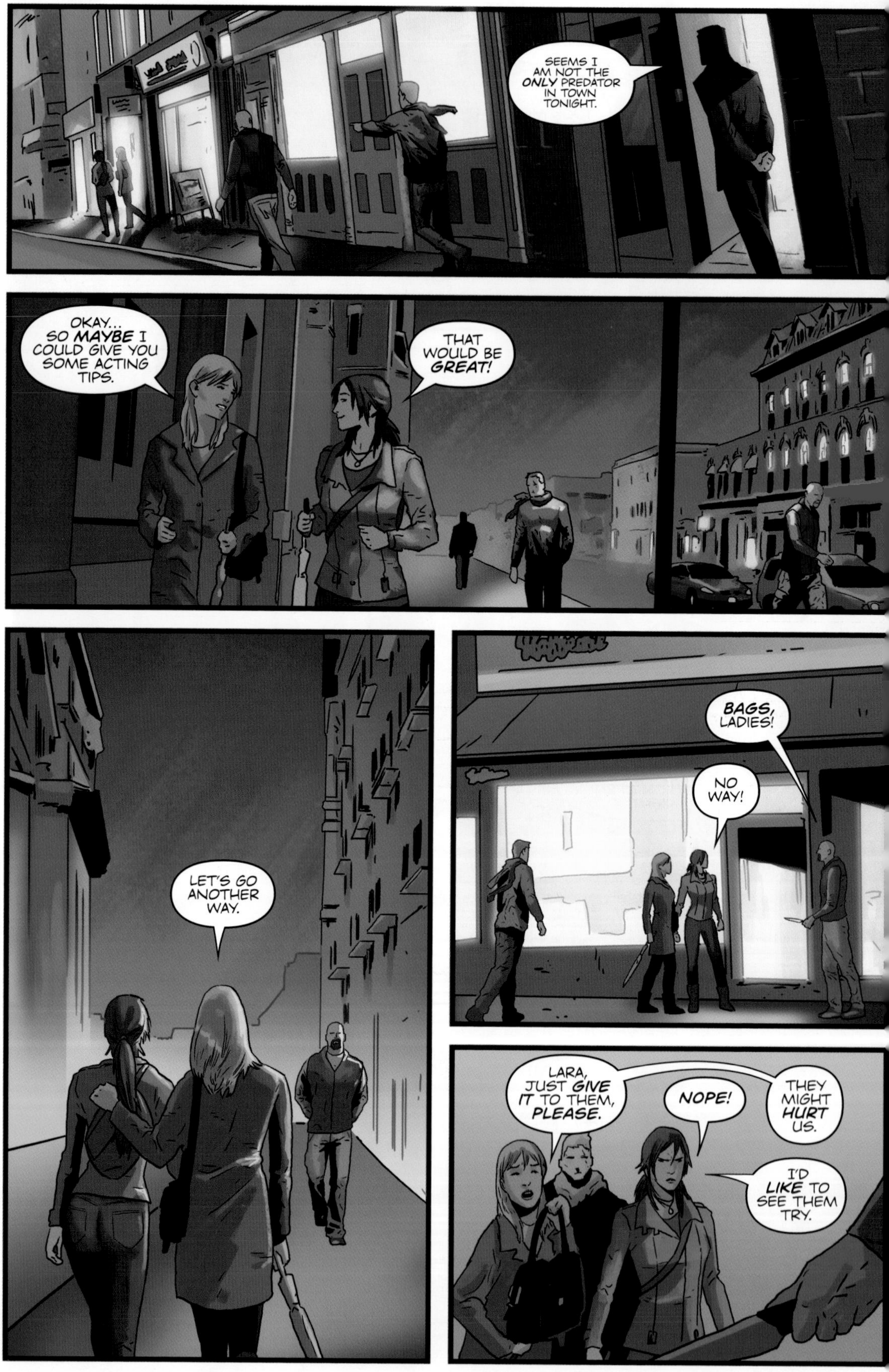
SEEMS I AM NOT THE ONLY PREDATOR IN TOWN TONIGHT.
OKAY... SO MAYBE I COULD GIVE YOU SOME ACTING TIPS.
THAT WOULD BE GREAT!
LET'S GO ANOTHER WAY.
BAGS, LADIES!
NO WAY!
LARA, JUST GIVE IT TO THEM, PLEASE.
NOPE!
THEY MIGHT HURT US.
I'D LIKE TO SEE THEM TRY.

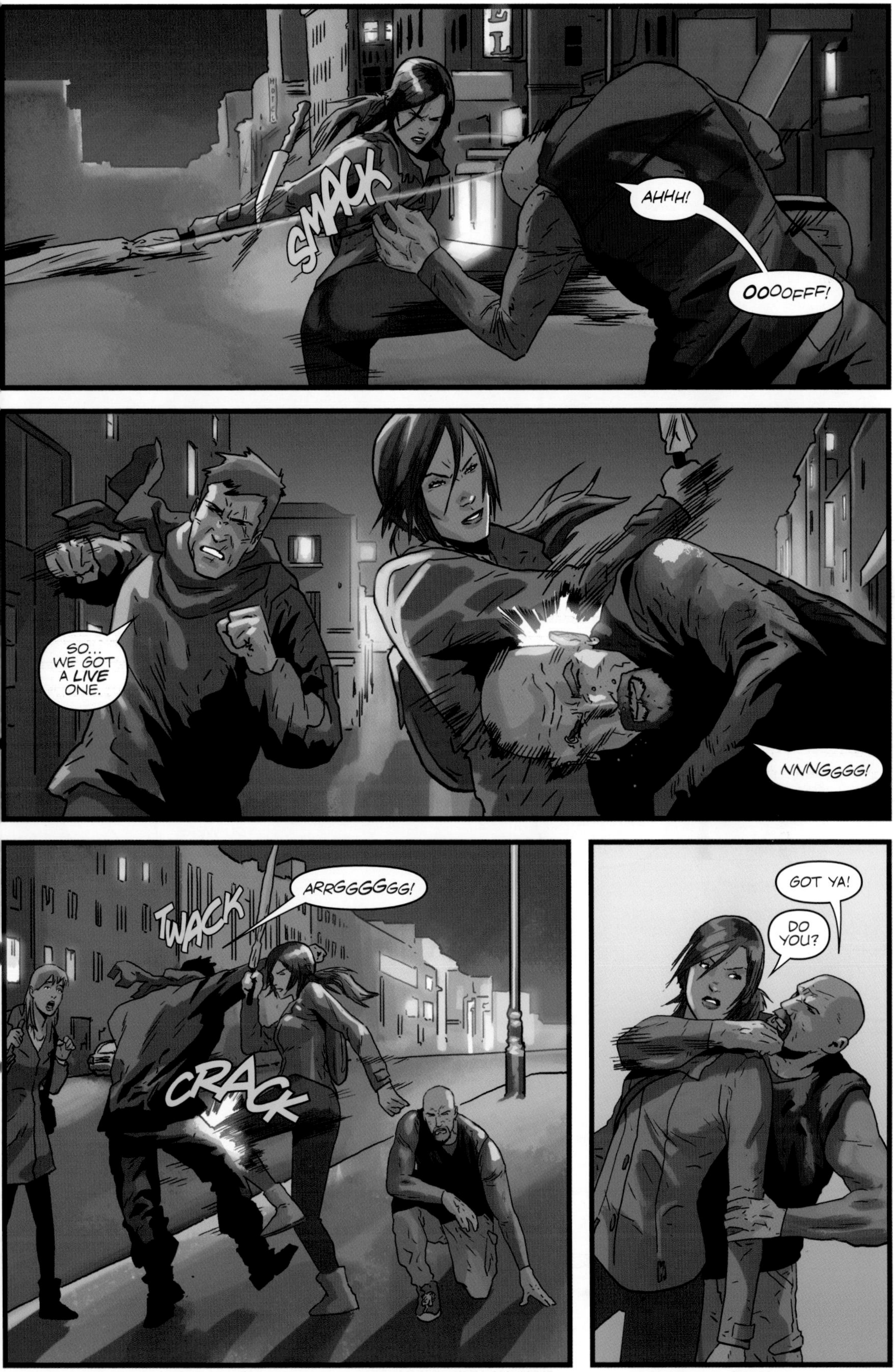
SMACK
AHHH!
OOOOFFF!
SO... WE GOT A LIVE ONE.
NNNGGGG!
ARRGGGGGG!
TWACK
CRACK
GOT YA!
DO YOU?

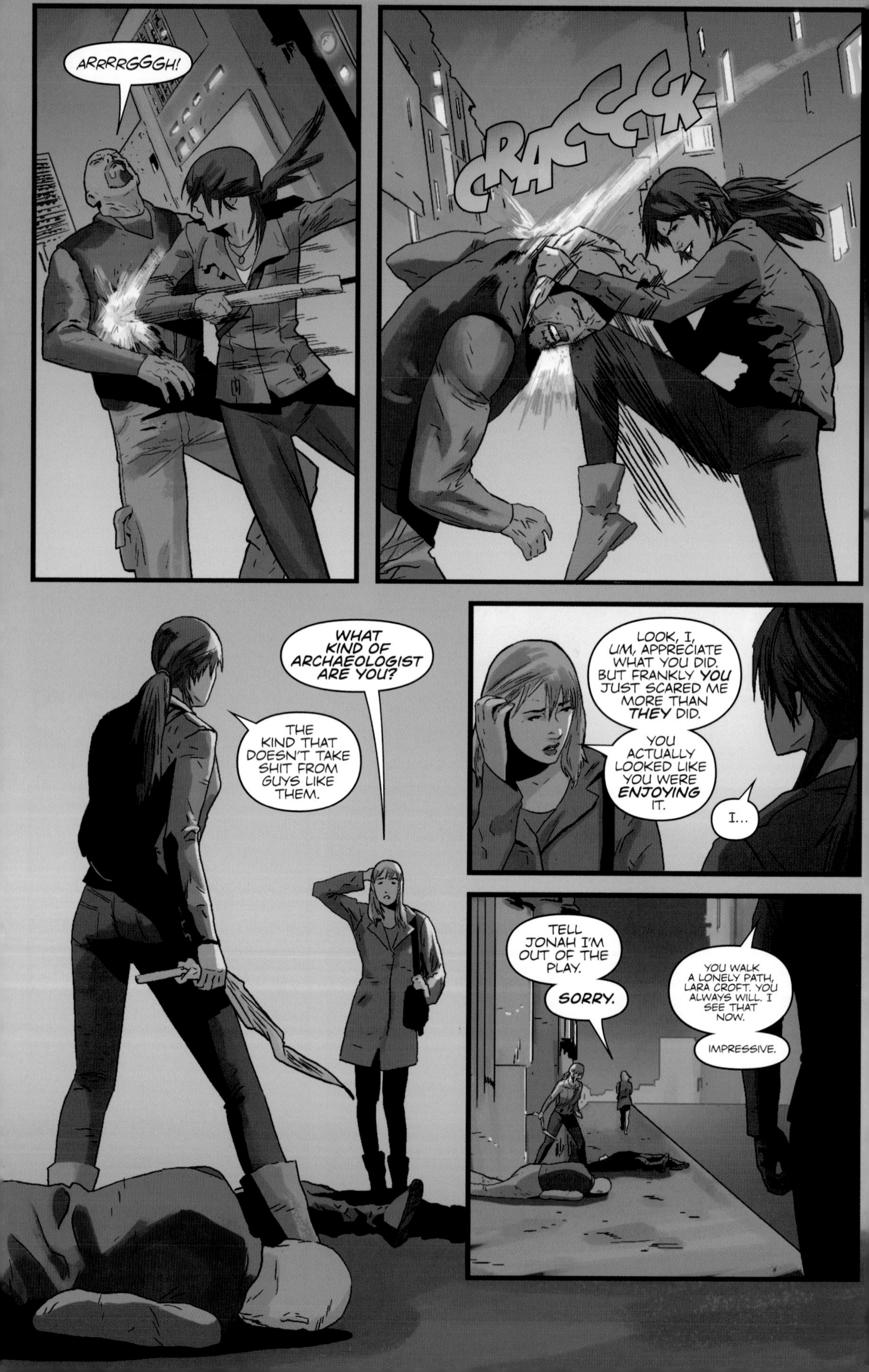
ARRRRGGGH!
CRACCCK
WHAT KIND OF ARCHAEOLOGIST ARE YOU?
THE KIND THAT DOESN'T TAKE SHIT FROM GUYS LIKE THEM.
LOOK, I, UM, APPRECIATE WHAT YOU DID. BUT FRANKLY YOU JUST SCARED ME MORE THAN THEY DID.
YOU ACTUALLY LOOKED LIKE YOU WERE ENJOYING IT.
I...
TELL JONAH I'M OUT OF THE PLAY.
SORRY.
YOU WALK A LONELY PATH, LARA CROFT. YOU ALWAYS WILL. I SEE THAT NOW.
IMPRESSIVE.

I always thought that brolly was ridiculous, anyway.

Jonah's going to KILL me.

BZZZT BZZZT BZZZT

YES?

DO BE QUICK, I'M QUITE BUSY.

MR. RAMILE? IT'S DR. PATEL, AT THE CLINIC.

OF COURSE, DOCTOR.

I'VE BEEN AWAITING YOUR CALL.

I'M LOATH TO SAY THIS OVER THE PHONE, MR. RAMILE, BUT I'M AFRAID THE PROGNOSIS IS WORSE THAN WE'D HOPED.

YOUR CANCER IS AGGRESSIVE.

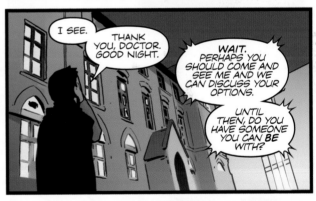

I SEE.

THANK YOU, DOCTOR. GOOD NIGHT.

WAIT. PERHAPS YOU SHOULD COME AND SEE ME AND WE CAN DISCUSS YOUR OPTIONS.

UNTIL THEN, DO YOU HAVE SOMEONE YOU CAN BE WITH?

"I SHOULDN'T HAVE THOUGHT SO, JUST A DAY AGO, DOCTOR.

"BUT YES. YES, I BELIEVE I DO.

"GOOD EVENING. WE WON'T SPEAK AGAIN."

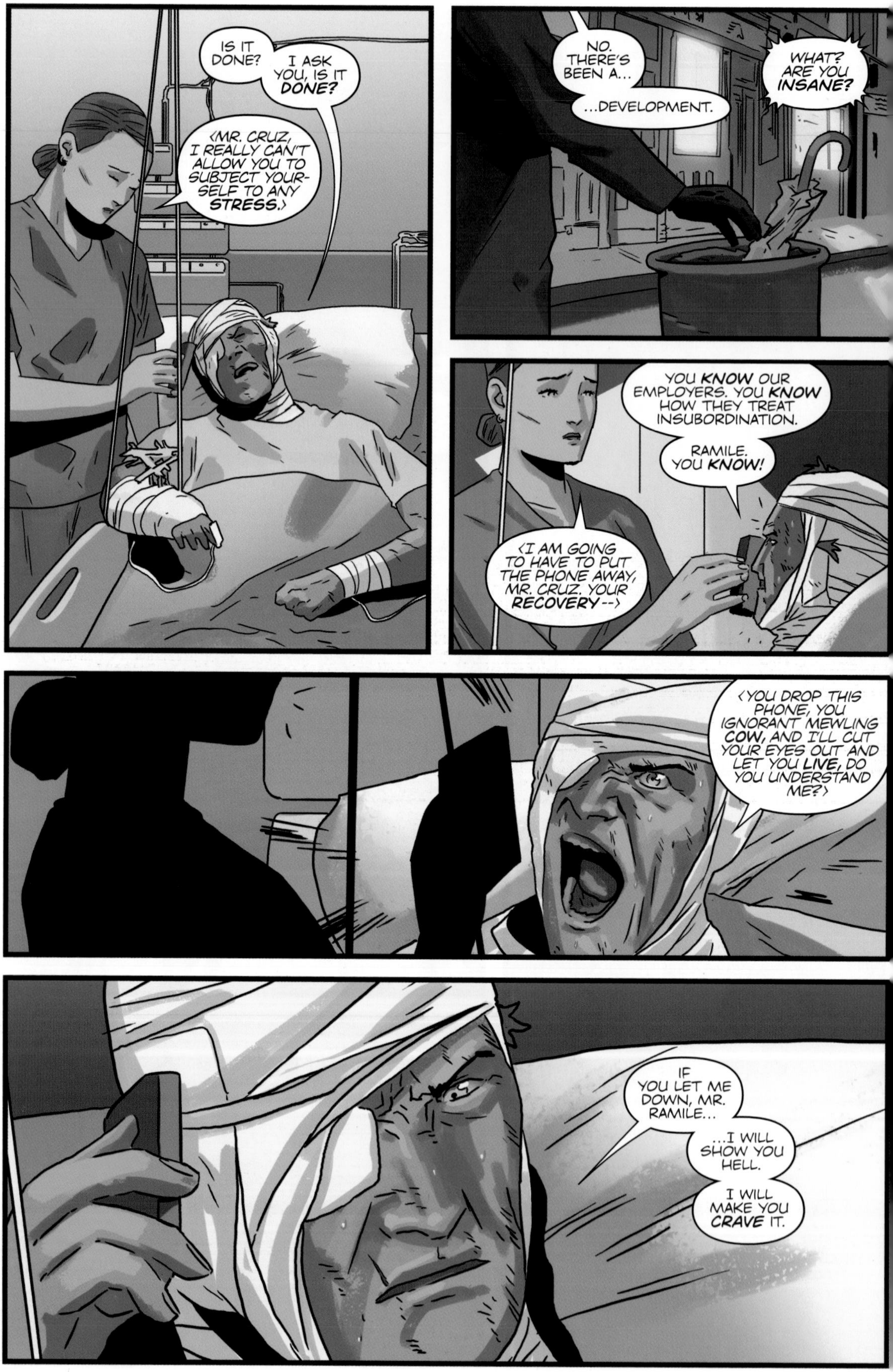
IS IT DONE?
I ASK YOU, IS IT DONE?
‹MR. CRUZ, I REALLY CAN'T ALLOW YOU TO SUBJECT YOURSELF TO ANY STRESS.›
NO. THERE'S BEEN A...
...DEVELOPMENT.
WHAT? ARE YOU INSANE?
YOU KNOW OUR EMPLOYERS. YOU KNOW HOW THEY TREAT INSUBORDINATION.
RAMILE. YOU KNOW!
‹I AM GOING TO HAVE TO PUT THE PHONE AWAY, MR. CRUZ. YOUR RECOVERY--›
‹YOU DROP THIS PHONE, YOU IGNORANT MEWLING COW, AND I'LL CUT YOUR EYES OUT AND LET YOU LIVE, DO YOU UNDERSTAND ME?›
IF YOU LET ME DOWN, MR. RAMILE...
...I WILL SHOW YOU HELL.
I WILL MAKE YOU CRAVE IT.

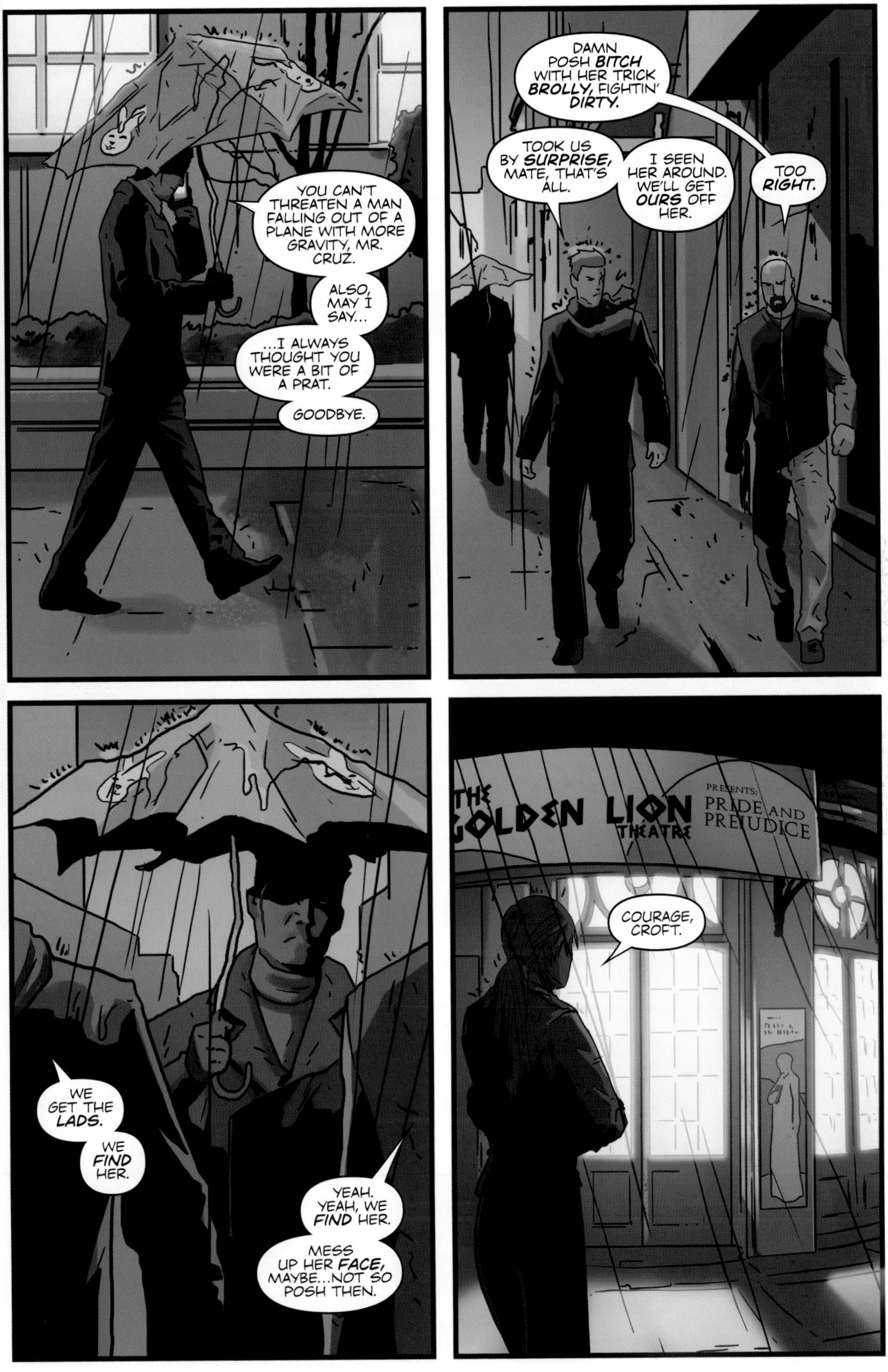
YOU CAN'T THREATEN A MAN FALLING OUT OF A PLANE WITH MORE GRAVITY, MR. CRUZ.
ALSO, MAY I SAY...
...I ALWAYS THOUGHT YOU WERE A BIT OF A PRAT.
GOODBYE.
DAMN POSH **BITCH** WITH HER TRICK **BROLLY,** FIGHTIN' **DIRTY.**
TOOK US BY **SURPRISE,** MATE, THAT'S ALL.
I SEEN HER AROUND. WE'LL GET **OURS** OFF HER.
TOO **RIGHT.**
WE GET THE ***LADS.***
WE ***FIND*** HER.
YEAH. YEAH, WE ***FIND*** HER.
MESS UP HER ***FACE,*** MAYBE...NOT SO POSH THEN.
THE GOLDEN LION THEATRE
PRESENTS: PRIDE AND PREJUDICE
COURAGE, CROFT.

UM.

JONAH?

I HAD A CHAT WITH ANDREA.

JUST A SECOND, LITTLE BIRD. THE THIRD ACT IS A *MESS.*

YOU DID?

EXCELLENT, THAT'S ONE THING SORTED. THANK YOU.

ACTUALLY--

I WAS WORRIED I WOULDN'T BE ABLE TO PULL THIS OFF, BUT THINGS ARE FINALLY STARTING TO TURN OUR WAY, YOU KNOW?

JONAH.

LARA, WHY ARE YOU STILL HERE? YOU AND ANDREA GET READY, WE'RE DOING SECOND RUN-THROUGH IN *TEN.*

JONAH!

SHE'S GONE, JONAH. SHE'S NOT COMING BACK.

I'M SO, SO SORRY.

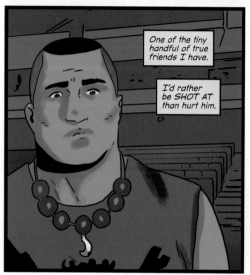

One of the tiny handful of true friends I have.

I'd rather be *SHOT AT* than hurt him.

YOU'LL TAKE THE LEAD, THEN, LARA.

YOU'LL BE ELIZABETH.

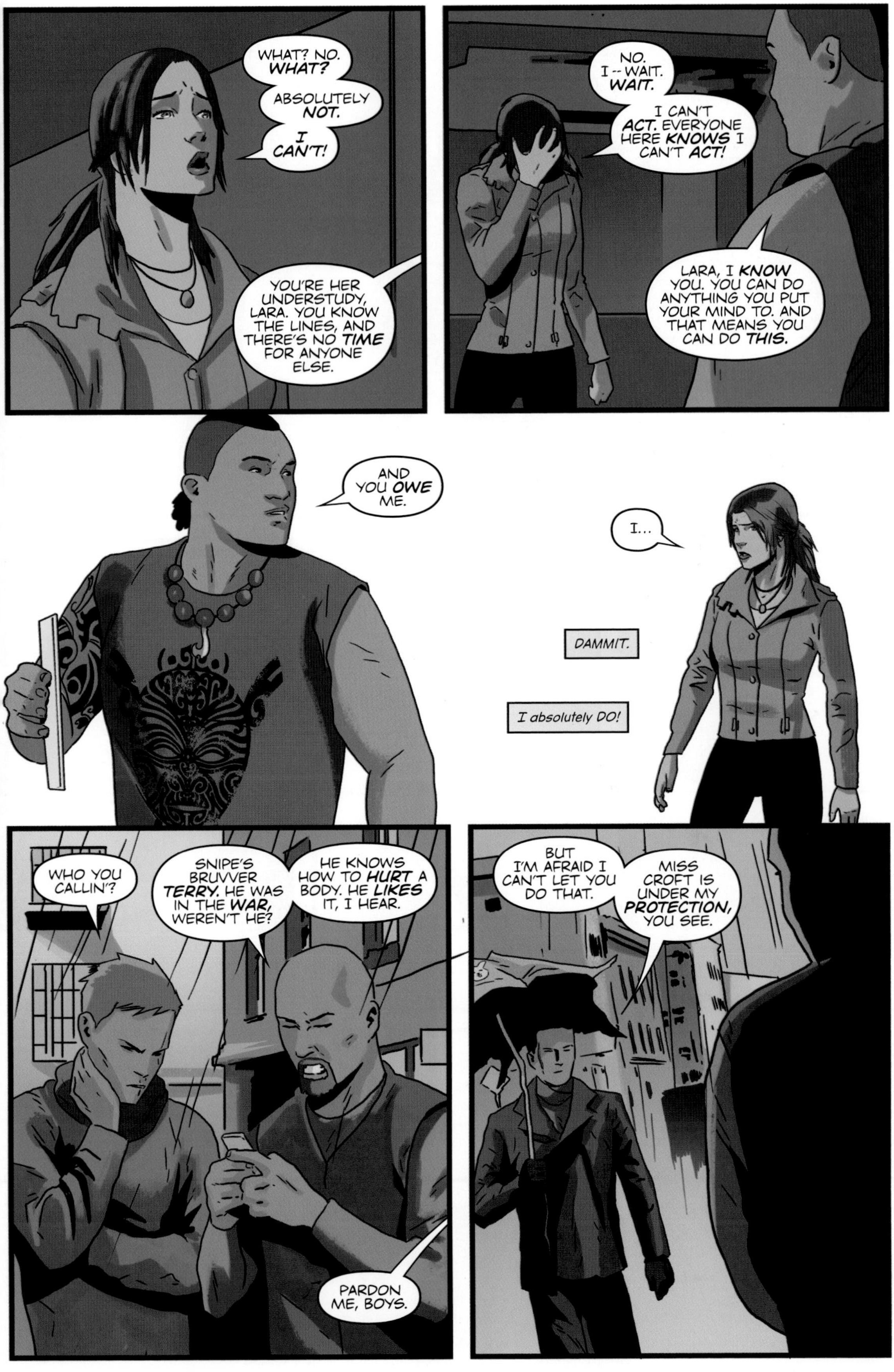
WHAT? NO. WHAT?
ABSOLUTELY NOT.
I CAN'T!
YOU'RE HER UNDERSTUDY, LARA. YOU KNOW THE LINES, AND THERE'S NO TIME FOR ANYONE ELSE.
NO. I -- WAIT. WAIT.
I CAN'T ACT. EVERYONE HERE KNOWS I CAN'T ACT!
LARA, I KNOW YOU. YOU CAN DO ANYTHING YOU PUT YOUR MIND TO. AND THAT MEANS YOU CAN DO THIS.
AND YOU OWE ME.
I...
DAMMIT.
I absolutely DO!
WHO YOU CALLIN'?
SNIPE'S BRUVVER TERRY. HE WAS IN THE WAR, WEREN'T HE?
HE KNOWS HOW TO HURT A BODY. HE LIKES IT, I HEAR.
PARDON ME, BOYS.
BUT I'M AFRAID I CAN'T LET YOU DO THAT.
MISS CROFT IS UNDER MY PROTECTION, YOU SEE.

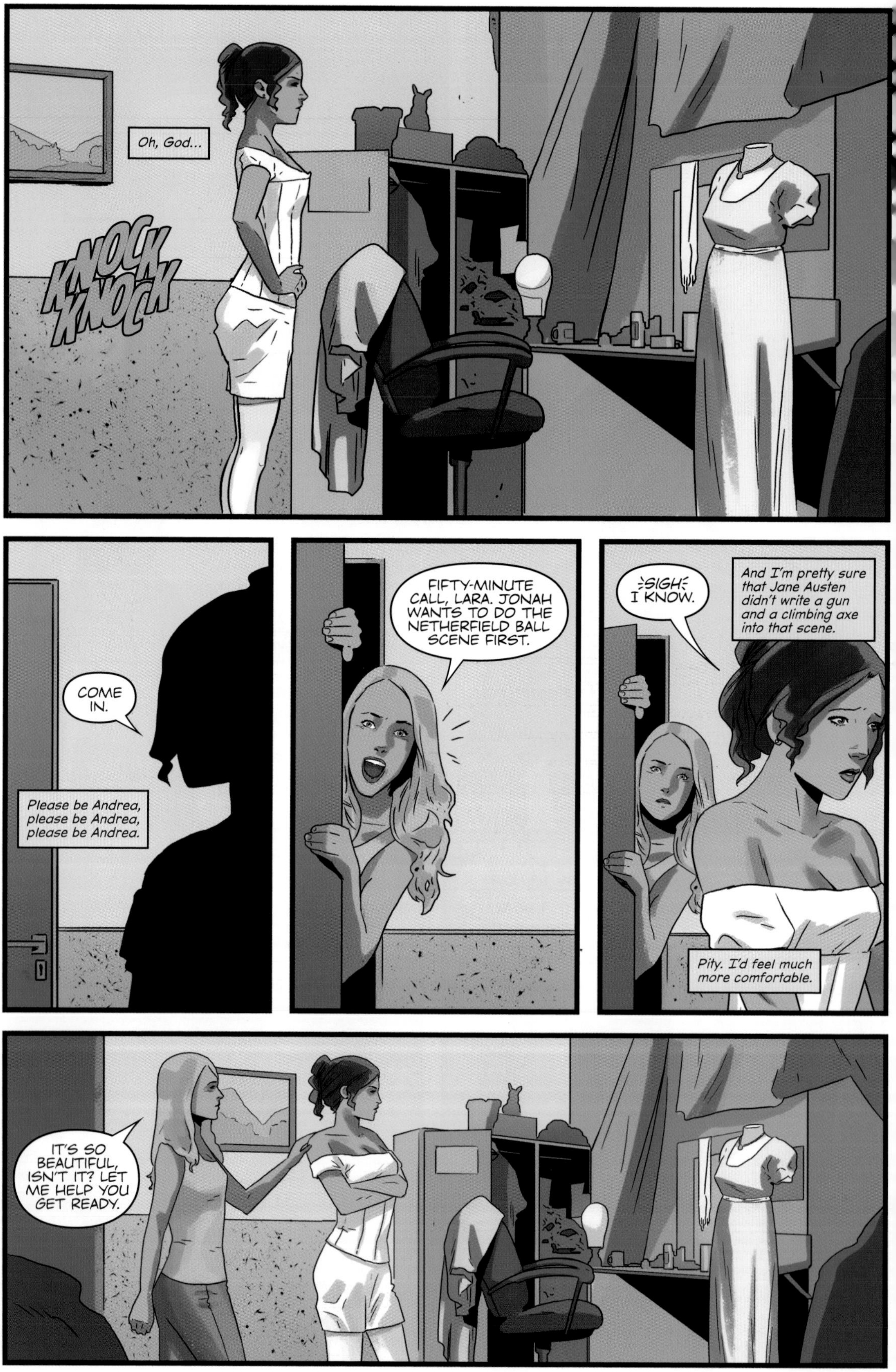
Oh, God...
KNOCK KNOCK
COME IN.
Please be Andrea, please be Andrea, please be Andrea.
FIFTY-MINUTE CALL, LARA. JONAH WANTS TO DO THE NETHERFIELD BALL SCENE FIRST.
SIGH I KNOW.
And I'm pretty sure that Jane Austen didn't write a gun and a climbing axe into that scene.
Pity. I'd feel much more comfortable.
IT'S SO BEAUTIFUL, ISN'T IT? LET ME HELP YOU GET READY.

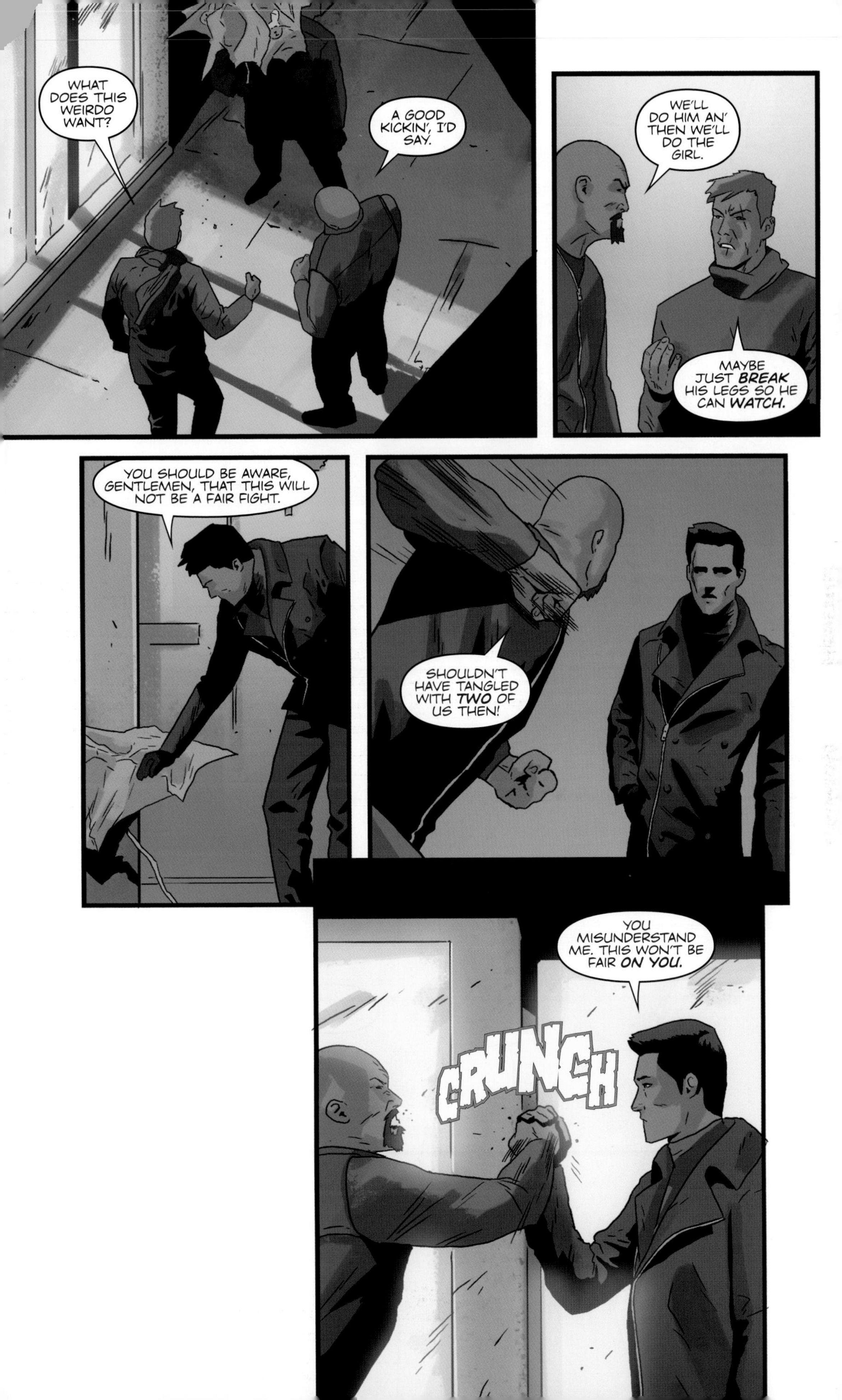

WHAT DOES THIS WEIRDO WANT?
A GOOD KICKIN', I'D SAY.
WE'LL DO HIM AN' THEN WE'LL DO THE GIRL.
MAYBE JUST **BREAK** HIS LEGS SO HE CAN **WATCH.**
YOU SHOULD BE AWARE, GENTLEMEN, THAT THIS WILL NOT BE A FAIR FIGHT.
SHOULDN'T HAVE TANGLED WITH **TWO** OF US THEN!
YOU MISUNDERSTAND ME. THIS WON'T BE FAIR **ON YOU.**
CRUNCH

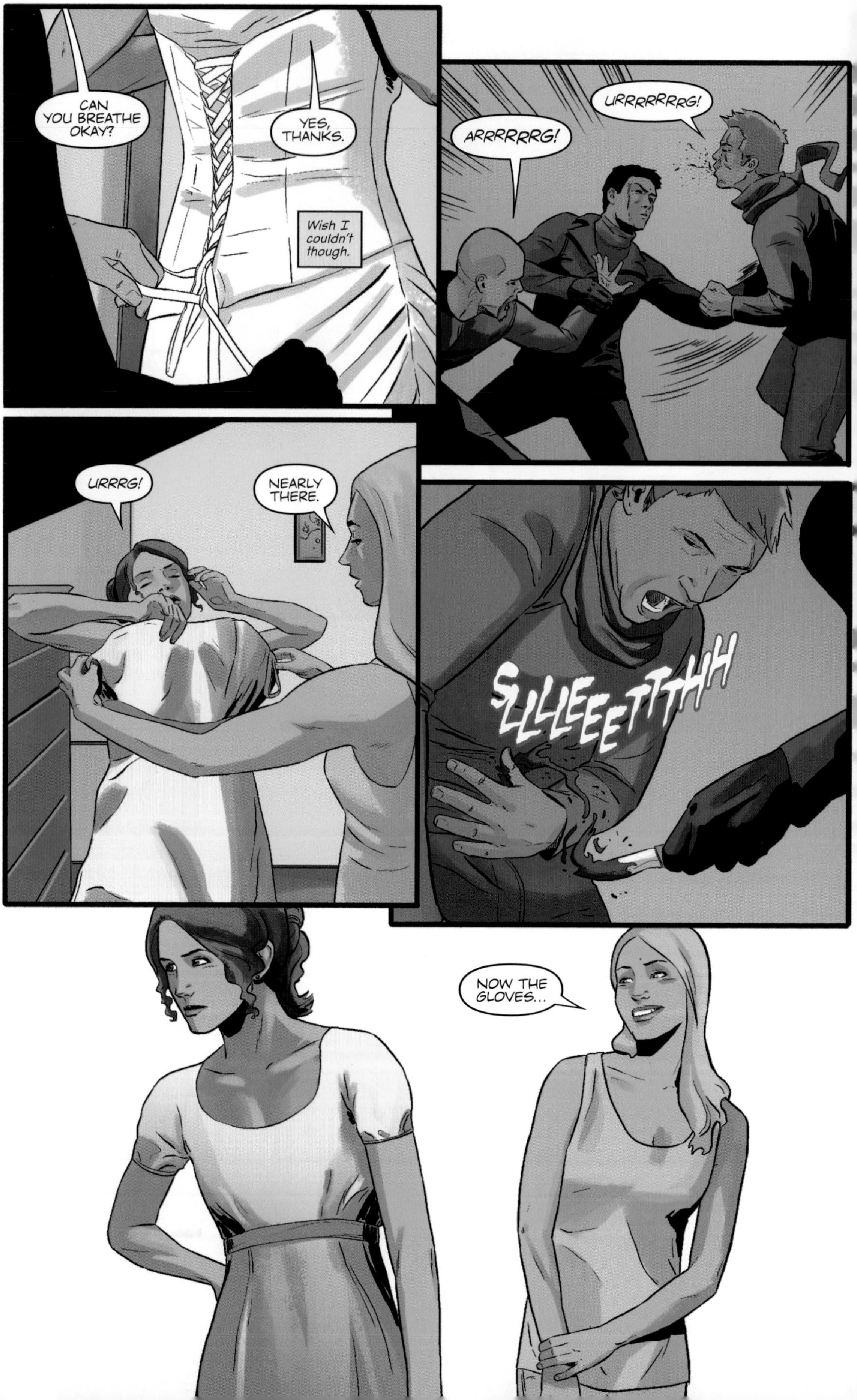

CAN YOU BREATHE OKAY?
YES, THANKS.
Wish I couldn't though.
ARRRRRRG!
URRRRRRRG!
URRRG!
NEARLY THERE.
SLLLLEEETTTHH
NOW THE GLOVES...

STOP, **STOP**. PLEASE.

I HAVE HEARD THAT MANY TIMES BEFORE. IT HAS NEVER WORKED.

AND IT NEVER WILL.

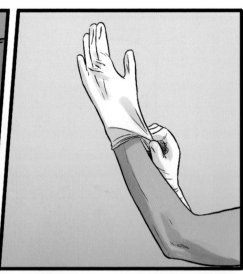

SCHHHUCK

URRRGGGGLLE...

DON'T TELL ANYONE I SAID THIS, BUT YOU LOOK BETTER THAN ANDREA.

YOU'RE AN OLD SOUL, LARA. USE IT.

It's just acting. I can do this. I CAN DO THIS.

MY ANGEL IS SAFE.

YOU SHALL NOT SPEAK OF HER AGAIN.

SHE IS THE ONE.

SHE WILL CONTINUE WHEN I CANNOT.

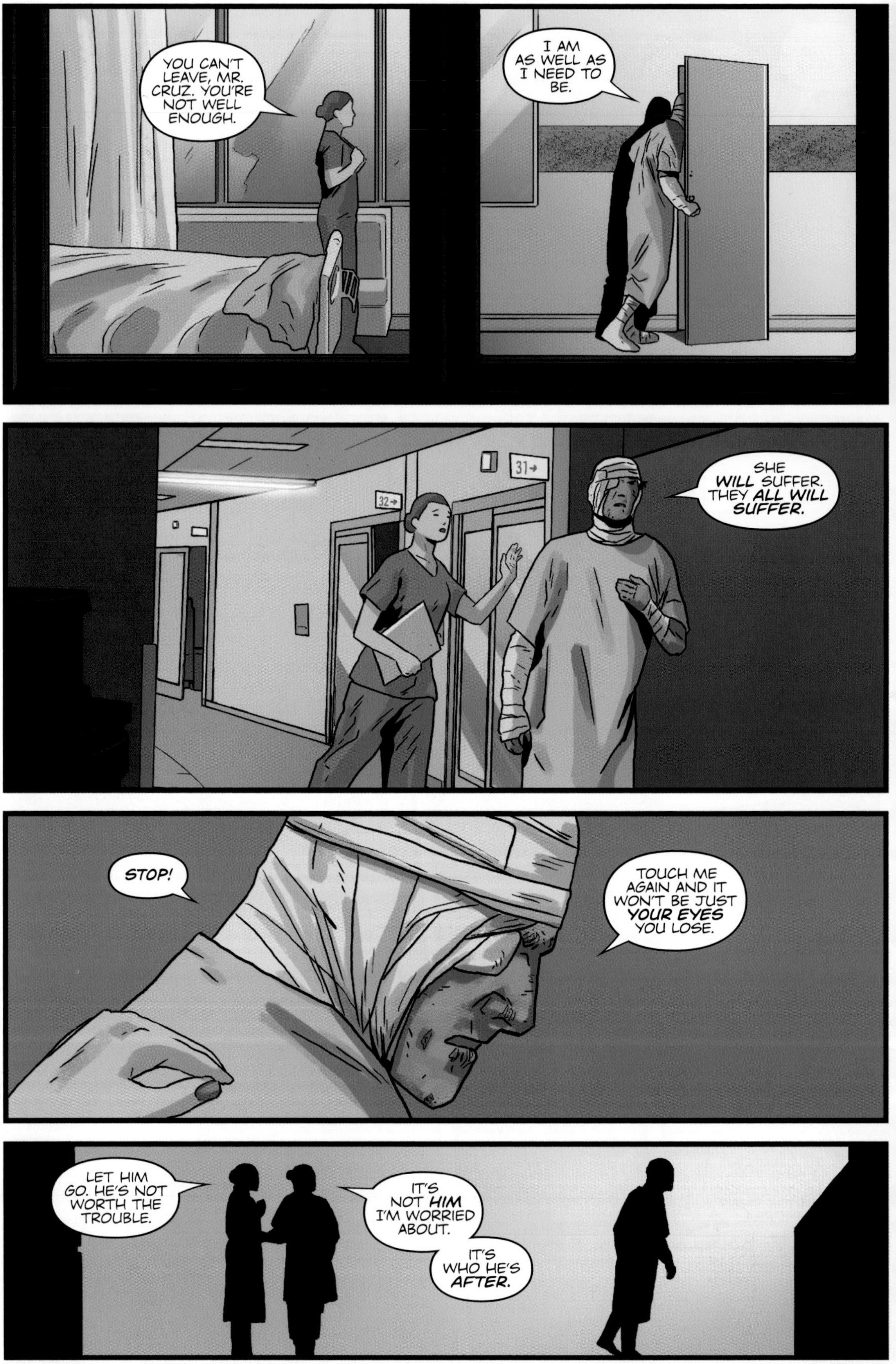
YOU CAN'T LEAVE, MR. CRUZ. YOU'RE NOT WELL ENOUGH.
I AM AS WELL AS I NEED TO BE.
SHE WILL SUFFER. THEY ALL WILL SUFFER.
STOP!
TOUCH ME AGAIN AND IT WON'T BE JUST YOUR EYES YOU LOSE.
LET HIM GO. HE'S NOT WORTH THE TROUBLE.
IT'S NOT HIM I'M WORRIED ABOUT.
IT'S WHO HE'S AFTER.

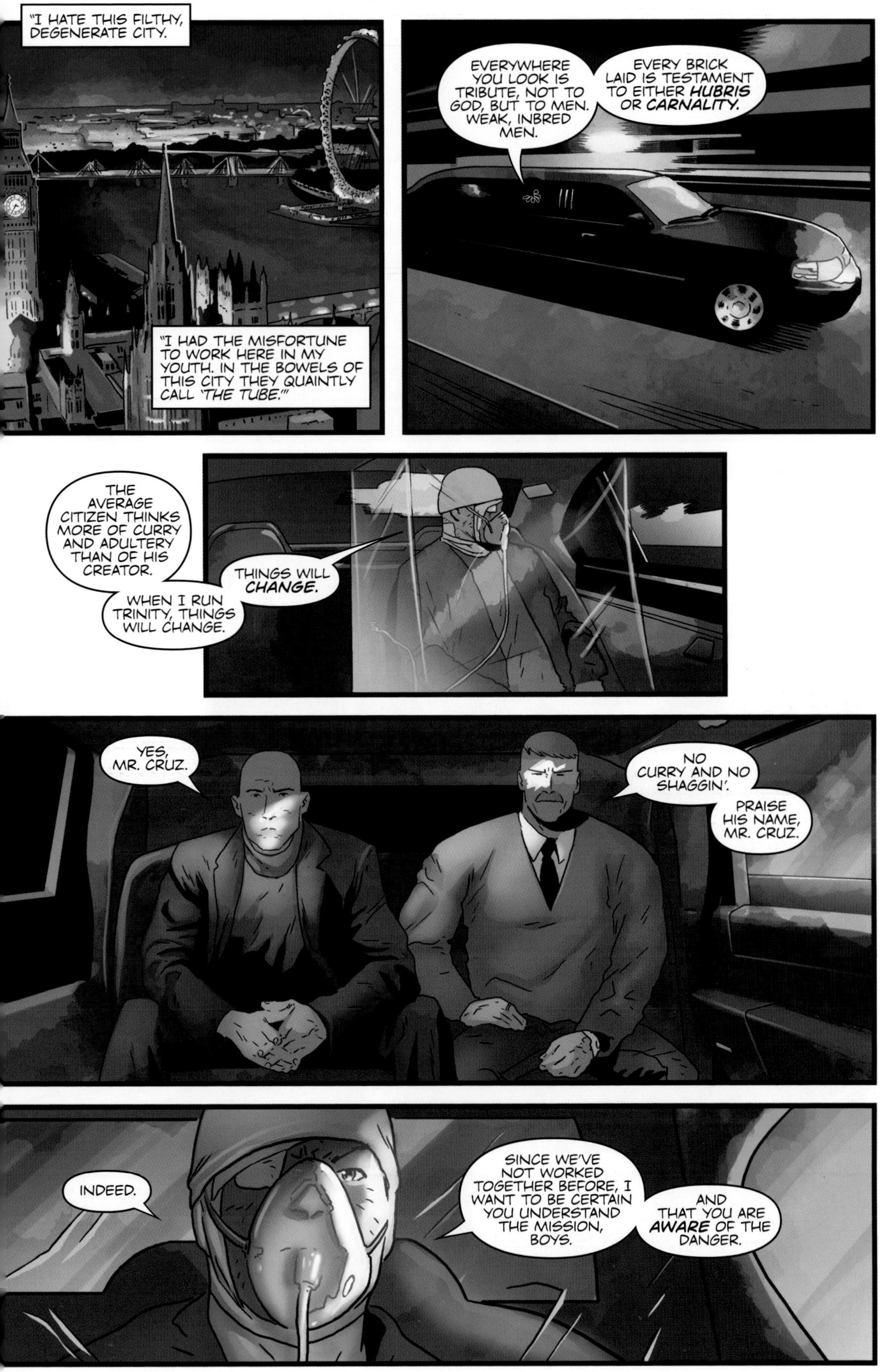
"I HATE THIS FILTHY, DEGENERATE CITY.
"I HAD THE MISFORTUNE TO WORK HERE IN MY YOUTH. IN THE BOWELS OF THIS CITY THEY QUAINTLY CALL 'THE TUBE.'"
EVERYWHERE YOU LOOK IS TRIBUTE, NOT TO GOD, BUT TO MEN. WEAK, INBRED MEN.
EVERY BRICK LAID IS TESTAMENT TO EITHER HUBRIS OR CARNALITY.
THE AVERAGE CITIZEN THINKS MORE OF CURRY AND ADULTERY THAN OF HIS CREATOR.
WHEN I RUN TRINITY, THINGS WILL CHANGE.
THINGS WILL CHANGE.
YES, MR. CRUZ.
NO CURRY AND NO SHAGGIN'.
PRAISE HIS NAME, MR. CRUZ.
INDEED.
SINCE WE'VE NOT WORKED TOGETHER BEFORE, I WANT TO BE CERTAIN YOU UNDERSTAND THE MISSION, BOYS.
AND THAT YOU ARE AWARE OF THE DANGER.

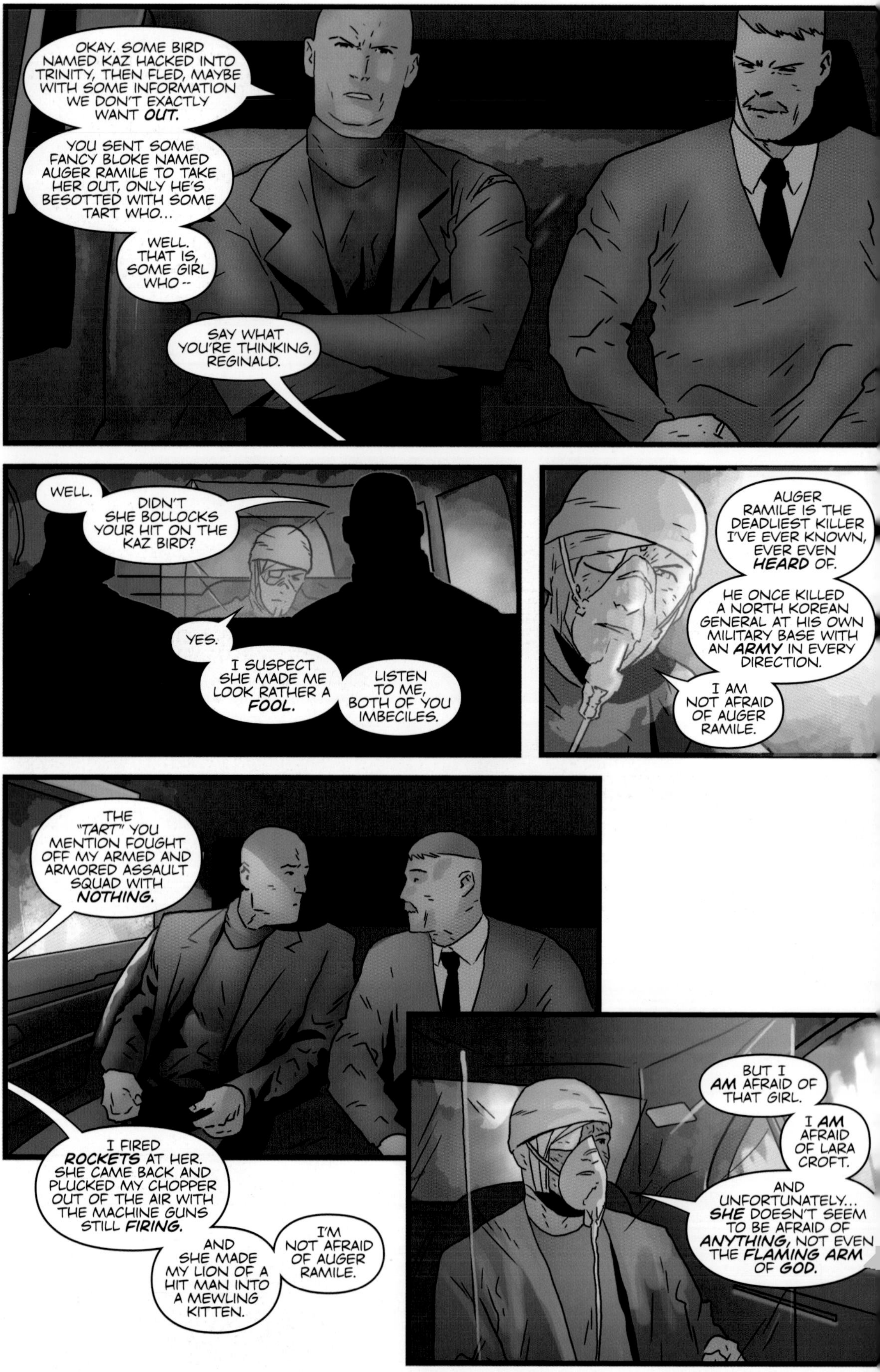

OKAY. SOME BIRD NAMED KAZ HACKED INTO TRINITY, THEN FLED, MAYBE WITH SOME INFORMATION WE DON'T EXACTLY WANT OUT.
YOU SENT SOME FANCY BLOKE NAMED AUGER RAMILE TO TAKE HER OUT, ONLY HE'S BESOTTED WITH SOME TART WHO...
WELL. THAT IS, SOME GIRL WHO --
SAY WHAT YOU'RE THINKING, REGINALD.
WELL.
DIDN'T SHE BOLLOCKS YOUR HIT ON THE KAZ BIRD?
YES.
I SUSPECT SHE MADE ME LOOK RATHER A FOOL.
LISTEN TO ME, BOTH OF YOU IMBECILES.
AUGER RAMILE IS THE DEADLIEST KILLER I'VE EVER KNOWN, EVER EVEN HEARD OF.
HE ONCE KILLED A NORTH KOREAN GENERAL AT HIS OWN MILITARY BASE WITH AN ARMY IN EVERY DIRECTION.
I AM NOT AFRAID OF AUGER RAMILE.
THE "TART" YOU MENTION FOUGHT OFF MY ARMED AND ARMORED ASSAULT SQUAD WITH NOTHING.
I FIRED ROCKETS AT HER. SHE CAME BACK AND PLUCKED MY CHOPPER OUT OF THE AIR WITH THE MACHINE GUNS STILL FIRING.
AND SHE MADE MY LION OF A HIT MAN INTO A MEWLING KITTEN.
I'M NOT AFRAID OF AUGER RAMILE.
BUT I AM AFRAID OF THAT GIRL.
I AM AFRAID OF LARA CROFT.
AND UNFORTUNATELY... SHE DOESN'T SEEM TO BE AFRAID OF ANYTHING, NOT EVEN THE FLAMING ARM OF GOD.

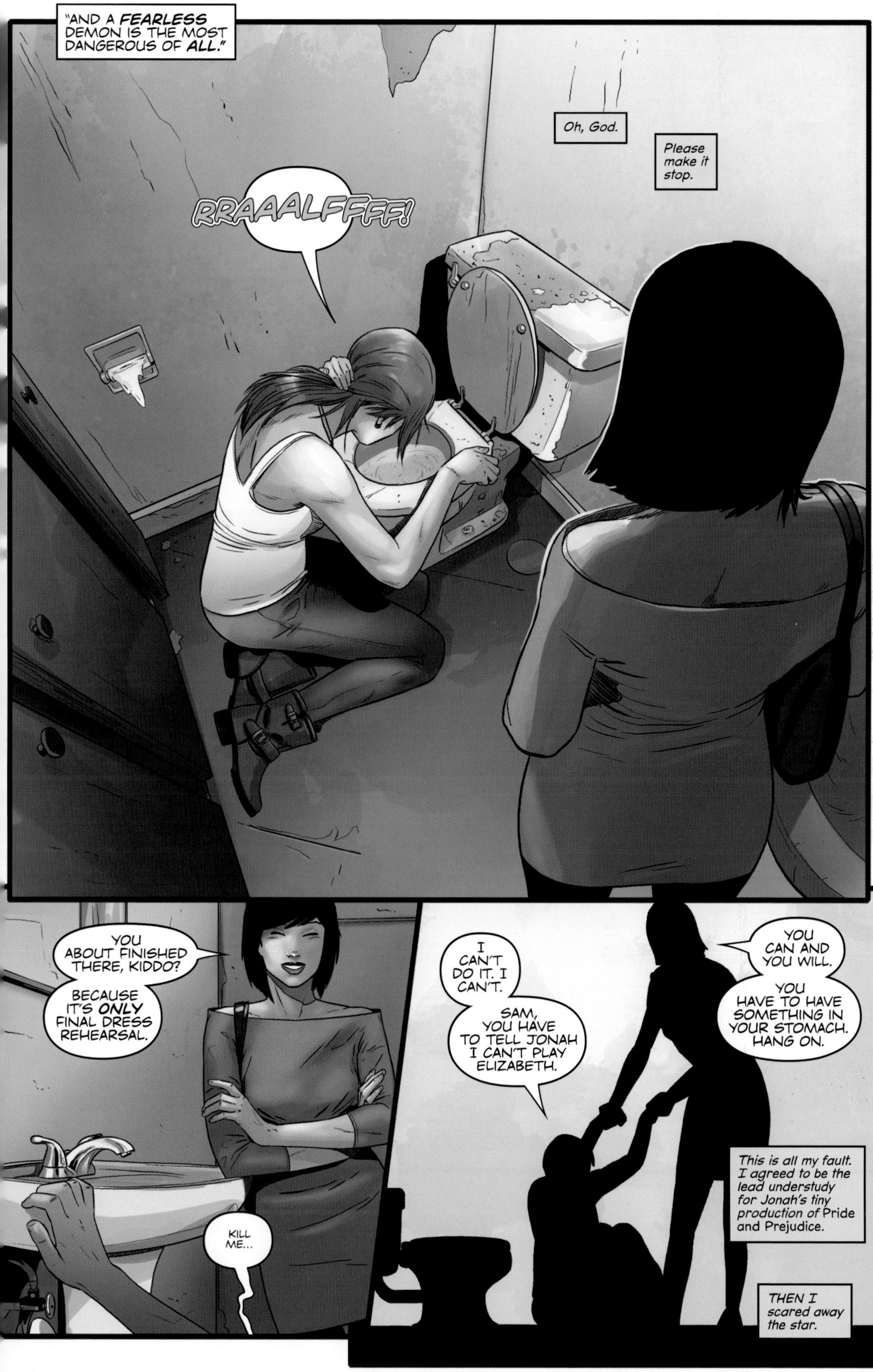
"AND A FEARLESS DEMON IS THE MOST DANGEROUS OF ALL."
Oh, God.
Please make it stop.
RRAAALFFFF!
YOU ABOUT FINISHED THERE, KIDDO?
BECAUSE IT'S ONLY FINAL DRESS REHEARSAL.
KILL ME...
I CAN'T DO IT. I CAN'T.
SAM, YOU HAVE TO TELL JONAH I CAN'T PLAY ELIZABETH.
YOU CAN AND YOU WILL.
YOU HAVE TO HAVE SOMETHING IN YOUR STOMACH. HANG ON.
This is all my fault. I agreed to be the lead understudy for Jonah's tiny production of Pride and Prejudice.
THEN I scared away the star.

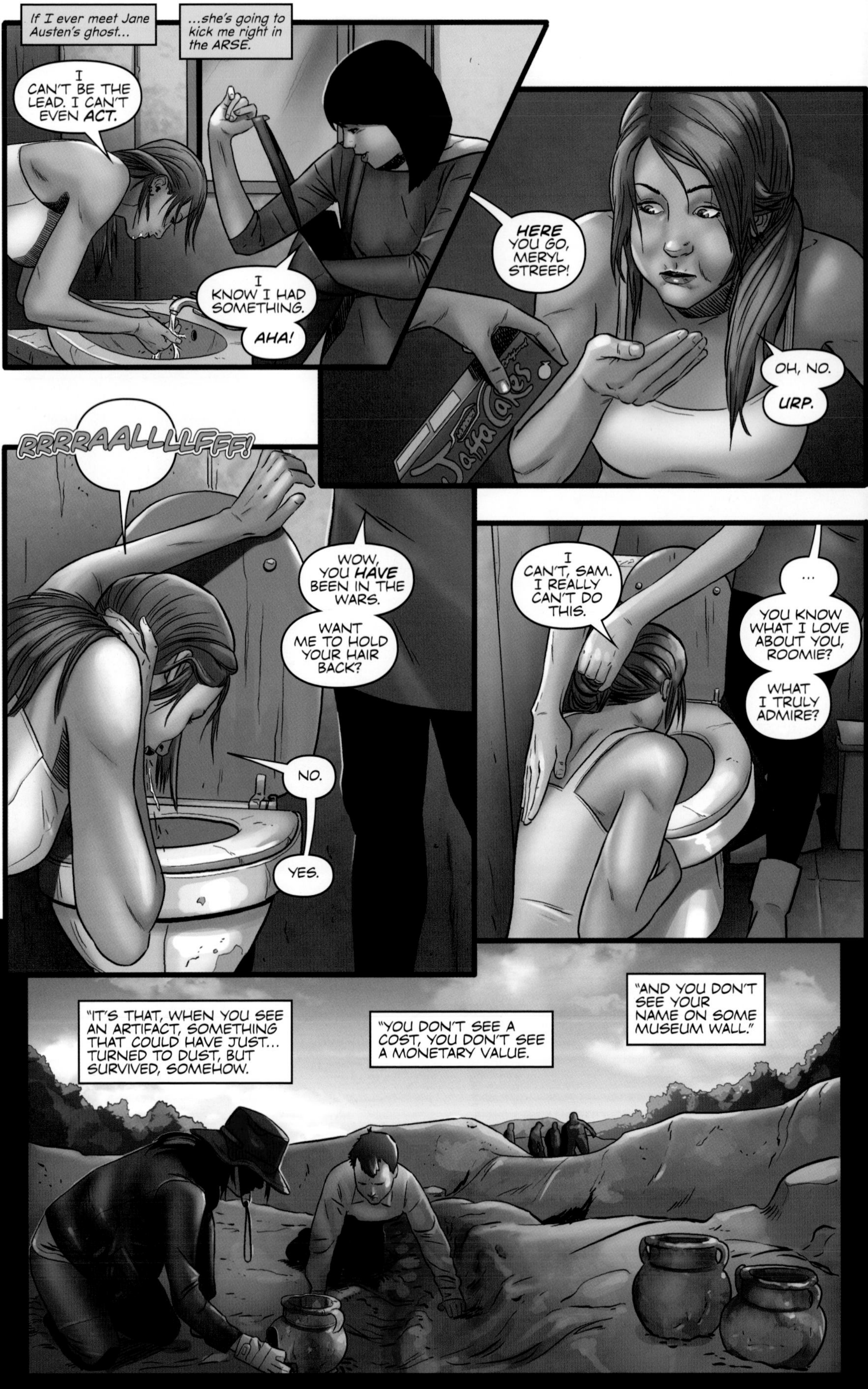

If I ever meet Jane Austen's ghost...
...she's going to kick me right in the ARSE.
I CAN'T BE THE LEAD. I CAN'T EVEN ACT.
I KNOW I HAD SOMETHING.
AHA!
HERE YOU GO, MERYL STREEP!
Jaffa Cakes
OH, NO.
URP.
RRRRAALLLLLFFF!
WOW, YOU HAVE BEEN IN THE WARS.
WANT ME TO HOLD YOUR HAIR BACK?
NO.
YES.
I CAN'T, SAM. I REALLY CAN'T DO THIS.
...
YOU KNOW WHAT I LOVE ABOUT YOU, ROOMIE?
WHAT I TRULY ADMIRE?
"IT'S THAT, WHEN YOU SEE AN ARTIFACT, SOMETHING THAT COULD HAVE JUST... TURNED TO DUST, BUT SURVIVED, SOMEHOW.
"YOU DON'T SEE A COST, YOU DON'T SEE A MONETARY VALUE.
"AND YOU DON'T SEE YOUR NAME ON SOME MUSEUM WALL."

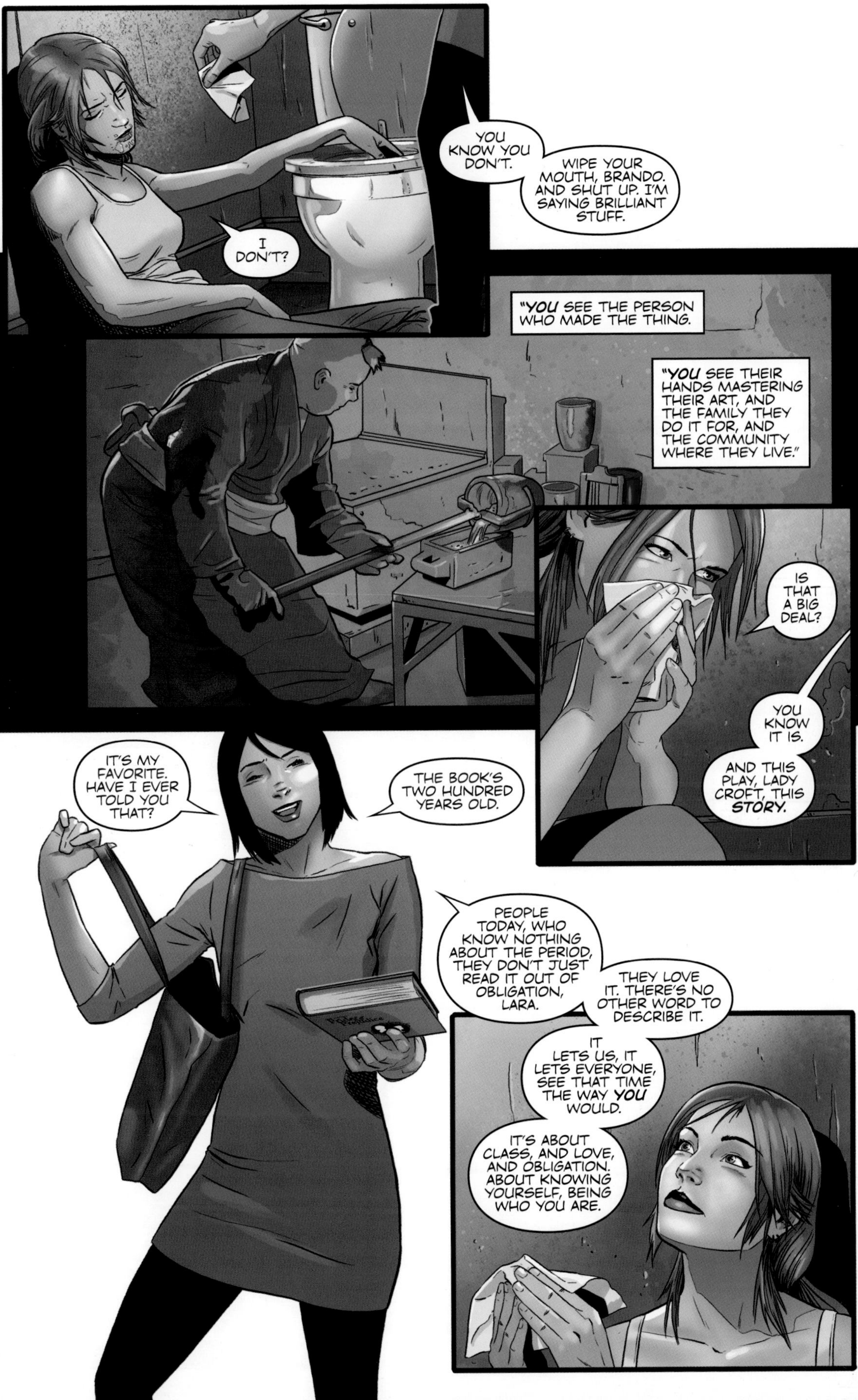

YOU KNOW YOU DON'T.
I DON'T?
WIPE YOUR MOUTH, BRANDO. AND SHUT UP. I'M SAYING BRILLIANT STUFF.
"YOU SEE THE PERSON WHO MADE THE THING.
"YOU SEE THEIR HANDS MASTERING THEIR ART, AND THE FAMILY THEY DO IT FOR, AND THE COMMUNITY WHERE THEY LIVE."
IS THAT A BIG DEAL?
YOU KNOW IT IS.
AND THIS PLAY, LADY CROFT, THIS STORY.
IT'S MY FAVORITE. HAVE I EVER TOLD YOU THAT?
THE BOOK'S TWO HUNDRED YEARS OLD.
PEOPLE TODAY, WHO KNOW NOTHING ABOUT THE PERIOD, THEY DON'T JUST READ IT OUT OF OBLIGATION, LARA.
THEY LOVE IT. THERE'S NO OTHER WORD TO DESCRIBE IT.
IT LETS US, IT LETS EVERYONE, SEE THAT TIME THE WAY YOU WOULD.
IT'S ABOUT CLASS, AND LOVE, AND OBLIGATION. ABOUT KNOWING YOURSELF, BEING WHO YOU ARE.

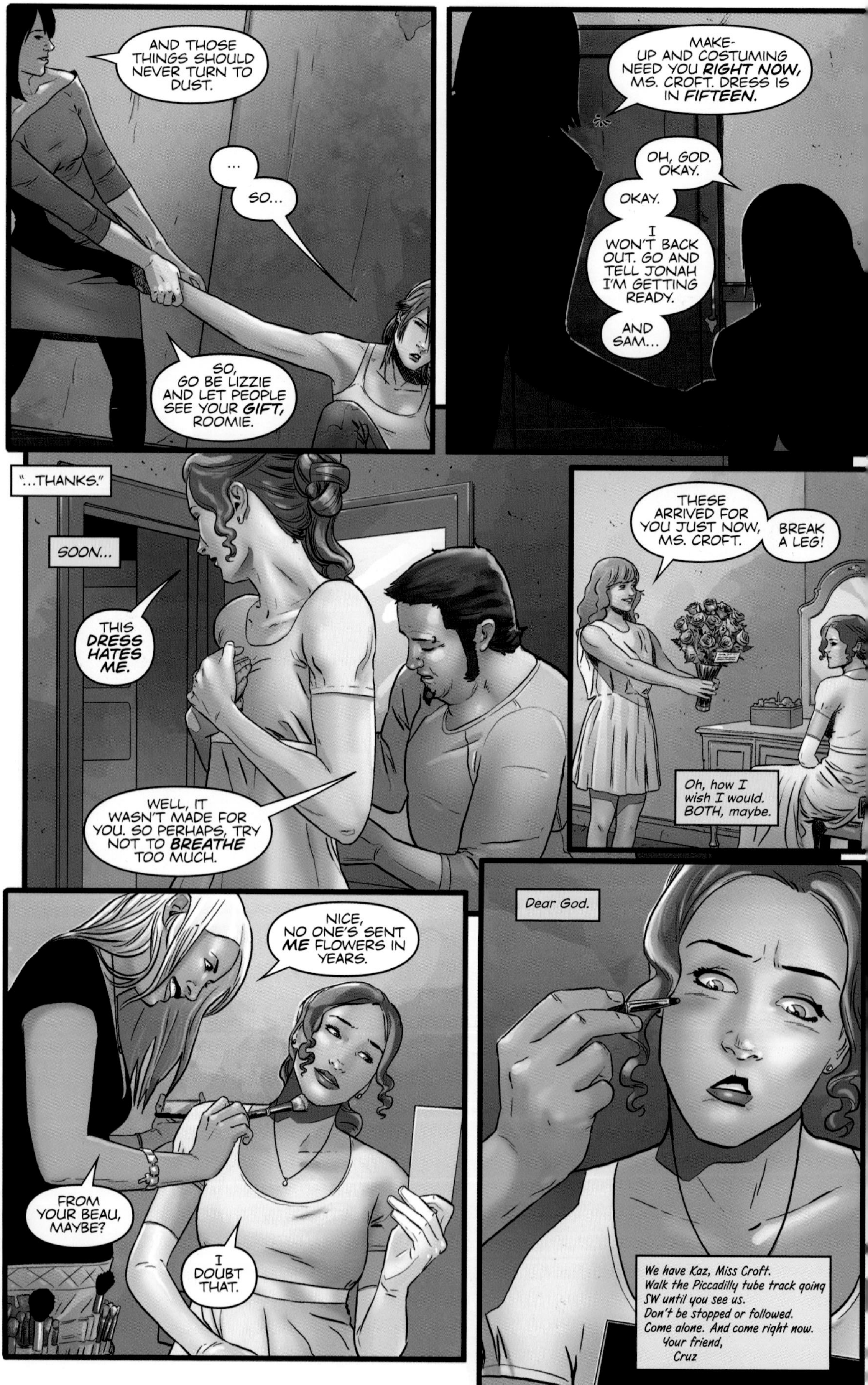

AND THOSE THINGS SHOULD NEVER TURN TO DUST.
...
SO...
SO, GO BE LIZZIE AND LET PEOPLE SEE YOUR **GIFT,** ROOMIE.
MAKE-UP AND COSTUMING NEED YOU **RIGHT NOW,** MS. CROFT. DRESS IS IN **FIFTEEN.**
OH, GOD. OKAY.
OKAY.
I WON'T BACK OUT. GO AND TELL JONAH I'M GETTING READY.
AND SAM...
"...THANKS."
SOON...
THIS **DRESS HATES ME.**
WELL, IT WASN'T MADE FOR YOU. SO PERHAPS, TRY NOT TO **BREATHE** TOO MUCH.
THESE ARRIVED FOR YOU JUST NOW, MS. CROFT.
BREAK A LEG!
Oh, how I wish I would. BOTH, maybe.
NICE, NO ONE'S SENT **ME** FLOWERS IN YEARS.
FROM YOUR BEAU, MAYBE?
I DOUBT THAT.
Dear God.
We have Kaz, Miss Croft. Walk the Piccadilly tube track going SW until you see us. Don't be stopped or followed. Come alone. And come right now. Your friend, Cruz

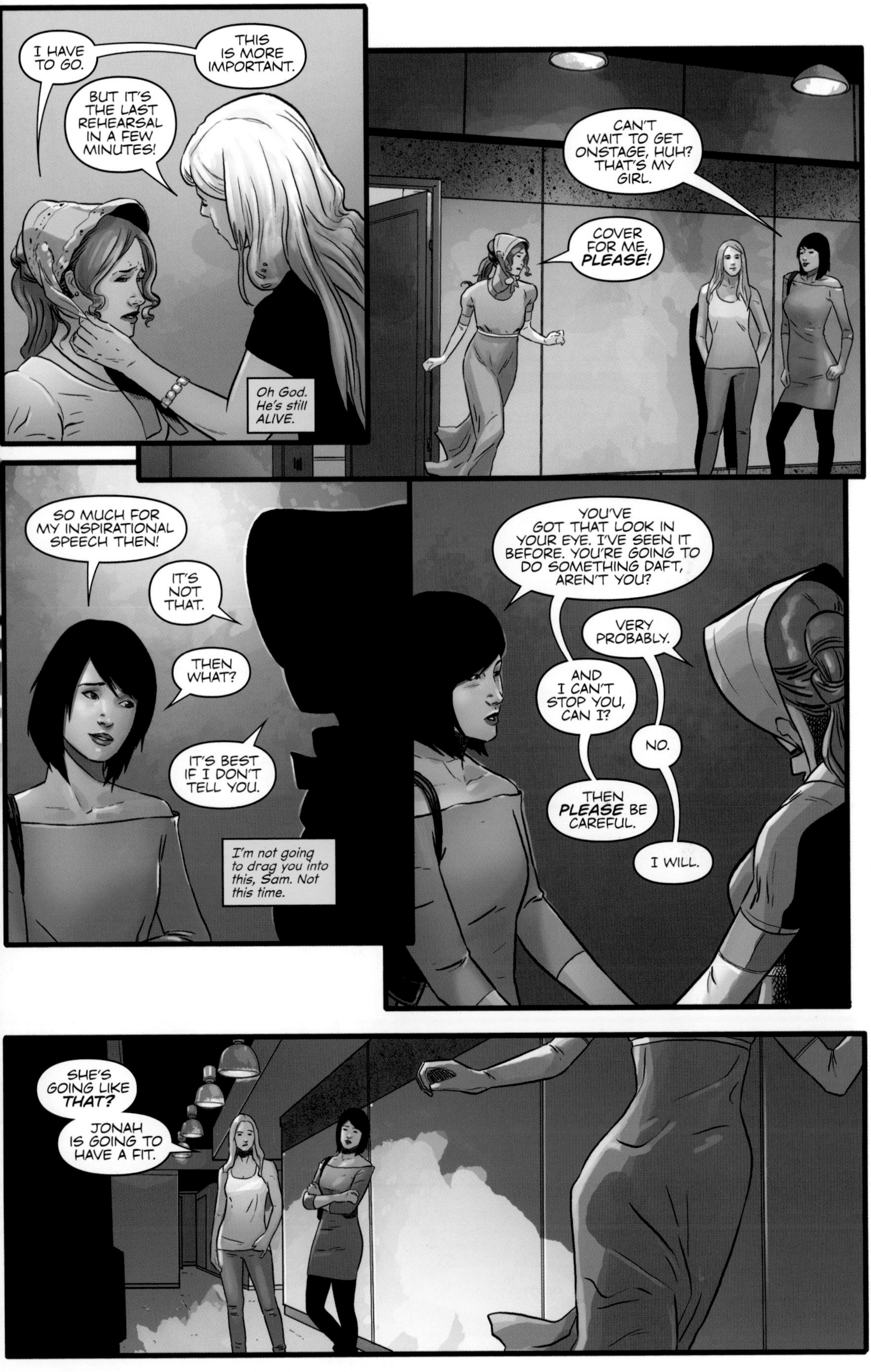
I HAVE TO GO.
THIS IS MORE IMPORTANT.
BUT IT'S THE LAST REHEARSAL IN A FEW MINUTES!
Oh God. He's still ALIVE.
CAN'T WAIT TO GET ONSTAGE, HUH? THAT'S MY GIRL.
COVER FOR ME, PLEASE!
SO MUCH FOR MY INSPIRATIONAL SPEECH THEN!
IT'S NOT THAT.
THEN WHAT?
IT'S BEST IF I DON'T TELL YOU.
I'm not going to drag you into this, Sam. Not this time.
YOU'VE GOT THAT LOOK IN YOUR EYE. I'VE SEEN IT BEFORE. YOU'RE GOING TO DO SOMETHING DAFT, AREN'T YOU?
VERY PROBABLY.
AND I CAN'T STOP YOU, CAN I?
NO.
THEN PLEASE BE CAREFUL.
I WILL.
SHE'S GOING LIKE THAT?
JONAH IS GOING TO HAVE A FIT.

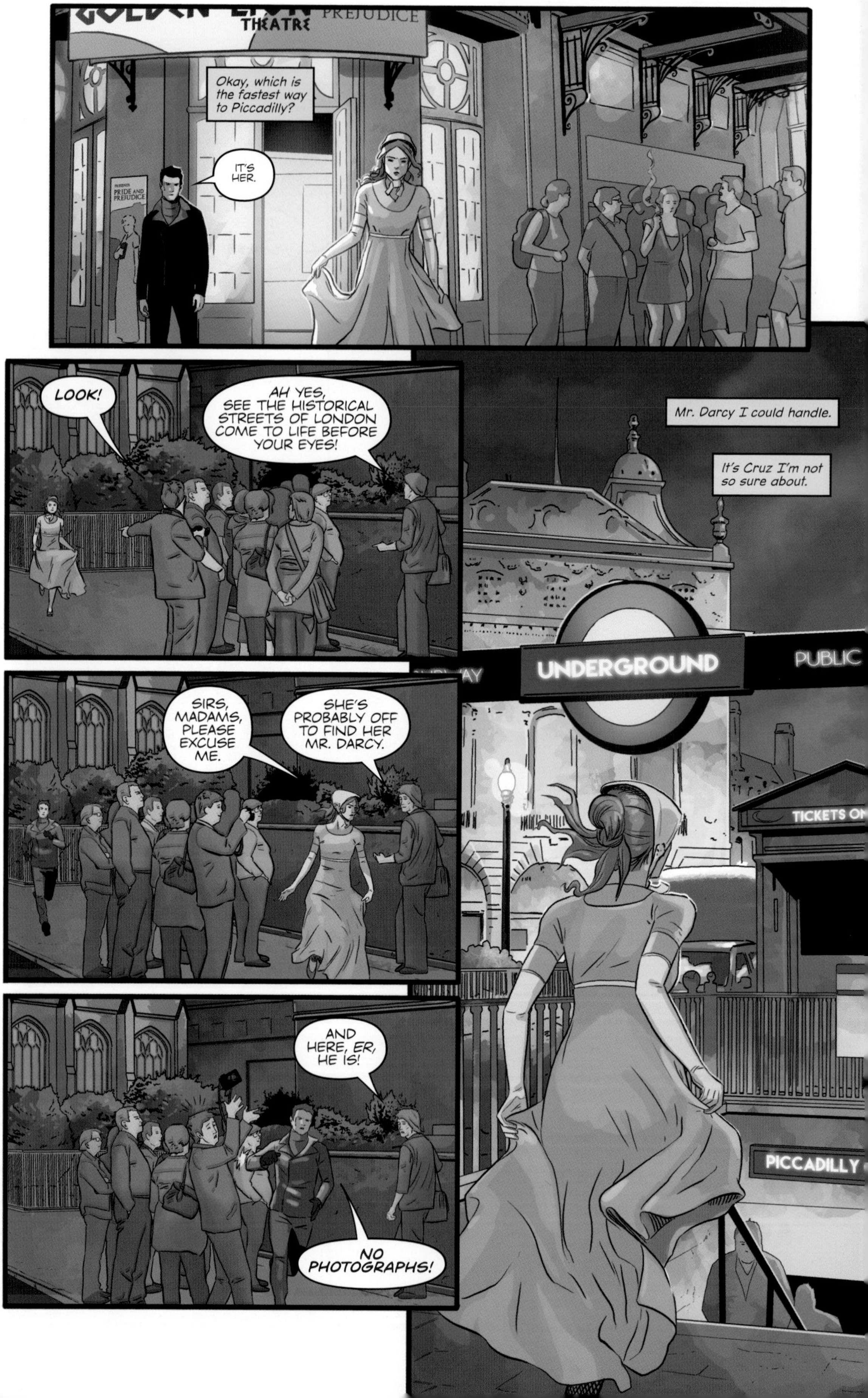
THEATRE
PREJUDICE
Okay, which is the fastest way to Piccadilly?
PRESENTS PRIDE AND PREJUDICE
IT'S HER.
LOOK!
AH YES, SEE THE HISTORICAL STREETS OF LONDON COME TO LIFE BEFORE YOUR EYES!
SIRS, MADAMS, PLEASE EXCUSE ME.
SHE'S PROBABLY OFF TO FIND HER MR. DARCY.
AND HERE, ER, HE IS!
NO PHOTOGRAPHS!
Mr. Darcy I could handle.
It's Cruz I'm not so sure about.
UNDERGROUND
PUBLIC
TICKETS ON
PICCADILLY

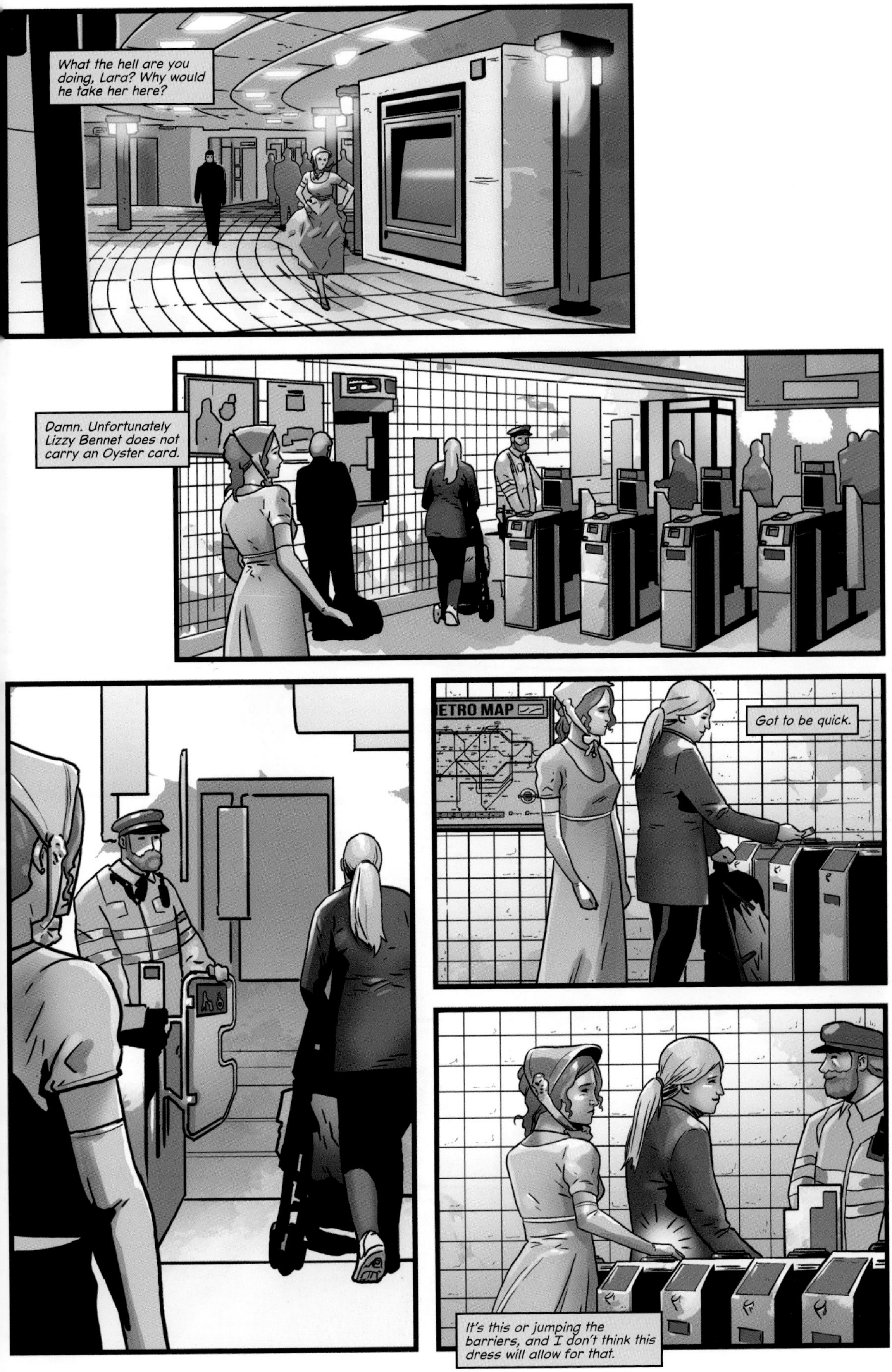
What the hell are you doing, Lara? Why would he take her here?
Damn. Unfortunately Lizzy Bennet does not carry an Oyster card.
METRO MAP
Got to be quick.
It's this or jumping the barriers, and I don't think this dress will allow for that.

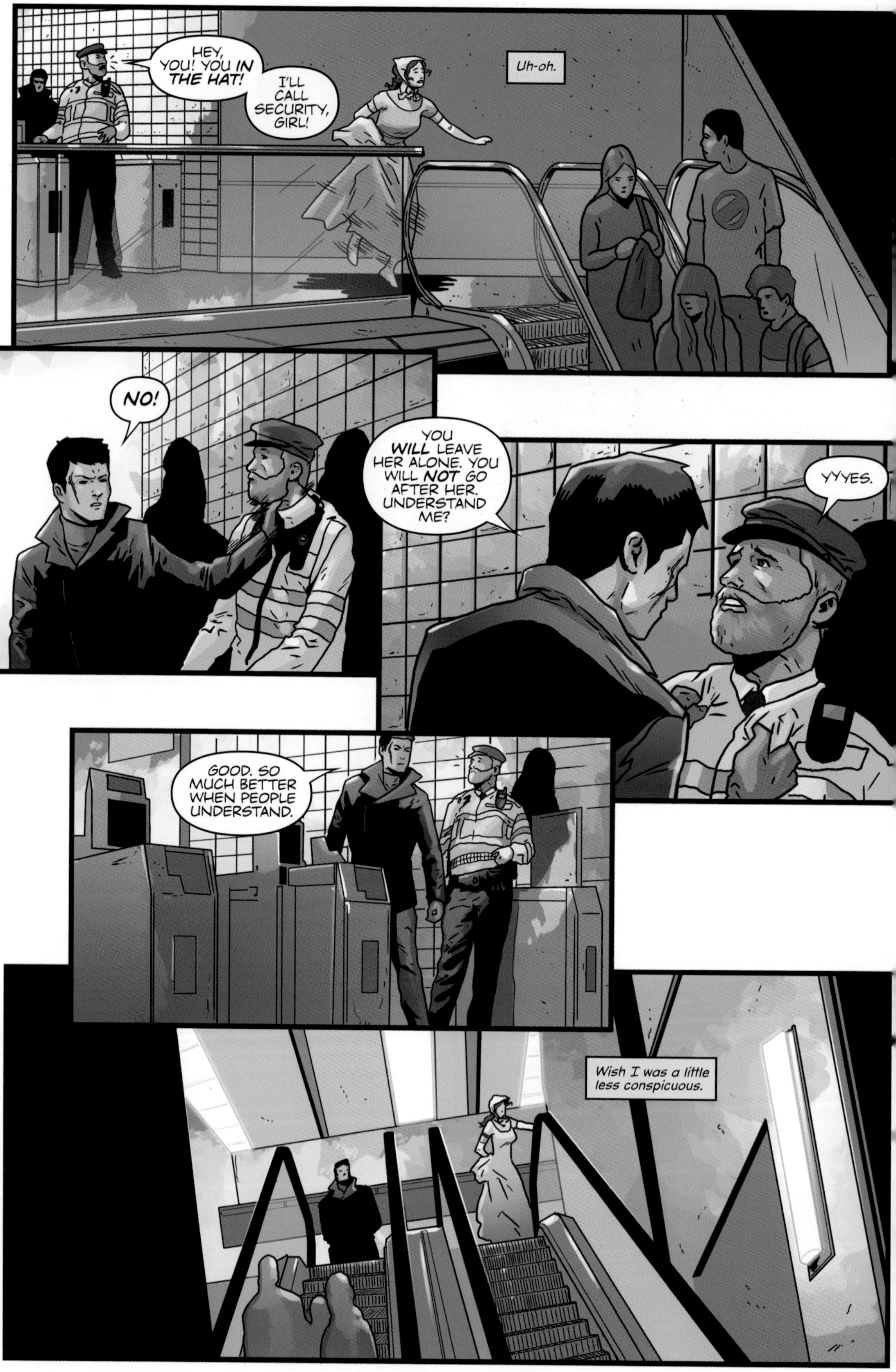
HEY, YOU! YOU IN THE HAT!
I'LL CALL SECURITY, GIRL!
Uh-oh.
NO!
YOU WILL LEAVE HER ALONE. YOU WILL NOT GO AFTER HER. UNDERSTAND ME?
YYYES.
GOOD. SO MUCH BETTER WHEN PEOPLE UNDERSTAND.
Wish I was a little less conspicuous.

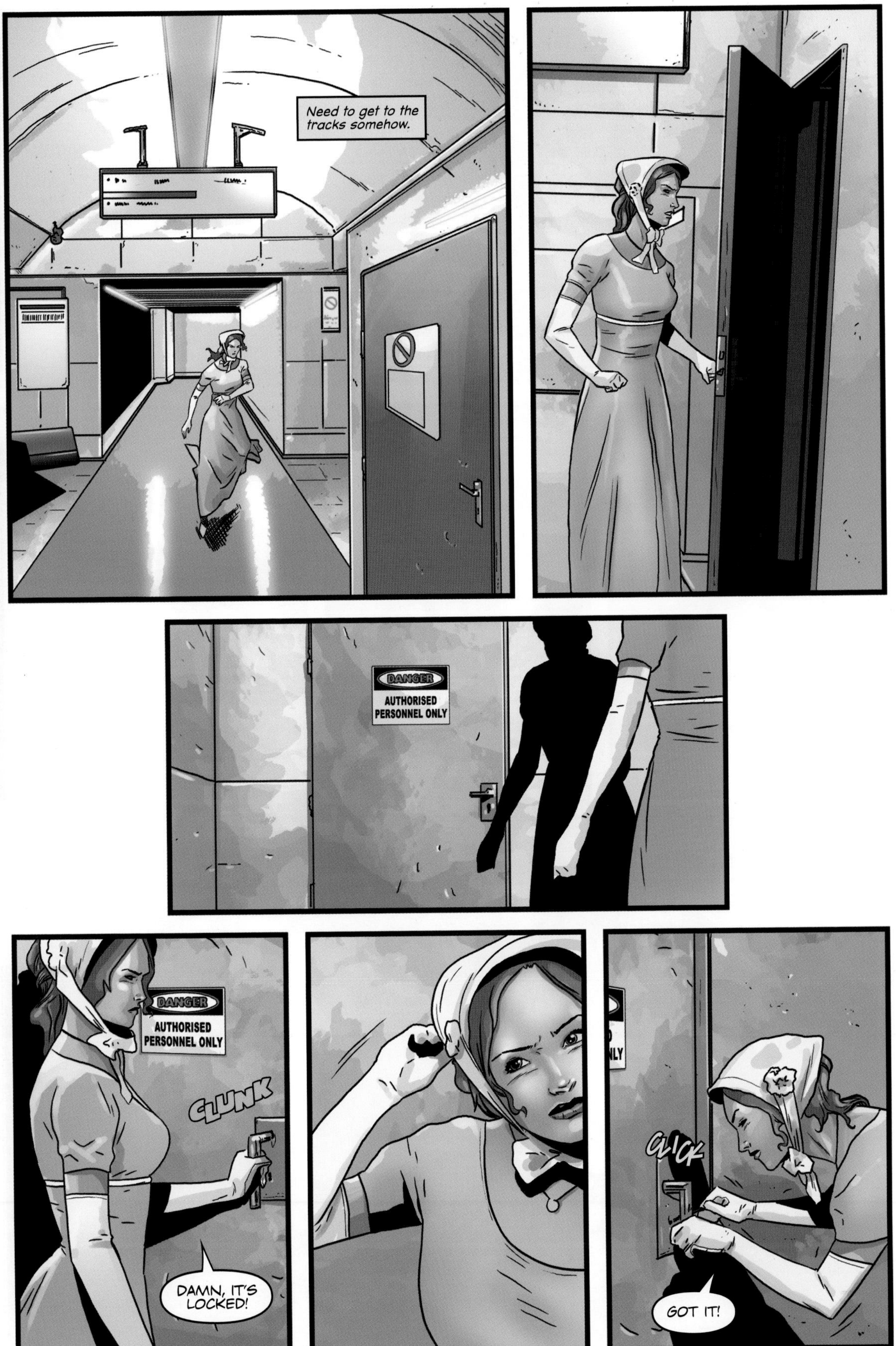
Need to get to the tracks somehow.
DANGER
AUTHORISED PERSONNEL ONLY
DANGER
AUTHORISED PERSONNEL ONLY
CLUNK
DAMN, IT'S LOCKED!
CLICK
GOT IT!

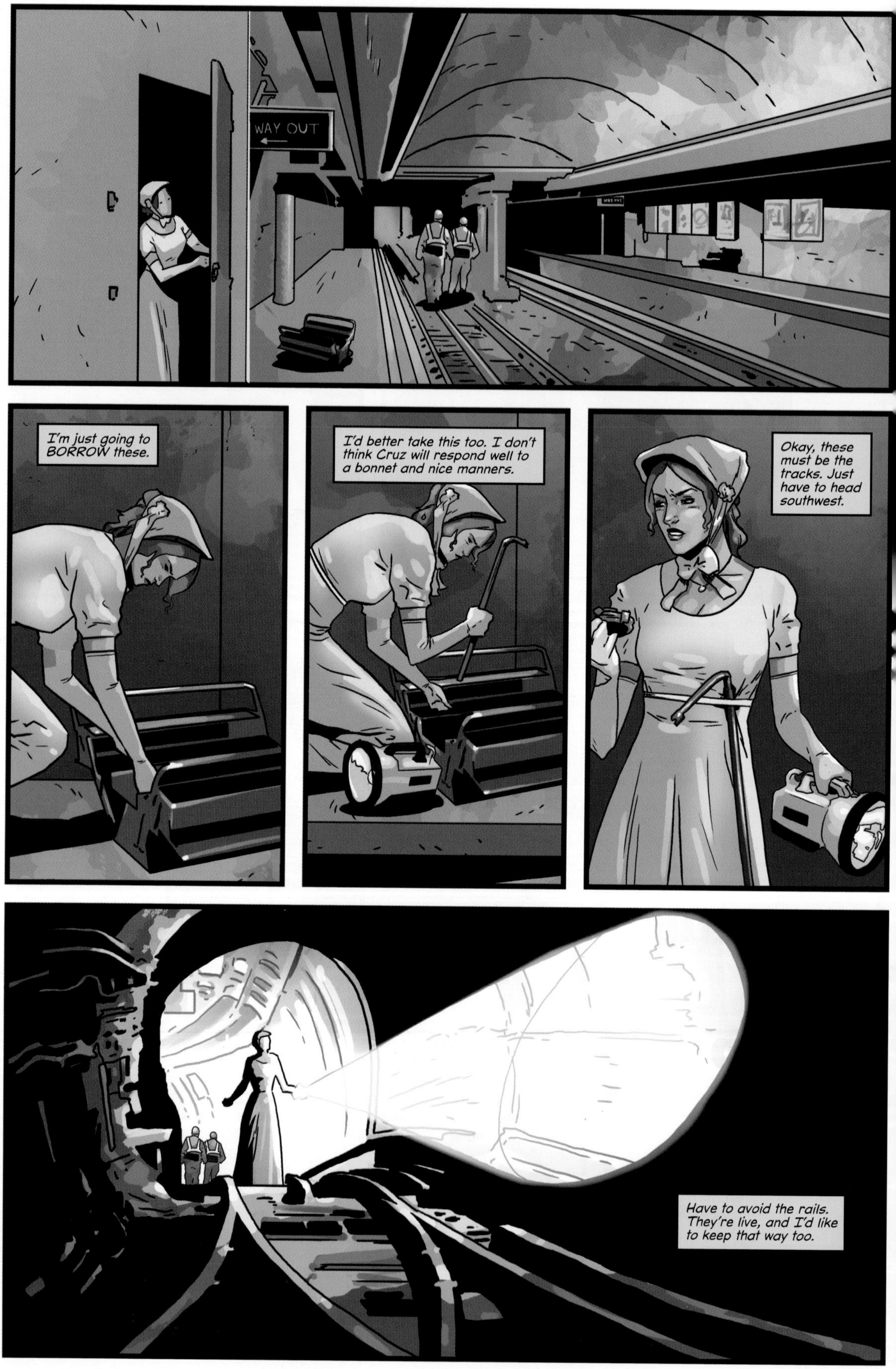
WAY OUT
I'm just going to BORROW these.
I'd better take this too. I don't think Cruz will respond well to a bonnet and nice manners.
Okay, these must be the tracks. Just have to head southwest.
Have to avoid the rails. They're live, and I'd like to keep that way too.

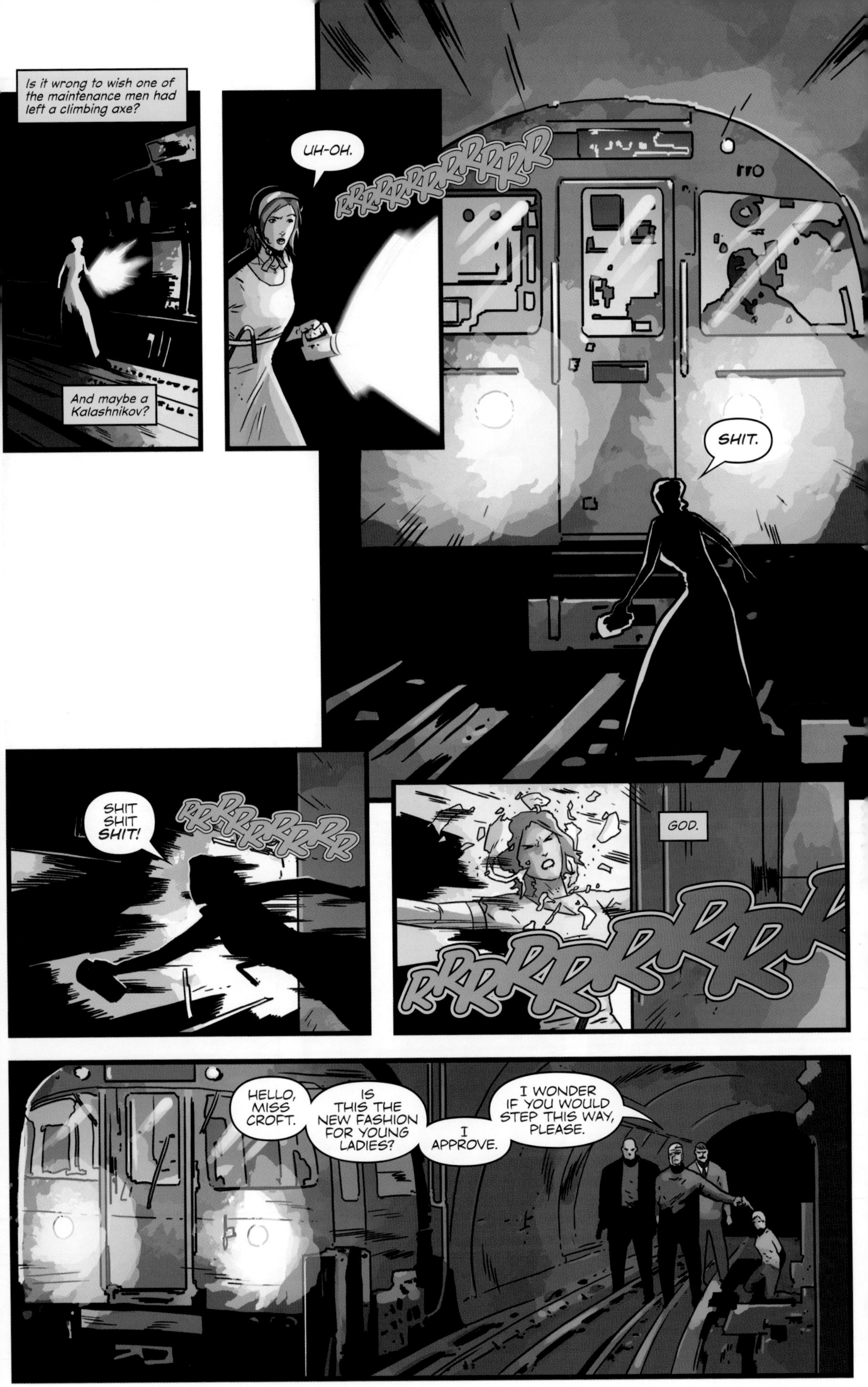
Is it wrong to wish one of the maintenance men had left a climbing axe?
And maybe a Kalashnikov?
UH-OH.
RRRRRRRRRRRRRR
SHIT.
SHIT SHIT SHIT!
RRRRRRRRRR
GOD.
RRRRRRRRRR
HELLO, MISS CROFT.
IS THIS THE NEW FASHION FOR YOUNG LADIES?
I APPROVE.
I WONDER IF YOU WOULD STEP THIS WAY, PLEASE.

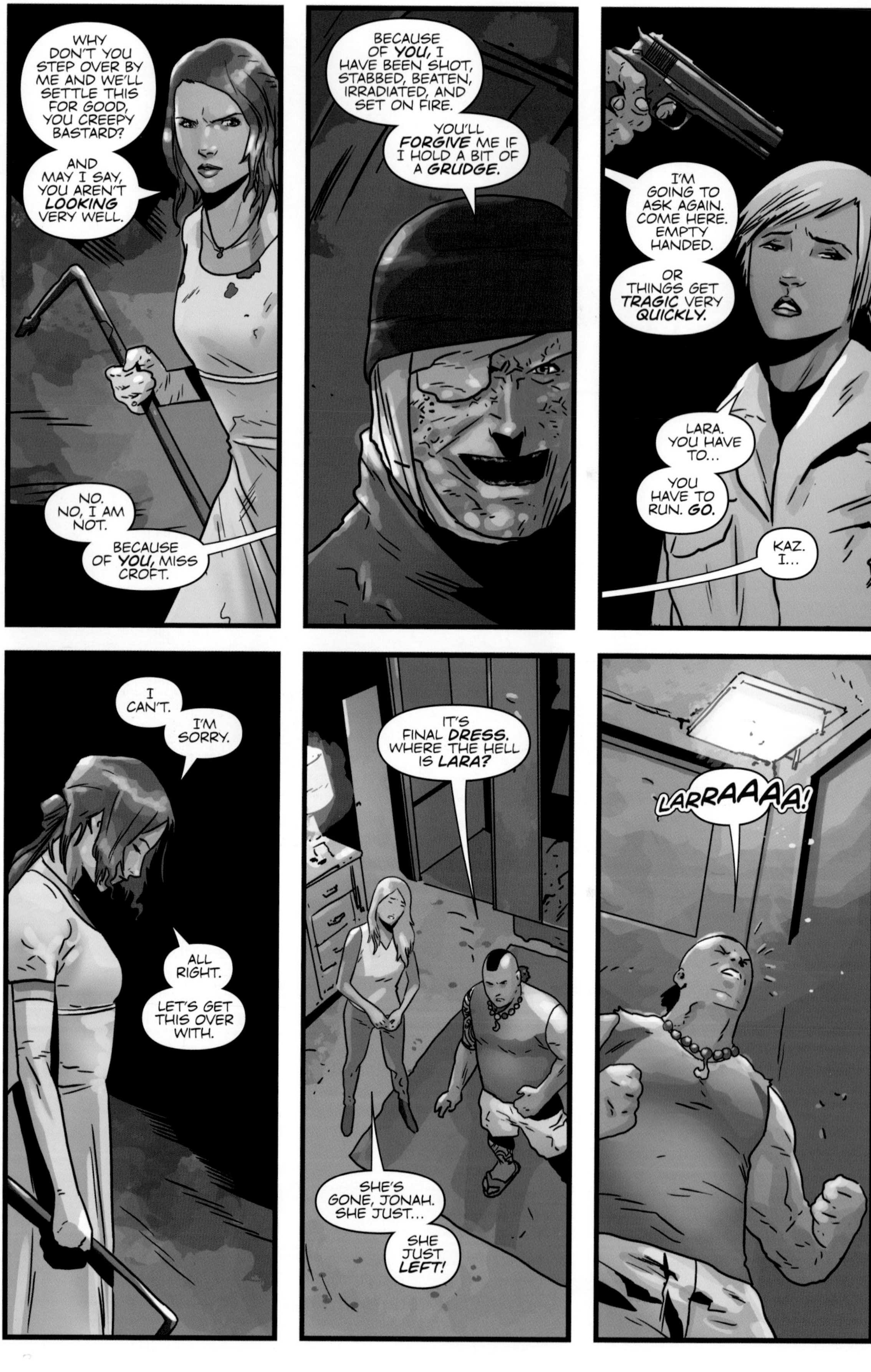
WHY DON'T YOU STEP OVER BY ME AND WE'LL SETTLE THIS FOR GOOD, YOU CREEPY BASTARD?
AND MAY I SAY, YOU AREN'T **LOOKING** VERY WELL.
NO. NO, I AM NOT.
BECAUSE OF **YOU,** MISS CROFT.
BECAUSE OF **YOU,** I HAVE BEEN SHOT, STABBED, BEATEN, IRRADIATED, AND SET ON FIRE.
YOU'LL **FORGIVE** ME IF I HOLD A BIT OF A **GRUDGE.**
I'M GOING TO ASK AGAIN. COME HERE. EMPTY HANDED.
OR THINGS GET **TRAGIC** VERY **QUICKLY.**
LARA. YOU HAVE TO...
YOU HAVE TO RUN. **GO.**
KAZ. I...
I CAN'T.
I'M SORRY.
ALL RIGHT.
LET'S GET THIS OVER WITH.
IT'S FINAL **DRESS.** WHERE THE HELL IS **LARA?**
SHE'S GONE, JONAH. SHE JUST...
SHE JUST **LEFT!**
LARRAAAA!

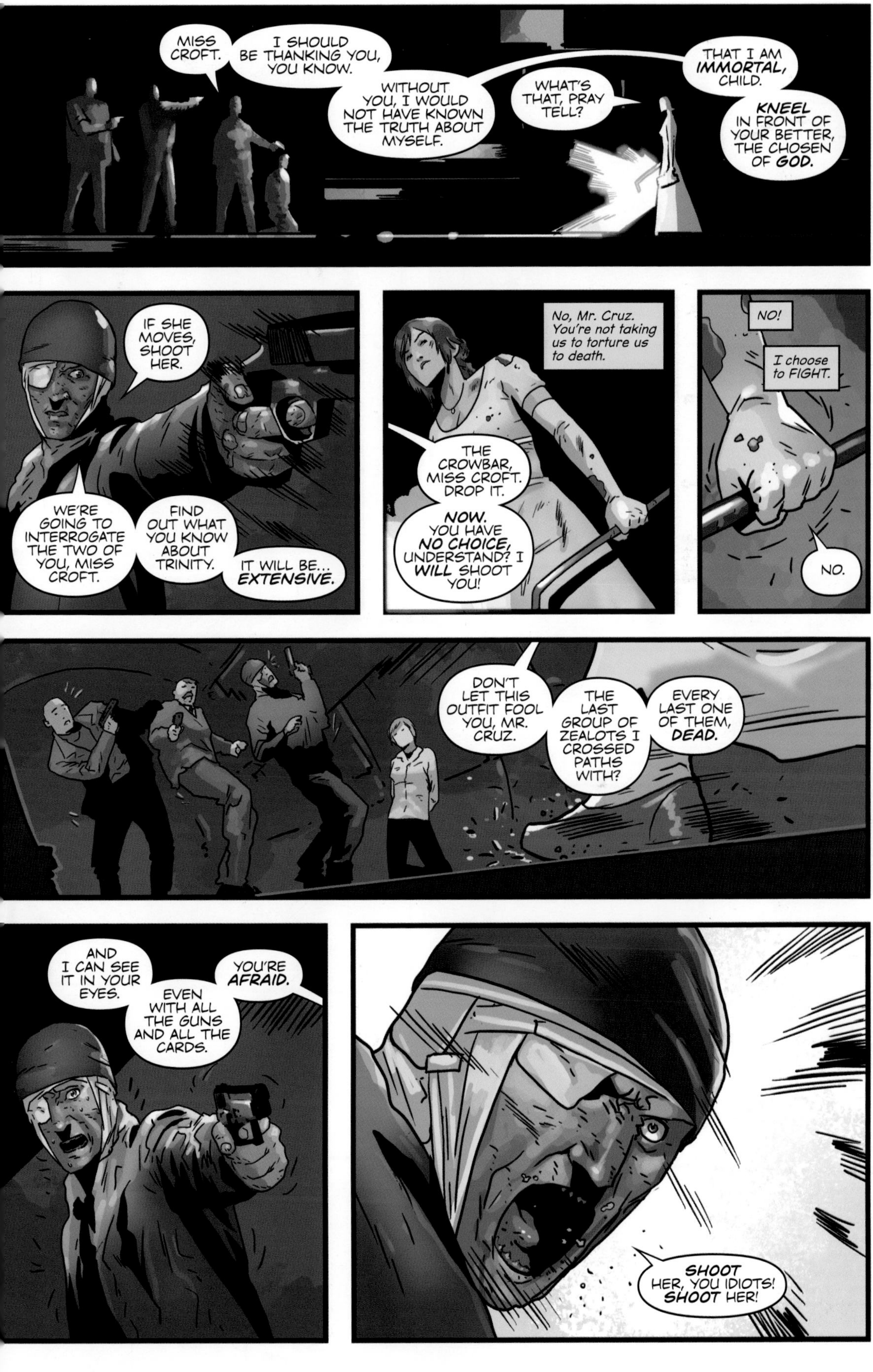
MISS CROFT.
I SHOULD BE THANKING YOU, YOU KNOW.
WITHOUT YOU, I WOULD NOT HAVE KNOWN THE TRUTH ABOUT MYSELF.
WHAT'S THAT, PRAY TELL?
THAT I AM IMMORTAL, CHILD.
KNEEL IN FRONT OF YOUR BETTER, THE CHOSEN OF GOD.
IF SHE MOVES, SHOOT HER.
WE'RE GOING TO INTERROGATE THE TWO OF YOU, MISS CROFT.
FIND OUT WHAT YOU KNOW ABOUT TRINITY.
IT WILL BE... EXTENSIVE.
No, Mr. Cruz. You're not taking us to torture us to death.
THE CROWBAR, MISS CROFT. DROP IT.
NOW. YOU HAVE NO CHOICE, UNDERSTAND? I WILL SHOOT YOU!
NO!
I choose to FIGHT.
NO.
DON'T LET THIS OUTFIT FOOL YOU, MR. CRUZ.
THE LAST GROUP OF ZEALOTS I CROSSED PATHS WITH?
EVERY LAST ONE OF THEM, DEAD.
AND I CAN SEE IT IN YOUR EYES.
EVEN WITH ALL THE GUNS AND ALL THE CARDS.
YOU'RE AFRAID.
SHOOT HER, YOU IDIOTS! SHOOT HER!

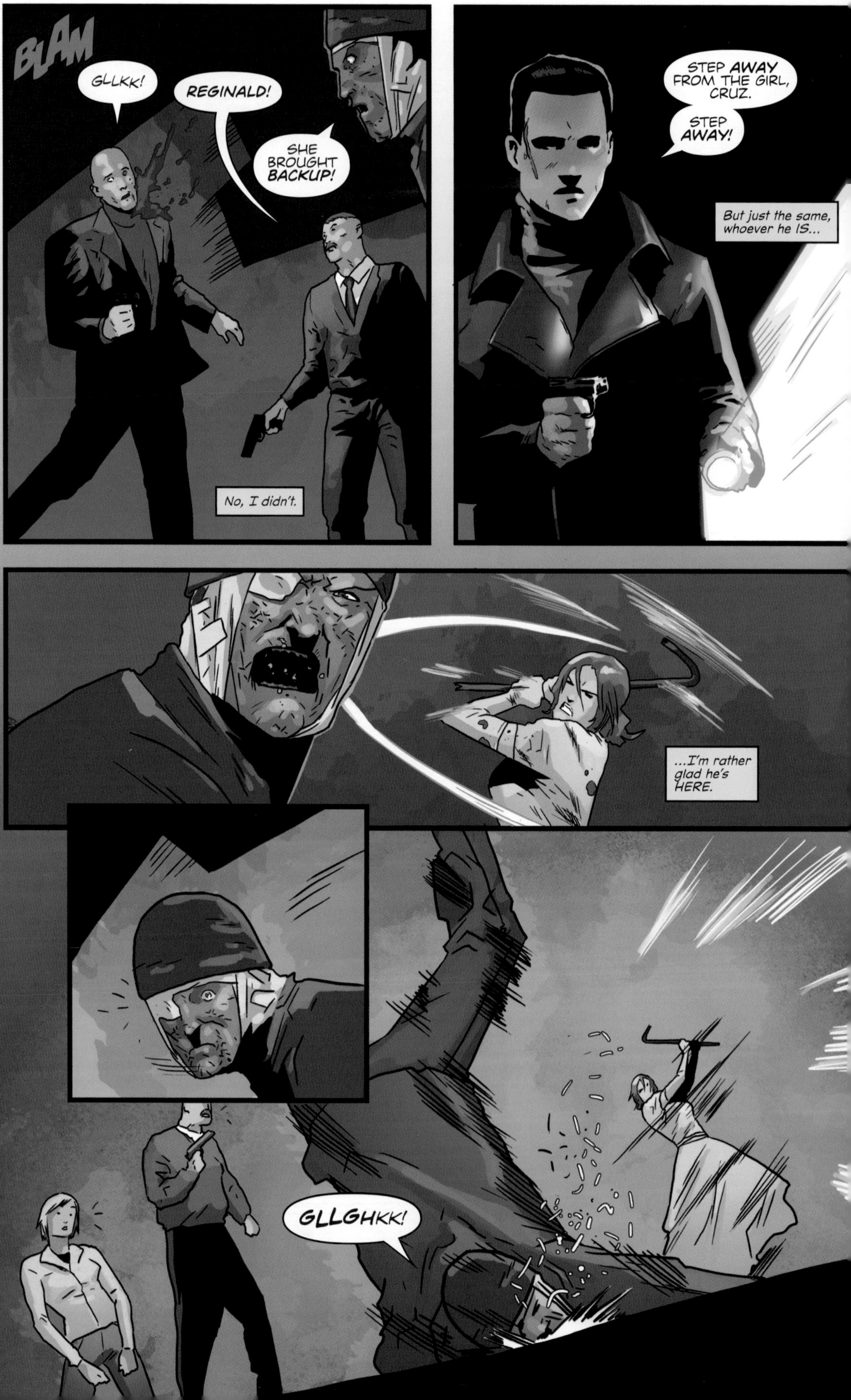
BLAM
GLLKK!
REGINALD!
SHE BROUGHT BACKUP!
No, I didn't.
STEP AWAY FROM THE GIRL, CRUZ.
STEP AWAY!
But just the same, whoever he IS...
...I'm rather glad he's HERE.
GLLGHKK!

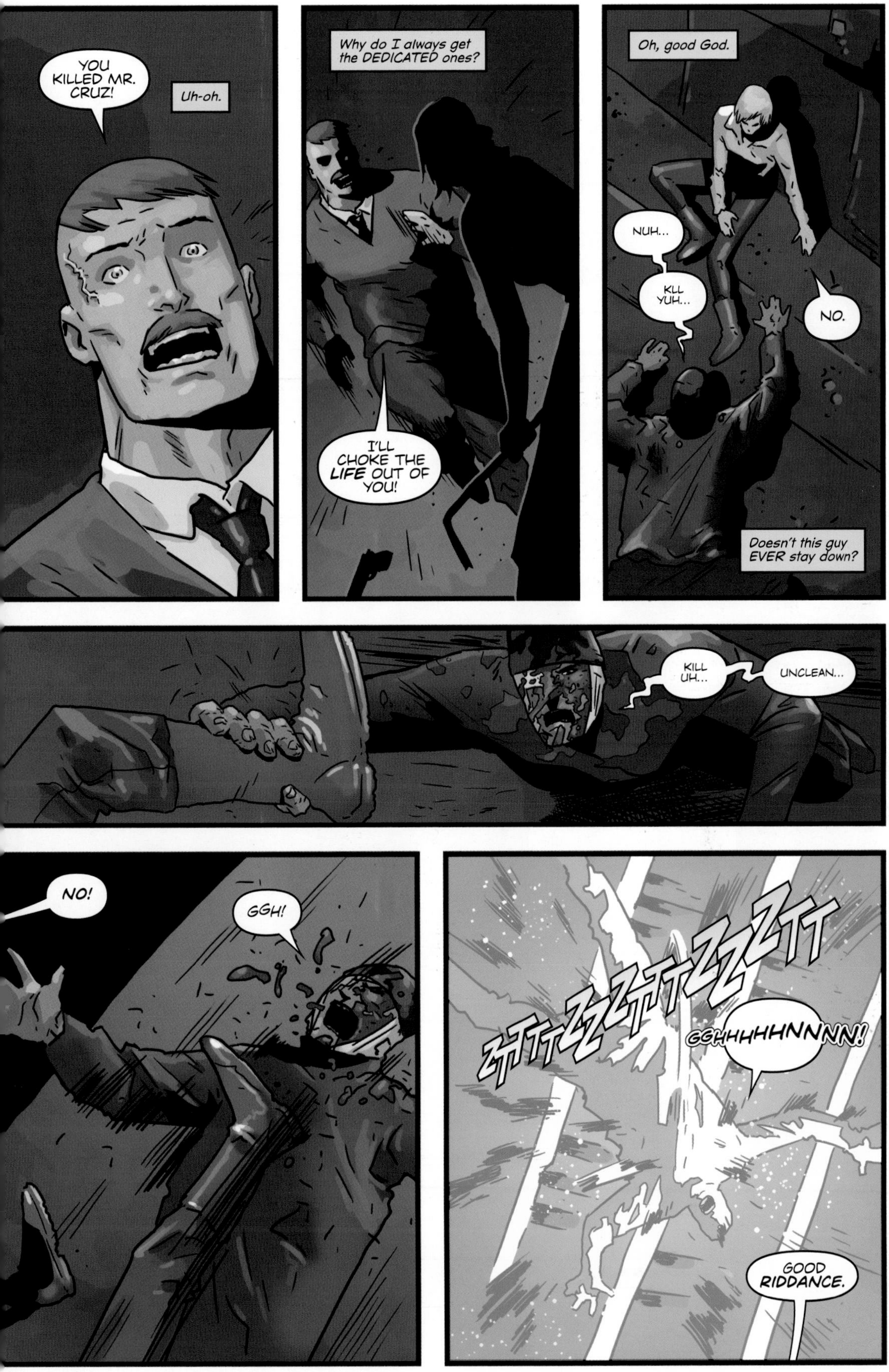
YOU KILLED MR. CRUZ!
Uh-oh.
Why do I always get the DEDICATED ones?
I'LL CHOKE THE LIFE OUT OF YOU!
Oh, good God.
NUH...
KLL YUH...
NO.
Doesn't this guy EVER stay down?
KILL UH...
UNCLEAN...
NO!
GGH!
ZTTTTZZZTTTZZZTT
GGHHHHHNNNN!
GOOD RIDDANCE.

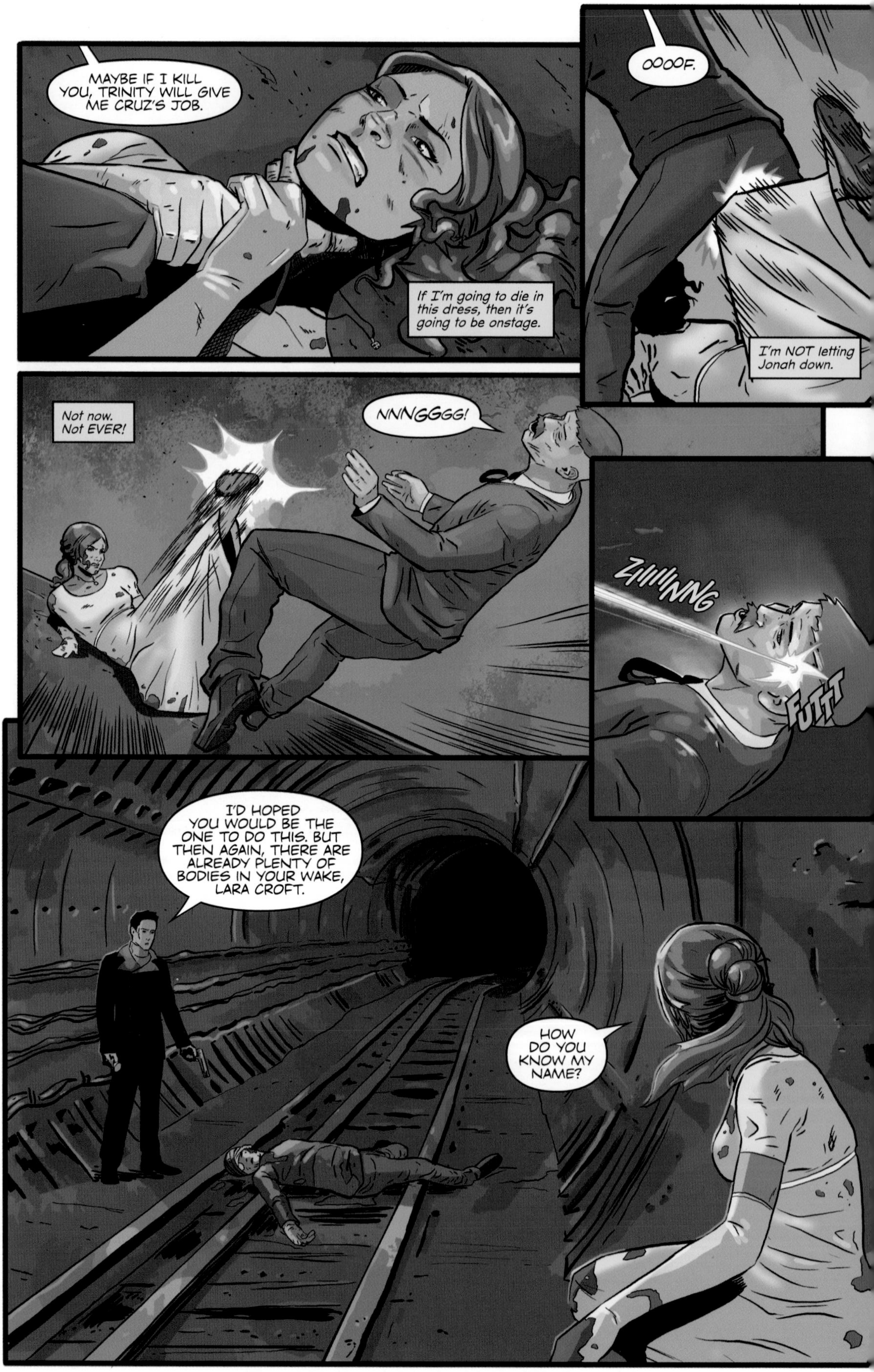
MAYBE IF I KILL YOU, TRINITY WILL GIVE ME CRUZ'S JOB.
If I'm going to die in this dress, then it's going to be onstage.
OOOOF.
I'm NOT letting Jonah down.
Not now. Not EVER!
NNNGGGG!
ZIIIINNG
FUTTT
I'D HOPED YOU WOULD BE THE ONE TO DO THIS. BUT THEN AGAIN, THERE ARE ALREADY PLENTY OF BODIES IN YOUR WAKE, LARA CROFT.
HOW DO YOU KNOW MY NAME?

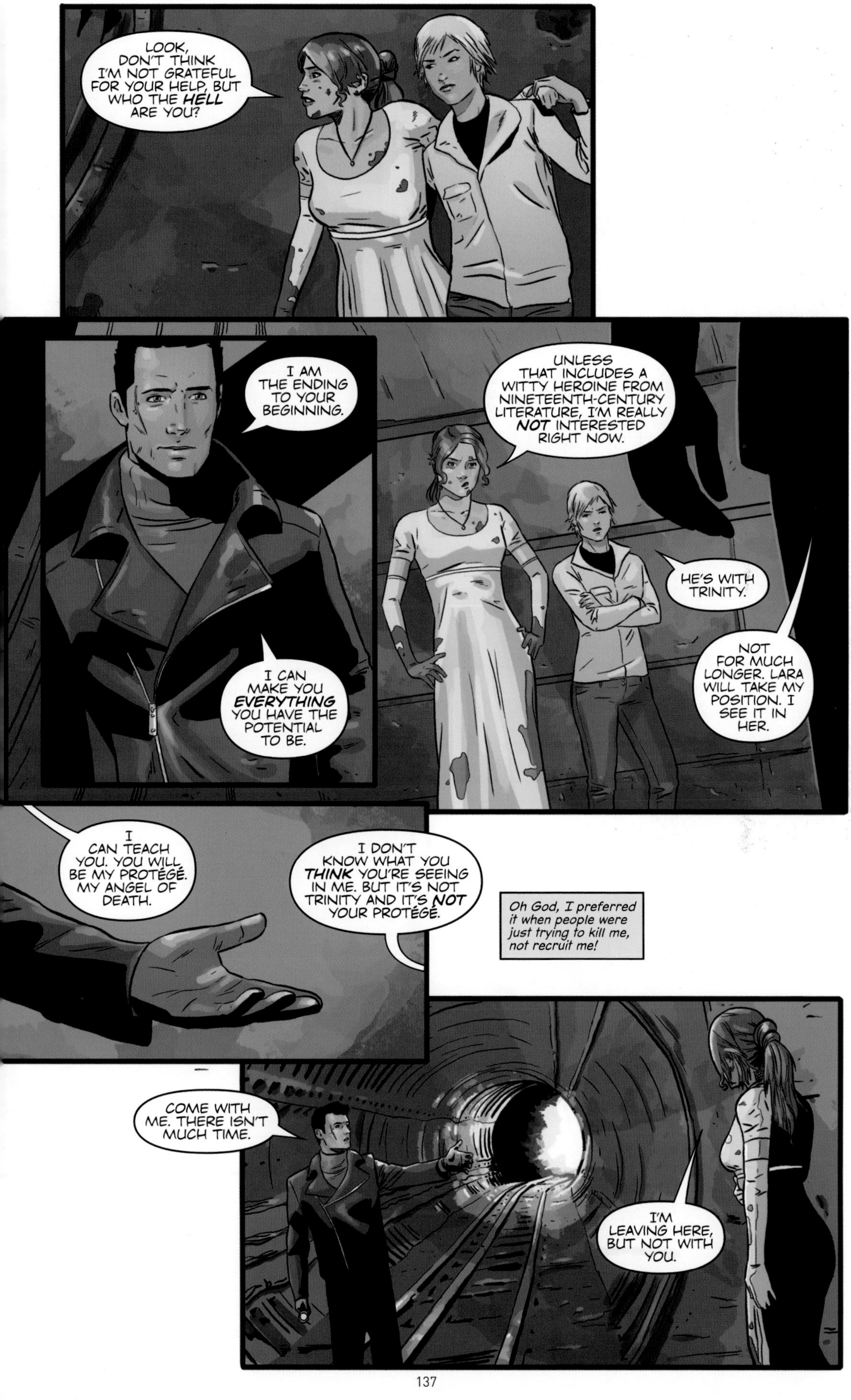
LOOK, DON'T THINK I'M NOT GRATEFUL FOR YOUR HELP, BUT WHO THE **HELL** ARE YOU?
I AM THE ENDING TO YOUR BEGINNING.
I CAN MAKE YOU **EVERYTHING** YOU HAVE THE POTENTIAL TO BE.
UNLESS THAT INCLUDES A WITTY HEROINE FROM NINETEENTH-CENTURY LITERATURE, I'M REALLY **NOT** INTERESTED RIGHT NOW.
HE'S WITH TRINITY.
NOT FOR MUCH LONGER. LARA WILL TAKE MY POSITION. I SEE IT IN HER.
I CAN TEACH YOU. YOU WILL BE MY PROTÉGÉ. MY ANGEL OF DEATH.
I DON'T KNOW WHAT YOU **THINK** YOU'RE SEEING IN ME. BUT IT'S NOT TRINITY AND IT'S **NOT** YOUR PROTÉGÉ.
Oh God, I preferred it when people were just trying to kill me, not recruit me!
COME WITH ME. THERE ISN'T MUCH TIME.
I'M LEAVING HERE, BUT NOT WITH YOU.

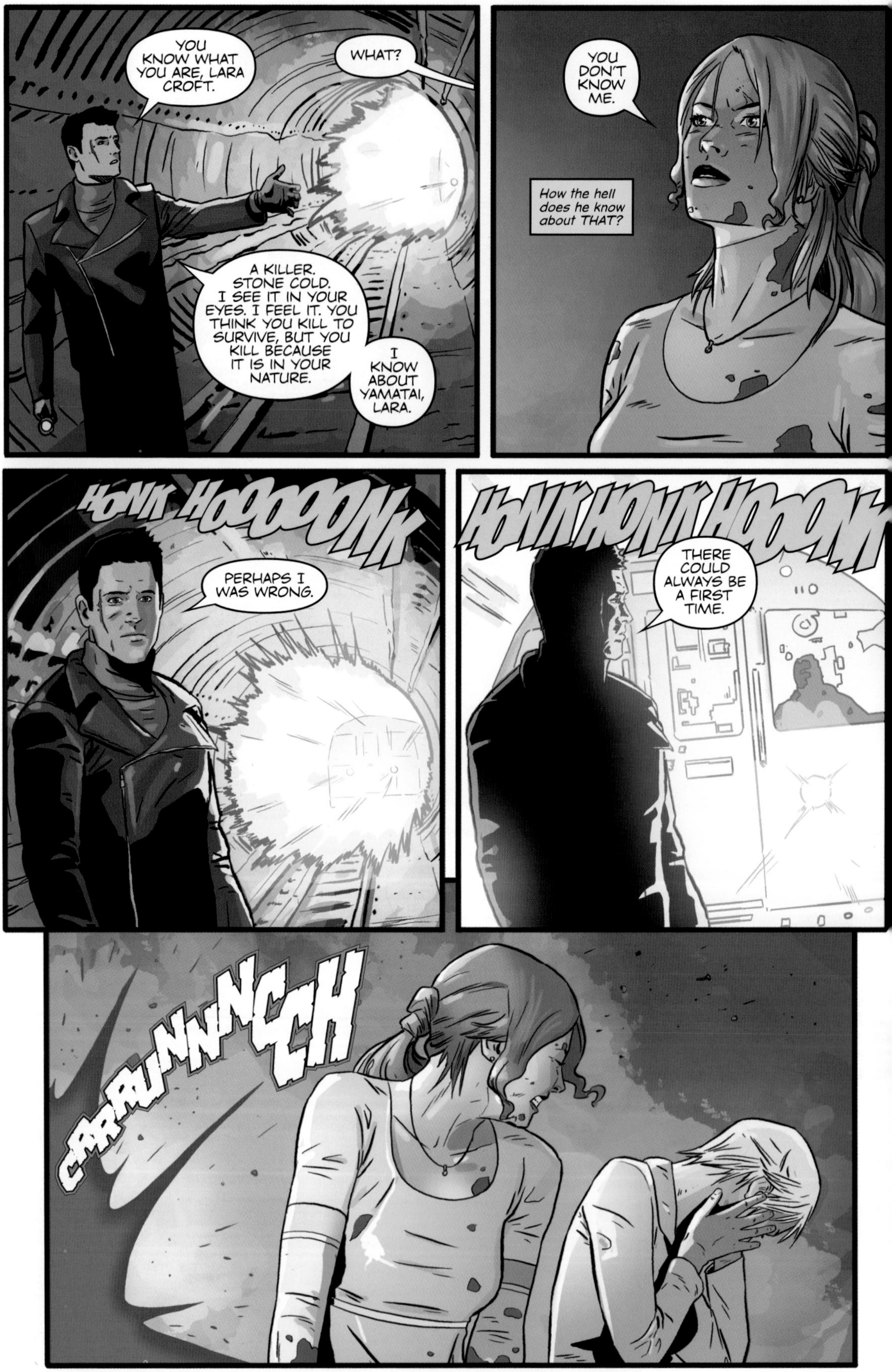
YOU KNOW WHAT YOU ARE, LARA CROFT.
WHAT?
A KILLER. STONE COLD. I SEE IT IN YOUR EYES. I FEEL IT. YOU THINK YOU KILL TO SURVIVE, BUT YOU KILL BECAUSE IT IS IN YOUR NATURE.
I KNOW ABOUT YAMATAI, LARA.
YOU DON'T KNOW ME.
How the hell does he know about THAT?
HONK HOOOOOONK
PERHAPS I WAS WRONG.
HONK HONK HOOONK
THERE COULD ALWAYS BE A FIRST TIME.
CRRRUNNNNCH

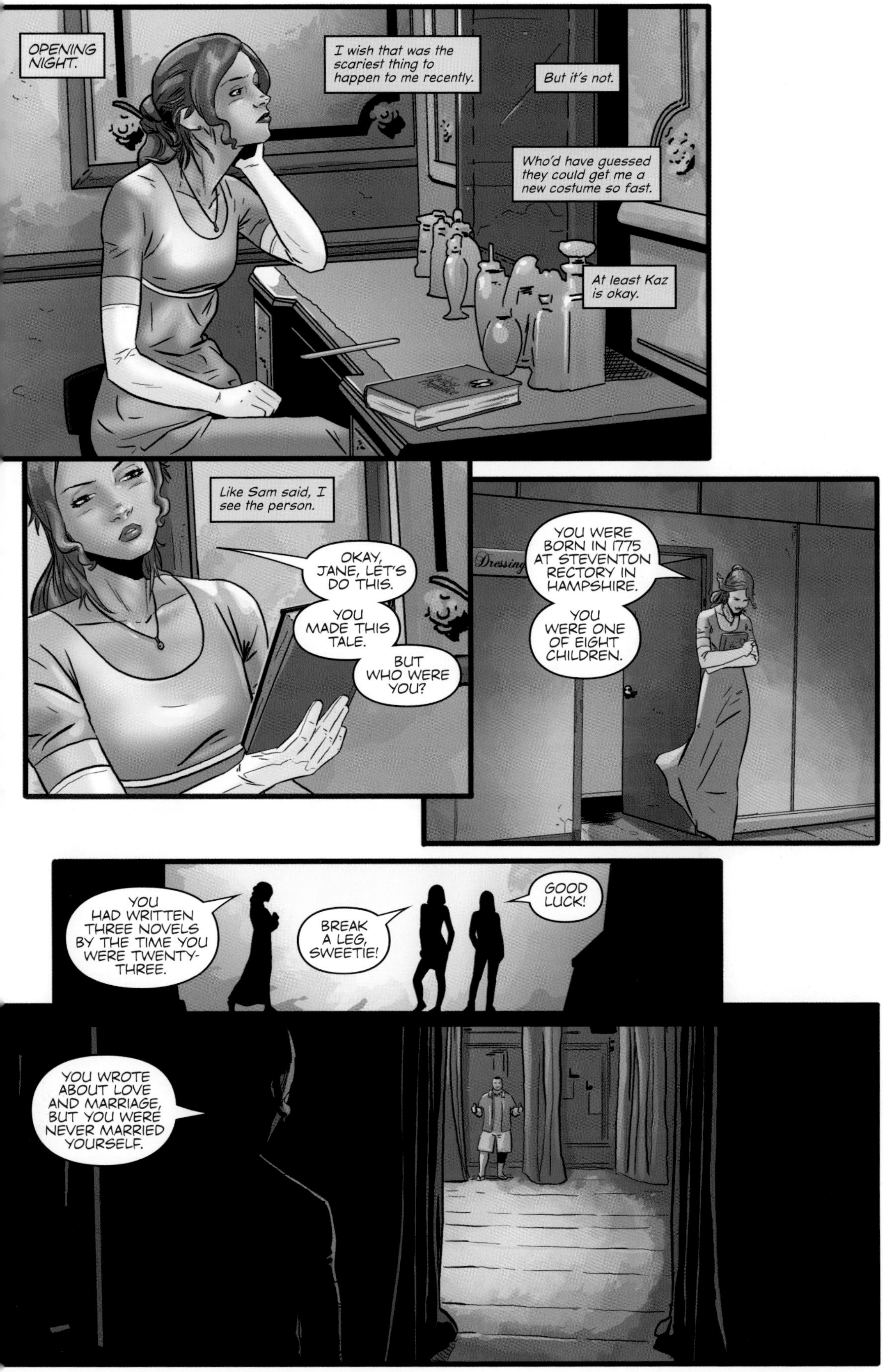

OPENING NIGHT.
I wish that was the scariest thing to happen to me recently.
But it's not.
Who'd have guessed they could get me a new costume so fast.
At least Kaz is okay.
Like Sam said, I see the person.
OKAY, JANE, LET'S DO THIS.
YOU MADE THIS TALE.
BUT WHO WERE YOU?
Dressing
YOU WERE BORN IN 1775 AT STEVENTON RECTORY IN HAMPSHIRE.
YOU WERE ONE OF EIGHT CHILDREN.
YOU HAD WRITTEN THREE NOVELS BY THE TIME YOU WERE TWENTY-THREE.
BREAK A LEG, SWEETIE!
GOOD LUCK!
YOU WROTE ABOUT LOVE AND MARRIAGE, BUT YOU WERE NEVER MARRIED YOURSELF.

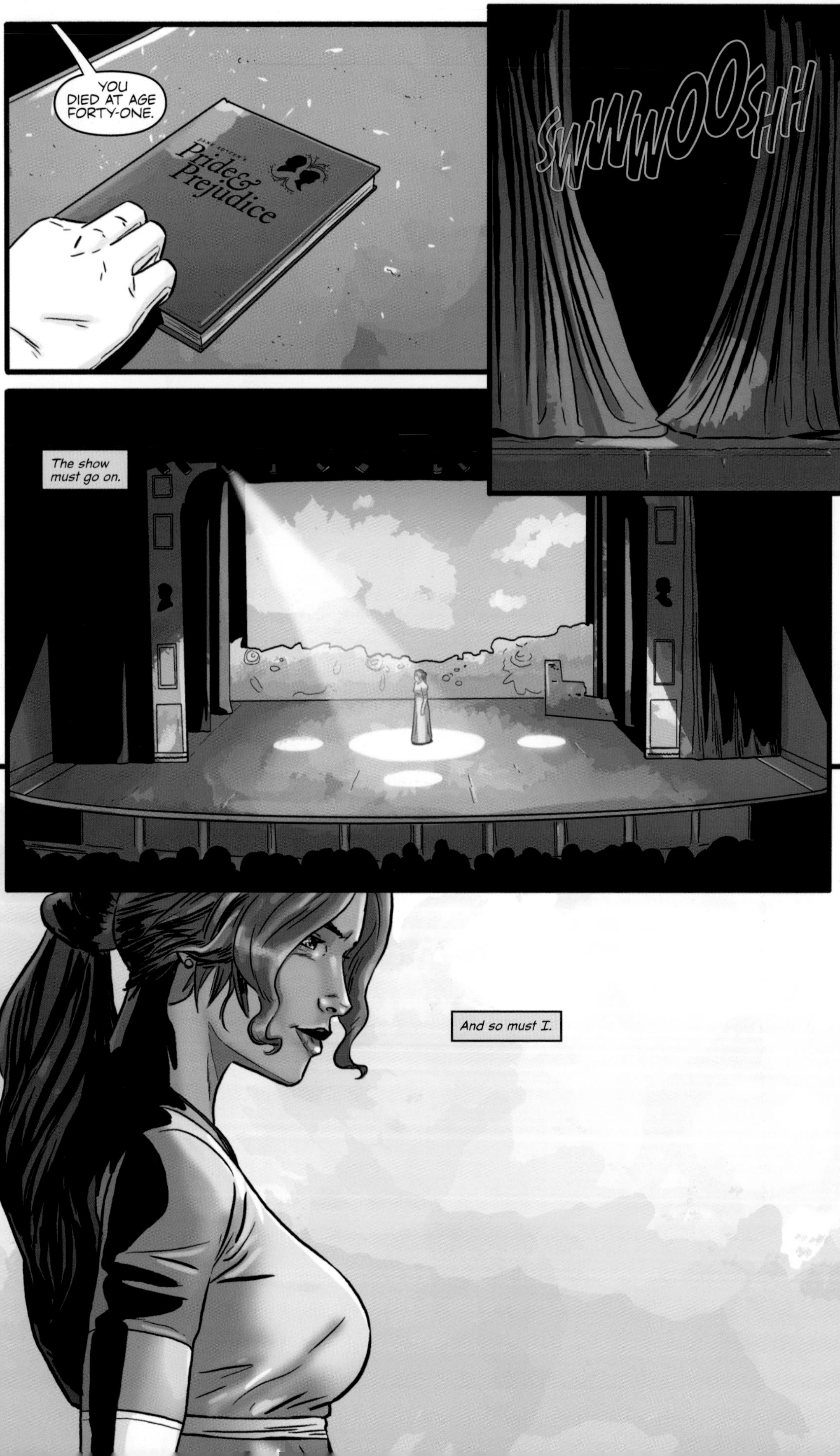
YOU DIED AT AGE FORTY-ONE.
JANE AUSTEN'S
Pride & Prejudice
SWWWOOSHH
The show must go on.
And so must I.

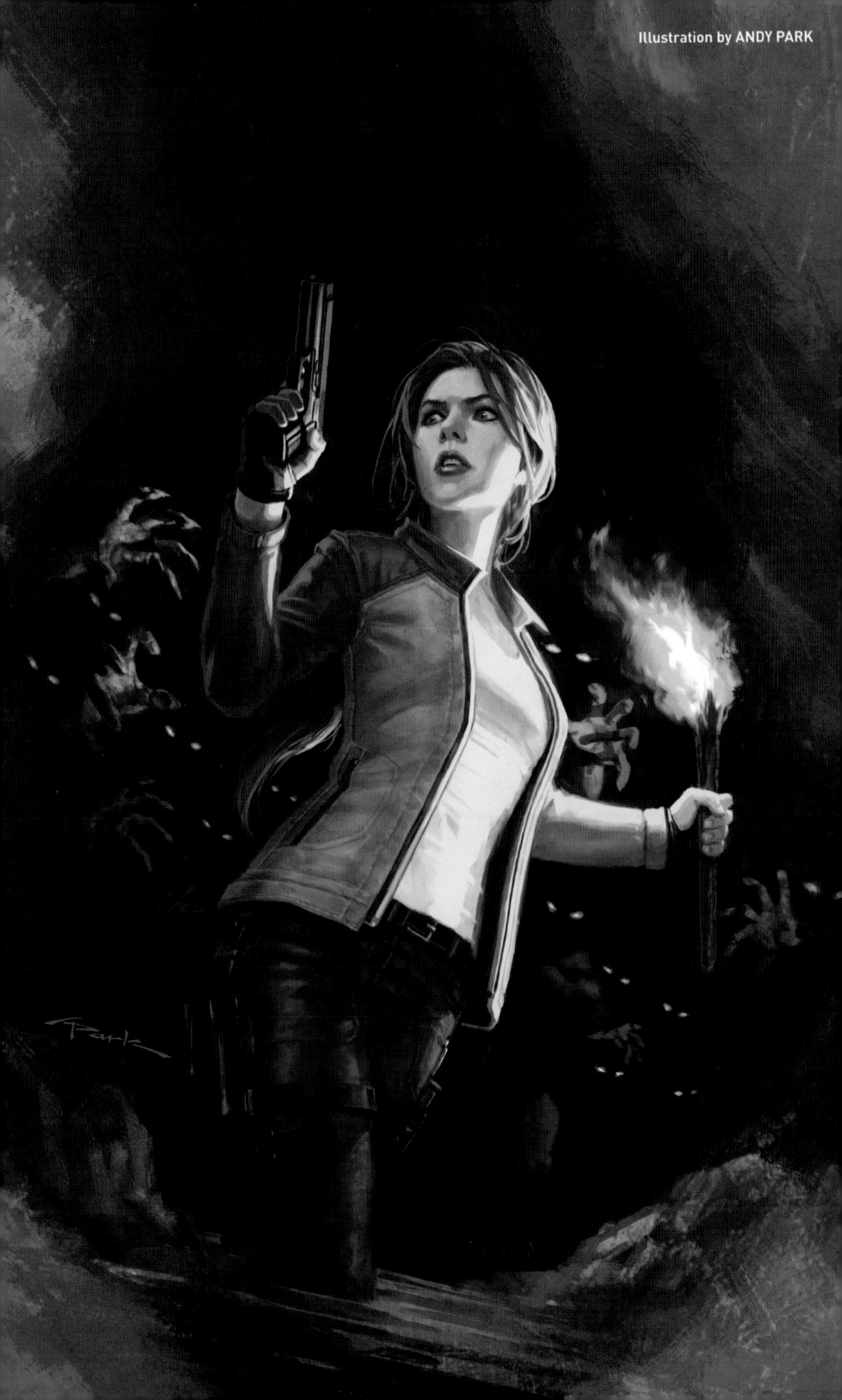

Illustration by ANDY PARK

Illustration by DAN SCOTT

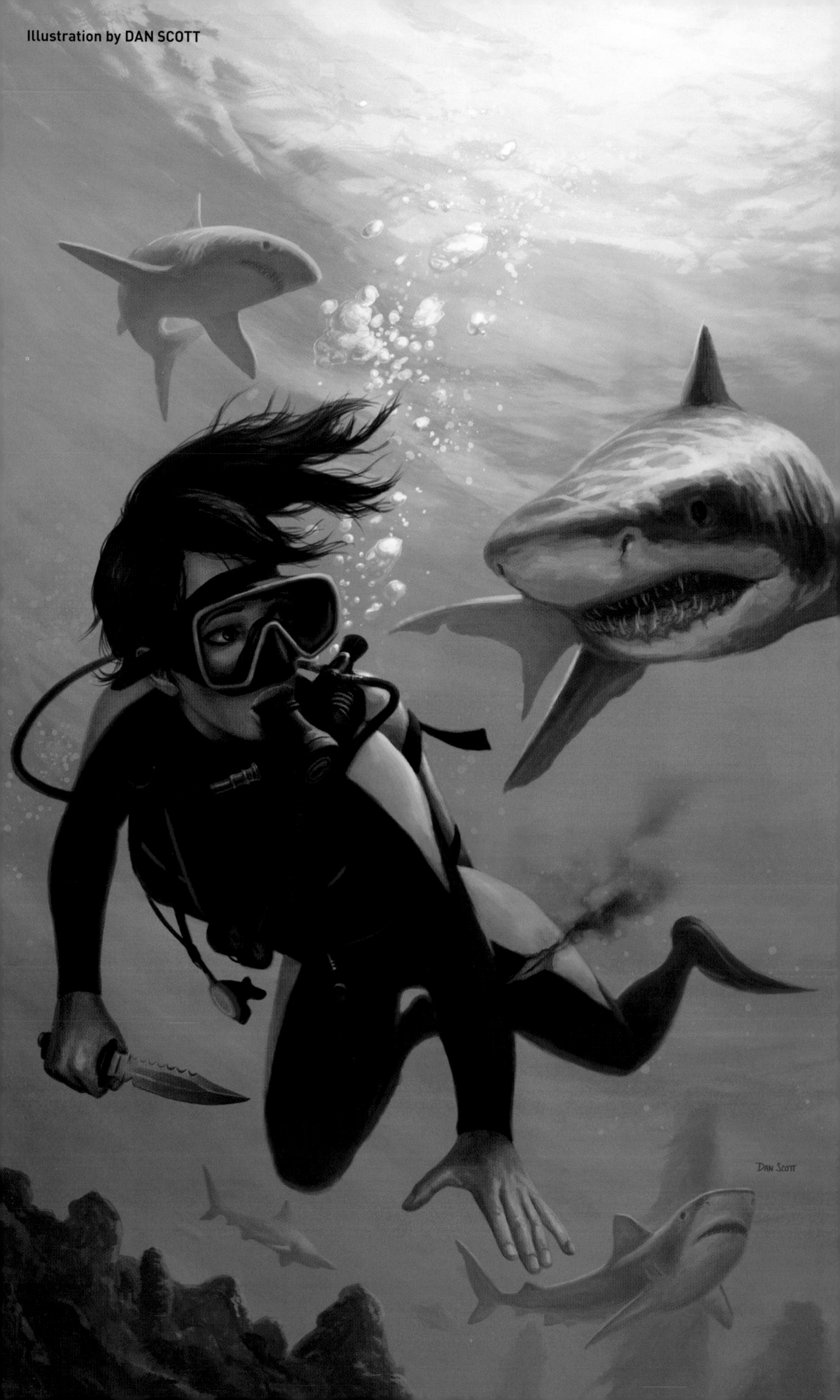
DAN SCOTT

TOMB RAIDER

In the wake of Yamatai's enduring evil, Lara is thrust into a dangerous web of mystery and intrigue in a frantic race to save her friend Sam.

TOMB RAIDER
THE TEN THOUSAND IMMORTALS
DAN ABNETT
NEW YORK TIMES BESTSELLING AUTHOR
& NIK VINCENT
CRYSTAL DYNAMICS
SQUARE ENIX

AVAILABLE NOW
WHEREVER BOOKS ARE SOLD

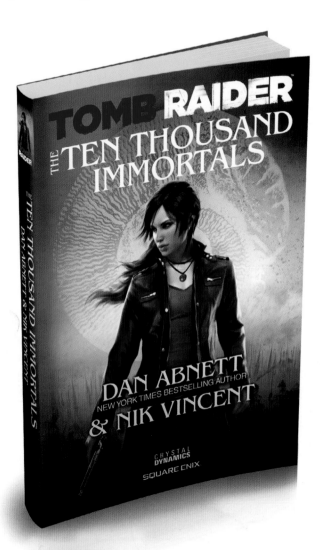